raindance writers'
lab: write + sell the hot
screenplay

To a master of storytelling
silenced too soon

Merlin Russell Grove
1929–1962

raindance writers' lab: write + sell the hot screenplay

ELLIOT GROVE

AMSTERDAM BOSTON HEIDELBERG LONDON NEW YORK OXFORD
PARIS SAN DIEGO SAN FRANCISCO SINGAPORE SYDNEY TOKYO

Focal Press
An imprint of Elsevier Science
Linacre House, Jordan Hill, Oxford OX2 8DP
200 Wheeler Road, Burlington, MA 01803

First published 2001
Reprinted 2003

Cover filmmaker Damjan Bogdanovic
Designer Dominic Thackray

British Library Cataloguing in Publication Data
A catalogue record for this book is available from the British Library

Library of Congress Cataloguing in Publication Data
A catalogue record for this book is available from the Library of Congress

ISBN 0 240 51636 2

For information on all Focal Press publications
visit our website at www.focalpress.com

Printed and bound in Great Britain by MPG Books Ltd, Bodmin, Cornwall

Contents

Stars – Television companies – Independent producers – DIY –
Playing piece – An original screenplay – The screenplay rights in writing, to a novel or short story – The screen rights to a living person's true
life story – The onanist's rash

Preface

Letters to Hollywood

I visited Los Angeles for the first time in 1997 as the guest of Dov S-S Simens. On my first day there he and I went to a Ralph's to get some food for the week. While in the checkout queue I saw the actor David Hasselblad, a couple of minor characters from *Friends*, and had a movie pitched to me by the checkout girl. Everyone, it seemed, was either in the movies or desperately trying to get in.

What makes a hot script? Purely and simply put, if someone offers you money for your screenplay, you have a hot script. If more than one person offers you money for your script, you are hot.

This book is about writing a hot script.

Part of selling your screenplay is learning how people in the movie business say No. On that same trip to Los Angeles, I was told by various people that yes, they loved what I was doing, that they would get back to me as soon as they had finished lunch, that yes, they wanted to work with me and so on.

Dazzled by the apparent success of my trip I returned to London and waited for the telephone to ring. Of course it didn't and I learned how people say yes in the film industry – when they give you a piece of paper with your name on it and some numbers that your bank recognizes. Then you have a hot script.

This book is about writing and selling the hot script.

Elliot Grove
London, January 2001

Acknowledgements

One of the great pleasures of being in the film industry is the privilege of working with countless gifted, vital people, some famous, others not. Through the collective work of gifted and talented individuals we make people laugh and cry, deceive them and inspire them in a rich tapestry of movie magic.

This book is the product of nearly ten years working at Raindance, and meeting and working with hundreds of people. Three stand out – my editor, Jennifer Welham of Focal Press, whose energy and vision inspired this book; Dominic Thackray, graphic designer and therapist extraordinaire; and my partner, Suzanne Ballantyne, whose support has nurtured me throughout.

I also thank the tireless staff at Raindance, past and present, whose suggestions and advice enrich this book, in particular Damjan Bogdanovic, Johanna von Fischer, Sandra Grant, Jamie Greco, Fred Hogge, James Knight, Talia Rogers, Chris Thomas and John Tobin.

The film business is tough, bruising and fiercely competitive. To the hundreds of talented writers, directors, producers and actors who have crossed my path and offered friendship, assistance and inspiration over the years I thank you for the wisdom and experience shared that has made this book possible.

About the Author

Mesmerized by the moving image from a young age, but unable to watch TV or films until his early teens due to the constraints of his Amish background, Canadian-born Elliot Grove followed formal art school training with a series of behind-the-scene jobs in the industry.

He worked for nine years as a scenic artist and set designer on sixty-eight feature films and over seven hundred commercials in his native Toronto, where he developed a distaste for the wasted resources on set and union red tape that prevented filmmaker wannabees like himself from getting their own features off the ground.

Elliot moved to London in the late 1980s and nine years ago, when the British film industry was drowning in self-pity, launched the Raindance Film Festival devoted to independent filmmaking and emerging talent.

Initially, Raindance catered mainly to American independents who understood that the combination of a positive mental attitude and a pioneering spirit provides the essential foundation upon which to produce and distribute films successfully. Happily, that attitude has now filtered through to the UK; independent filmmaking, once a small organism, has become a global phenomenon. Elliot is proud of the fact that last year's Raindance line-up included seventy-eight independent features from twenty-two countries.

Upholding the ethos of Raindance, Elliot wrote, produced and directed the feature, *Table 5*, for just over £200. He also lectures on screenwriting and filmmaking throughout the UK and Europe, and in 1992 set up the training division of Raindance which now offers over two dozen evening and weekend masterclasses on writing, directing, producing and marketing a feature film. Elliot firmly believes that success in the moviemaking business is a simple matter of demystifying the process of breaking into the film industry and allowing individual talent to prosper.

In 1998 Elliot founded the British Independent Film Awards to promote British talent.

Elliot lives in London with his partner and two girls.

1 Introduction

Before I start let me make it clear that I don't know anything about screenwriting – I am in fact totally self-trained. I didn't go to any script or film school. In fact, I never saw a single movie or television program until I was sixteen.

I was born into an Amish Mennonite community outside Toronto. As a child I was taught that the Devil lived in the cinema. One day while in town waiting for a farm repair at a blacksmith, I saw the cinema on the high street. I had noticed the cinema before, but ignored it, because of what my family had taught me. But on that hot spring day – it sat there, beckoning. I paid my ninety-nine cents to see what the Devil looked like and entered totally unprepared for what I saw.

My first cinematic experience was *Lassie Comes Home* and when I sat in the cinema I was so totally convinced, so totally tricked by the images on the screen that I was swept away. I had no prior warning of what the cinema was, I had no education or knowledge of the technology of the cinema and I could just as easily have been on the moon. Not only was I pondering at 'How did they do that?' but I believed then, as I do now, that cinema contains a special form of magic. My next encounter with the Devil was *The Sound Of Music* followed by hundreds of other movies. I will never forget that first experience.

My childhood was thus void of any movies and my personal history of cinema did in fact start when I was sixteen. I missed many of the classic films of European and American cinema. Even now, I force myself to watch certain black and white classics I missed as a youth. To compensate for my lack of classic cinema, I have inherited a strong oral tradition through the Bible stories I was told as a child. I was enthralled by the farming and gardening stories that were recounted each night at family dinner: a table that could easily consist of twenty people – children, relatives and travelling farmhands. I was also forced to learn all of the Greek myths, not because of the religious tone of my upbringing, but because my mother thought I should broaden my education.

Much later, I read many of the Chinese books on spirituality and warfare and noted that those stories stirred in me the same primal emotions as the stories from my childhood.

I base my script expertise on two things:

Firstly, what I have learned about screenplays I learned by reading them, and what I learnt about screenwriters I learned by working with them at Raindance Film Festival: hundreds of writers since 1991, and from reading over 2,500 scripts – an average of one script per day since the beginning of 1992.

Secondly, my Amish Mennonite upbringing – a strict upbringing with a strong oral tradition. My early childhood memories are of being cajoled, frightened into righteousness, to the point of total fear after hearing the story of Daniel being eaten alive in the Lion's Den.

Biblical reference

I envy screenwriters. I would consider myself an average writer at best, but the reason I envy screenwriters so much is that there is a Biblical reference to screenwriting. The ancient prophets who wrote the Bible were able to predict the film industry, and hidden in that revered tome is a useful reference for screenwriters:

In the beginning was the Word and nothing but the Word and the Word was God.

All movies start with the written word – the script.

My screenwriting training started as a script reader. I read scripts for a modest fee and wrote up to five pages of critique on dialogue, characterization, plot, structure and so on. I realized fairly soon in my reading that most new writers tend to make the same mistakes. In fact it became so obvious that when I started a new critique I often just typed in the new script's different character names on the critique templates on my computer!

If nothing else, this book will show you the common errors of first time writers and will show you how to avoid them. Of course, it is my intention to show you much more, and to give you the most advanced tools for screenwriting currently available.

The first half of this book contains the prevailing theory in all of those other expensive screenwriting books and seminars, and compresses them into a few short chapters. By showing you all of those so-called rules, I will try to give you a simple new paradigm that will enable you to plan your script and your career for the new millennium. Lastly, and throughout this book, I want you to remember that there are no rules. Rules are only the attempts by others to explain a fact with examples they choose that prove their theory. By showing you the theorems and the facts, you should be able see how to transcend these rules and develop your own unique and highly personal screenwriting style.

Remember too, that I do not consider myself an expert in scriptwriting – I only have a few observations, which I would like to share with you in the hope that they are useful. Or, if you like, I will propose a method to follow that will enable you to get your story onto paper. But please remember that everyone has instinctive storytellers lurking inside themselves. Learn to let it out!

I hope you enjoy this workbook, and please let me know how we can make it clearer and more helpful.

It then follows that the entire movie making process is one of originating ideas, finding the right words to express the idea on paper and then transferring them to the screen. No movie ever starts without words. This process is what distinguishes the movie industry from, say, the property business, where deals start with measurements, financial calculations and an artist's impression of the finished project.

Screenwriters can be certain that they have this biblical ordination, this biblical recognition, which separates them from us mere mortals. Trust me. In a business as fiercely competitive as screenwriting, you need all the help that you can get.

What is a Hot Script?

A screenplay those elusive script buyers are offering to buy. The more buyers chasing your script, the hotter it is, and by association, the hotter you are. Writers never get paid for writing a screenplay. The only way you get paid is when you sell your screenplay. And finding a screenplay good enough to buy is very difficult. Producers in the industry today moan constantly about the lack of quality scripts in circulation. Write a script that's hot, and the film production companies, the producers and the agents will send the limos.

Original ideas

Of the 2,500 screenplays I have read as a script reader, I never read a script that was a bad idea. What I did read, on a daily basis, were scripts that were a poor execution of these ideas.

Consider the story of the British feature *Shallow Grave*. Written by John Hodge and directed by Danny Boyle, it had circulated throughout the industry to lukewarm interest, because Danny was considered a TV drama director, not a feature director. Learning that David Aukin, then the head of Channel Four, was due at the Edinburgh Film Festival to give a talk, Danny found out from Aukin's office that he was staying for a few hours and catching the 7pm flight back to London. He then found the taxi driver who was hired to stand and wait for Aukin and take him to the airport. He bribed the driver with a five-pound note to simply hand the screenplay to Aukin when he got in the cab to go to the airport. The flight to London lasts an hour. What would you do if you were in Aukin's shoes with an hour to kill? Needless to say, the deal for *Shallow Grave* was done days later, and Boyle launched his career.

Before I start with some specific information that you will need to cut the odds against success, let me define some basic principles so we both know what we are talking about.

The Seven Basic Requirements of a Screenplay

1. Entertainment

The film business's only product is entertainment. By entertainment I do not mean solely to divert. The film business has many examples of films like this. Films which sadly create needless sex and violence to divert the attention of the audience, but which make no attempt to use any of the other tools at the disposal of the screenwriter and filmmaker – setting, action, characterization, plot, structure and dialogue.

Entertainment comes from the Latin root to intertwine. This is the task of the screenwriter – to intertwine all of the elements available to a screenwriter and weave them together to create an entertaining story.

In well-crafted screenplays, the weaving should be tight and invisible. Setting, action, characterization, plot, structure and dialogue should be combined so that the seams do not show. A writer who has learned how to do this is mastering the craft of screenwriting. For an exercise, list three films you feel were created solely to divert:

Now, list the three films you feel came closest to successfully weaving these tools together:

Tools not rules

There is no such thing as a screenwriting rule. I present tools that are designed to assist you in writing your script. These are not rules.

Can you find any common elements that link the films in each area?

Hint Try to answer these questions when you look at a film – What made you get interested in the story? At which minute did you first get bored? At which minute did you first get interested? Were there any common elements in the setting, the action, the characterization that connect the films? What did you like most about each film? What did you like least?

There is no science to this approach, but if you deconstruct a story you may discover techniques that you can use (or avoid!) in your own work.

2. Commerce

Orson Welles said 'A poet needs a pen, a painter needs a brush, but a filmmaker needs a whole army.'

Like it or not, it is the film business and it is a complex business at that. Writers tend to be drawn by the making of the film – the technicians, the actors, the scoring, the cinematography, design of the costumes and props. But these are the actions of the film industry (read car industry, agricultural industry, aerospace industry). The actual creation and making of a film is the role of the film industry.

Writers who forget the business side of the industry do so at their peril. The bankers and financiers, the marketing and public relations people, the owners and employees of the cinemas, the accountants with their complex procedures, the tax lawyers, the copyright and royalty collectors are a few of the silent faces who are employed by the film industry.

Add in the more glamourous roles of the actors, the directors, the editors, make-up artists, scenic artists, lighting and sound specialists and you really have an army of people involved in the making of a film.

Each area is really a sub-industry, and the people in each sub-industry tend to dislike the people in the other sub-industries. But money and collaboration govern the entire movie business. Therefore, a writer who includes camera directions in a screenplay, or is too specific in stage directions is precluding the possibility of collaboration with the cameraman and the actors – two very important categories of collaborators. The trick is to write a screenplay that inspires each and every category of person likely to be involved in the making of the movie. A successful writer learns how to do this, and to incorporate the creativity of everyone into the movie. Thus a finished screenplay should be considered a blueprint for a movie, or suggestions for a movie, and not a carefully bound package of precisely typed paper that represents the death of a few trees! Writers who ignore this, or who fail to research and educate themselves about the intricacies of the movie business will encumber their chances of success by this lack of knowledge.

Writers must learn as much as possible about the industry.

Hint Read the trade papers. Read the film magazines. Read the trashy weeklies. Scour these various publications for hard news and juicy gossip that will arm you with knowledge.

As a writer, you are inevitably going to spend long hours writing alone, and the commercial and collaborative aspects of the film business can be easy to forget. Also remember that as a writer, you are basically setting up your very own business where you manufacture products (scripts and treatments) and for which the cost of manufacture (paper, some ink and some envelopes) is minuscule compared to the possible sale price of a script.

A writer friend of mine once boasted to a dinner table of light industrialists that he had started a business with a 10,000 percent mark up. The table went dead, and finally, one of the more arrogant businessmen asked him what it was and my friend offered 'I'm writing a screenplay.'

Oddly enough, many astute businessmen recognize the financial limitations of their own businesses, even though they look financially secure and wealthy beyond belief. I have met several highly successful businessmen who know to a cent how much their business will earn this next year and the year after. Whereas their businesses crank out a profit at a predictable rate, affected only by basic economic factors such as employment and interest rate rises, only in the world of athletics or movies can an individual turn from pauper to multi-millionaire literally overnight. Writing a well-crafted and commercially viable screenplay will catapult you straight into the movie business at the very highest level. But before we get too dreamy-eyed thinking of riches and before we order the Rolls Royce catalogue, remember the following. You will never get paid for writing a script. You only get paid if you sell it. And only a hot script sells.

The bottom line in the film industry is the movie. If you have that one idea that no one else has, but which someone thinks they can make money with, the movie business will send the limos. But only for a well-crafted commercially viable script.

3. Contrivance

There is nothing more contrived than the film business. Everything about the industry from the way we view the images on a screen, to the way that films are created by groups of technicians shows the movie business to be the most contrived of any art form in the world. As a screenwriter, we must learn to fill the vacuous void of the screen with images and voices that follow the contrivance in the cinema.

Remember too, that as children we all looked forward to the bedtime stories that our parents told us. Now that we are adults, we are still going to the cinema for a bedtime story. The fact that the filmmakers used a series of contrivances to bring us the story is something that we expect and accept.

For example, it is common knowledge that films are shot out of sequence. Suppose the script calls for the first scene to be in her bedroom downtown, getting dressed, and the second scene with her at the airport, flinging herself into the arms of her lover whom she hasn't seen for two days. We all know that the director doesn't film the first scene, yell 'Cut', and drag everyone out to the airport for the second scene, and so on. We know that films are shot out of sequence for matters of economy. Yet we accept this when we sit in front of a screen and watch a movie.

Remember when we go to the cinema we expect one of two things – that the story that we are going to see will change our lives forever, or we don't fall asleep.

4. Peeping Tom

Human beings are fixated by what happens to others. Walk down any street and notice the crowd gathered around an accident victim, or feel your head turn while walking down a street at night and see the shadow outline of a naked body against a bedroom curtain.

Let's face it – we love to gape.

For screenwriters, the challenge is to create a world that people want to stare at, and to make the screen characters, dialogue, setting and action so compelling that they cannot wrench themselves away from the screen until the very last frame, the very last words in the script.

5. Maximize, in minimal circumstances

Creative economy is the big challenge. To achieve this, a screenwriter has to maximize everything that they have at their disposal. Remember too that as a screenwriter you are denied many of the literary tools. Alliteration, simile and metaphor are devices best left to poets, lyricists or novelists.

Also, a screenwriter can only write what you actually see on the screen. Therefore, you can't say 'It's very cold' – because how do you show cold? You could say 'Hail bounces off the windscreen'.

But I don't mean just the creative tools. I mean that as a writer you need to maximize your own personal life, to be able to take the energy and patience to explain to those with whom you share your life that what you are doing is very important to you. Know when to pull back and when to involve them which is also a big challenge.

Earning their keep

Each word must earn its keep on the page. Thus, a description like 'a late Victorian sixteen-room country house overgrown with perennials' would be better stated as 'a run-down mansion'.

One of the worst things about writing is sneaking into your workspace and turning on the computer. Something about the click of the switch, or the chime the machine makes when you switch it on creates a black hole of energy. Energy that sucks in all sorts of things – the telephone rings, a pet (if you have one) needs attention, or worst of all, if you share your life with someone else, a human being tries to help you. It usually goes like this – 'Honey, I'm going to write now for forty-five minutes.' Fifteen minutes later, the love of your life walks behind you and starts massaging your neck and cooing words like 'You look really tired' or 'You really should do something about those bags under your eyes' and before you know it you have stopped writing and gone to bed!

Handling your personal life so that your family and friends know that while you are writing you must not and cannot be disturbed takes a special skill. You have to learn how to do this too, if you want to write the hot script.

6. Hollywood, love it or leave it?

First of all, let me explain that by Hollywood I mean the professional film and television community centred in Los Angeles – yes, Hollywood is the major centre of film production. But by Hollywood I also mean the centres of film production in other major cities – New York, Toronto, Hamburg, Vancouver, Barcelona, and London.

In these cities, and others, professional film production companies also turn out movie after movie, although perhaps not on the same scale as in Los Angeles. These film production companies vary in size from mini-majors like FilmFour, Canal Plus, Pathé or Kinoveldt to small companies producing a picture or two directly for TV or the home video market.

Personally I love Hollywood films.

This always gets me into problems. Running the Raindance Film Festival, which is noted for its cutting-edge and aggressive films, my acquaintances ask me 'But how could you possibly like Hollywood films? Most Hollywood films suck!'

True. But so do most ballets, most novels, most operas, most paintings, most poems, most symphonies and most rock songs.

By saying I love Hollywood films I mean that I love seeing vast expanses of scenery, sparkling special effects, snappy and crisp dialogue, gorgeous costumes and settings, ambitious and grand camera movements that make up typical Hollywood films. And when Hollywood succeeds and tells a story that compels the viewer, that elicits emotion in the audience, that brings a lump to the throat, or a gasp of laughter, Hollywood is fantastic. It also follows that one of the best ways to write for the screen is to study Hollywood films.

Hint Go and see as many Hollywood films that you possibly can.

Pay or Play

Producers agree that the main reason so many substandard screenplays are shot is because of the negotiating logistics foisted on them and screenwriters by 'Pay or Play'.

The only way to secure major talent is to book them for a specific time slot, and then agree to pay them whether or not the project actually starts shooting at that time.

So, if the screenplay needs to be rewritten or revised at the expense of the start date and the accompanying onerous financial penalties, producers push unfinished screenplays into production knowing that they are minimizing their exposure.

There are some acquaintances of mine attempting to make a career in the film industry who belabor the Hollywood point and say that they are tired or bored of Hollywood films.

To them, or to you, if you find yourself sharing this sentiment, I respectfully suggest that you are in the wrong business. If you say that you are fed up with glitz, with glamour, and fatigued by sparkle, then I think that you are really in the wrong business.

If you are in this category, then view this book as a simple book designed to increase your understanding of the movie business, and use it as something that will increase your enjoyment of the films you chose to see, but please, don't pretend to be a part of it. You are just setting yourself up for hurt and disaster.

By Hollywood I also refer to the time-honored tradition of passing each script through a series of filters. The Hollywood filtering system is not without fault. Hollywood makes many poor scripts. The reason for this is more to do with the politics of the film business than anything else, and more specifically, the pay-or-play deals that predominate the industry.

The Hollywood system spends hundreds of millions of dollars each and every year on developing screenplays, and in the process creates opportunities for writers to write and get paid.

Since 1999, a whole new breed of production company has leapt out of nowhere. Their remit is to produce moving pictures for the Internet, and they produce dramatic films for distribution on this exciting new platform. I would also call these companies 'Hollywood'. This is another medium demanding scripts.

In summary, the films produced by Hollywood companies are created for the sole purpose of earning money for the producers and investors who have financed the production budget (and the writers' cheque).

7. Audience

The biggest mistake a writer can make at the outset of writing a screenplay is imagining his or her screenplay turned into a movie and playing at hundreds or thousands of cinemas around the world. To write with this goal is demonstrating a fundamental lack of knowledge about the film business and confusion of the roles of scriptwriter and filmmaker.

A filmmaker makes a film to play to an audience in a cinema or in front of a TV screen. The filmmaker's goal is to elicit emotion in an audience.

The goal of a screenwriter is entirely different. The audience of a screenwriter is just one person – a reader. Usually in the film industry, this reader is male and late fifties, overweight with a tight silk shirt tucked into a pair of expensive slacks, secured by a crocodile skin belt. The reader's body is adorned with gold rings and bracelets. Very often, this reader has absolutely no training in film, but they are reading your script, and they have one thing that you want – a chequebook.

Because the role of the audience is so important, let's take a closer look at the status of the observer.

Suppose that I am a DJ and my job is to attend the radio station and choose music for my show, which airs every morning from 3am to 4am. Hardly a favorable time, but in addition to my paycheck, the other benefit is that I can choose any music I want. Many people would consider this an ideal job, albeit with unsociable hours.

figure 1.1
Audience Chart A

The model looks like this:

Suppose one evening, as I am about to leave for work, the radio producer calls and says that there is conclusive proof that this evening during my show, absolutely no one will be listening. Is there any point in my attending the studio to play my favorite records? Surely I can do this in the comfort of my own home.

figure 1.2
Audience Chart B

Let's look at the model again, only now from the perspective of a writer:

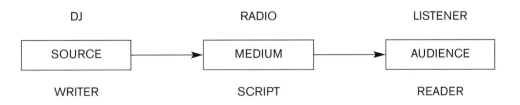

The writer writes for the reader. This is where the biblical quote becomes so vital. I call it the Screenwriter's Leap of Faith.

How do you know that each time you start to write a script that you will be able to write a good script? Screenwriting is an art form, and you may not be able to hit it every time you try.

If you write a good script, how will you know how to get it to the right reader, the reader with a checkbook? And if you get it to the right reader or producer, how do you know if this producer will hire the right director, the right actors, the right editor, music supervisor and so on?

You don't. You might get lucky and write a superb screenplay, send it to a great producer, have it directed by the hottest director and cast, and still find that you cannot get your film onto any screen in the world.

How do you know what is going to happen? From the moment that you have that great idea for a film you decide to commit endless hours of time and energy to writing it. And you do so without having any idea whatsoever about the final fate of your screenplay.

The screenwriter's leap of faith is that amazing belief in yourself and your idea that will carry you through all of the barriers to success – the Biblical quote has never been more applicable.

Hint The goal of a filmmaker is to elicit emotion in an audience. The goal of a screenwriter is to elicit emotion in a reader.

There are four times during this book that I am going to go into *bummer*. This is the first and it relates to that miserable word called misfortune. There is nothing I can do to teach you about the word misfortune except to try to educate you as much as possible about the savvy needed for the industry, and then hope that you are able to minimalize the odds against you.

Consider these two questions – Is every hit movie good? Is every good movie a hit?

Every year at the Raindance Film Festival, I find a sweetheart, darling, cute film that I really believe is right for the British audience. The film plays to a packed house, including several distributors. After the screenings of these films, the audience bursts into rapturous applause, and the audience files out talking excitedly about the movie.

Usually in cases like this, I sidle up to one of the Acquisition Executives that I recognize at the screening and ask them what they think of the film. They know that what I am really asking is whether or not they think it suitable for a UK release. I am usually told 'It's too American for a British audience' or 'I don't think the British public is ready for something as controversial as that.' Misfortune can and will befall you. Learn to recognize it, and move on. There is nothing you can do about it.

From this, however, can be learned one of the most fundamental rules of screenwriting – learn when to let go. Not everything you do is going to work. Your job as a writer is to inspire the teams of other creatives that are involved in the filmmaking process and not every idea, every time is going to work. There is nothing you can do about this. Learn when (and how) to let go.

Hint *Grant me the strength to change what I can, to accept the things I cannot and the wisdom to know the difference.*   St Francis of Assisi

---

The role of violence and sex

What writers can control

The actors' actions: through description in the screenplay.

Dialogue: through the script.

Setting: where a story is told.

The story, the story, the story.

But, once the screenplay has left your hands, everything can be changed.

What writers can't control

Casting and performance.

Editing.

The vision of the director.

Cinematography and ability of the cameraman/woman.

Production Design, Set, Wardrobe and Special FX: artistry of the craft people.

Score and suitability of music.

Marketing, poster, and trailer: the skill of the market makers and publicists.

The success of the film: Hey! Who does? It is a crapshoot.

Successful writers write to inspire everybody else, and know when to let go.

Every scene, every line, every word in your script should be brimming with violence. In terms of violence, think of the following words – taunt, tense, violent emotion, contradiction, conflict – in each and every scene, every line of your script.

There are three types of violence:

Physical violence – the arming of our fellow citizens, the escalation of global conflicts leave me cold. I hate it, even though it is a part of every-day life and likely to remain that way.

Sociological violence – the violence caused by the loss of one's place in society, at work, at home. This violence fascinates me, partly because I am a voyeur, and partly because I love to study the structures that cause such moves, both failure and success.

Psychological violence – which terrifies me. Being put in a position where all my values and beliefs are challenged to the point where I am unable to function is my personal nightmare.

How one treats violence is important. The cinema is rooted in theatre Let us look at the history of cinema to see how they used violence. Take the ancient story of *Oedipus Rex*. How would you describe this story to someone? Write down how would you pitch this story to a development executive in ancient Greece.

What did you come up with? A story about revenge? About jealousy? About destiny? Did you mention the violence? Most pitches don't mention the violence in a specific way.

If I were pitching *Oedipus Rex* to an artsy film company, it would be like this – A young man, heir to the throne of Greece, discovers that he has travelled both ways through his mother's birth canal, and is so distraught that he pierces his eyes. The violence here is both physical and psychological.

Hint If you are unsure how this story goes, look it up. The Greek classics are wonderful stories that can provide inspiration for your story.

Screenwriters are artists and do have a responsibility for the work they create. To create a screenplay that glamorizes and condones gratuitous violence or sex is irresponsible.

The recent court case of Oliver Stone being sued successfully by the families of victims killed by copycat killings from *Natural Born Killers* is a good example.

How about *Medea*? Another extremely violent story where the Queen of Greece discovers she is being two-timed by her husband. She butchers their children, cooks them and serves them to her husband for dinner. Can you imagine pitching this story to PBS? The violence here is mainly physical with psychological violence at the very end.

Those are ancient stories. Let's move up to Shakespeare, considered one of the greats, and *Hamlet*. Again, this is a story with epic themes of destiny, revenge, and guilt. At the end of the story, the stage is littered with the bodies of the dead and dying. Even children's stories are extremely violent. Consider *Bambi*. Poor Bambi, the cute little deer sees her mother blown away by evil hunters!

Hint Screenwriters merit attention of the audience through skillful use of violence and sex.

In conclusion, never forget what we expect when we go to the cinema. The most we expect is that our lives are changed forever. The least we expect is that we don't fall sound asleep. Anywhere in the middle is fine!

Finally, everything in the film industry that I have observed comes down to one thing – a script that can attract a reader will find an audience. To attract, a script must be great, not good.

Summary

1. Nobody knows anything – remember that this book is designed to give you a practical plan, a method, to getting your idea onto paper.

2. The quickest way into the film industry is with a script – a hot script.

3. Never forget the writer's role – to inspire everyone else, then let go.

4. You are an intuitive storyteller. Let nothing inhibit you.

Now, let's start getting that idea out of your head and onto paper.

2   Getting Your Idea on to Paper

For most writers this is the moment you have been dreading. If you're like me you probably remember announcing the fact that you want to write a screenplay to your family and friends. Did you make that specific announcement at some point during the last eighteen months? Do you remember the warm glow of well-wishers patting you on the back saying 'Naturally you could write a screenplay – a great screenplay. I can hardly wait until I can read it.' They know you have talent. You have spent the next eighteen months doing nothing about your screenplay. It's just stuck in your head eating your waking moments, and fear upon fear, suppose you meet one of those well-wishers at a party or on the street? The first thing they say is 'How is your screenplay going?' And you have to lie and say it's going really well, even thought it's not.

Take the plunge.

Hint *A barn full of hay is going to be emptied fork by fork. And one forkful has to be first.*   Old Amish saying

---

Getting Started – the Basic Premise

Many new writers I meet at the Raindance Writers Lab and through the teaching I do are ready to give up completely on writing. The reason they feel unable to continue is because their stories have become wandering and confused, which in turn has made them feel confused and unfocused. They feel this way because they did not start with the plan.

Writing a screenplay is a complex job, and a successful screenplay has hundreds of different elements in it. Simply typing FADE IN: at the top of page one and hoping that ninety to a hundred and twenty pages later, you can type FADE OUT, with a marketable script, is unrealistic.

In order to write a screenplay, you need to build a plan, a blueprint. The blueprint has to consider the elements of a screenplay – characterization, plot, action, dialogue and setting. Then, you have to plan how to incorporate these elements in a bold, fresh and original way, in order to enhance the commerciality of your screenplay. Consider this as the business plan for your story – the who, what, where, why and when.

Another way to look at the plan is as the method to writing a screenplay. A process that allows you to combine your creative energy with proven formulas.

Successful screenwriters also understand what the market is looking for, and learn what sorts of stories the people who buy screenplays are looking for. There are two ways of looking at this – developing the savvy to market your script or developing the savvy to hone your literary skills.

New writers hate the planning part of writing because they want to get straight into the fun bits of writing the first two words of a screenplay FADE IN:, their first slug line INT: WRITERS GARRET - DAY, a line or two about the setting and then the dialogue.

Hint If you start writing your script without a plan, it will certainly fail.

In general, the more you plan, the better your script will be. I will show you later in Chapter 15 how to capture those impetuous and exciting creative moments and incorporate them into your script.

A page of screenplay, properly typed, creates approximately one minute of screen time. Thus a ninety-page script would end up as a movie around ninety minutes long.

To write without a plan is a bit like this – have you ever agreed to meet a friend or two after work, say at 6:15 and maybe go and do something? Your office might be in an exciting and trendy part of town, close to bars, restaurants, nightclubs and cinemas. The theory of meeting after work is that surely in the centre of a playground like this, a few adults can have some fun. Everyone is excited about the prospect of a night out and the hours at work fly by.

Then you meet. The reality, however, is far different from what you had dreamt about. First of all, one of your friends is a few minutes late. You have just missed the movie! You all agree that it is a little early to go for dinner – another reasonable option – so instead you pop into the local bar for a quick drink. A few good jokes sidetrack you. Suddenly you realize that you have missed the theatre as well, and the next showing of that darling film you all wanted to see. Never mind, you decide to go out for dinner. But what kind of cuisine? Chinese, Japanese, Taiwanese, Cantonese, Vietnamese? How about Latin, Mexican, Tex-Mex? Maybe it should be German, or Italian or French. Or ethnic? How about some good Jewish or… Before you know it all of the really good restaurants are booked out for the night, and you have to settle for a milkshake at Macdonald's and a bus ride home. If this has happened to you, can you remember the feeling of defeat that awaited you when you got home?

This is exactly the same feeling you will have if you attempt to write a screenplay without planning, but with one difference. On the failed night out, your friends will share the blame with you. With screenwriting, you have no one to blame but yourself. And your friends will blame you. Which will lead to a deep-seated lack of confidence. Which will cause you to stop writing.

Three reasons you won't write your screenplay

1. Lack of confidence

2. Self-destruction

3. Procrastination

Of all the writers I met who have now given up, lack of planning is the primary reason that they have stopped writing. Don't let it happen to you, and allow me to show you in the next few pages how simple it is to formulate a really good plan. The more work and care you put into planning your movie, the better it will be.

If you decorate a room without filling and sanding all the little holes, your paint job isn't going to look too good. In decorating, like screenwriting, preparation is everything.

Hint Be prepared to bend and rebend your ideas in the planning stage. Prepare to be confused. It is so much easier than trying to do it in the finished draft.

Creating a Workable Blueprint for Your Movie

1. The premise

One of the first tasks in writing a script is to distil your idea and discover what is at the core of your story.

Write the idea that you have for your story in a few simple lines. This will be one of the most difficult tasks in the entire process and it is important that you take the time to understand this task fully. You should aim to have a paragraph roughly three to four lines long that works like this:

This is a story about [describe your hero] who [what she wants more than anything else does] but [name the overwhelming obstacles preventing the realization of your goal] and [tease us with the ending].

You will hear a saying in the film business – 'Tell me your movie in twenty-five words or less.' What they want is the three to four lines above.

Hint Don't name the hero, describe the hero. Unemployed banker, lonely housewife or young football player is better than Mary or Bill.

Hint Make the paragraph a tease, you are writing an ad for your movie.

Hint Phrases such as 'situations dictate' or 'only to discover' are useful in shaping your paragraph, but are hackneyed and should be avoided if possible in the final draft.

As a screenwriter, the twenty-five words are essential. It is the road map that you will tack on the wall where you write, to remind yourself every step of the way what your story is about.

Without the plan, you will meander all over town in a fruitless and ultimately frustrating exercise that may force you away from writing forever.

2. Twenty-five words or less

The historical root of the twenty-five words or less phrase is the TV guide in America that only accepts twenty-five words per movie. The theory is that with so many movies and so many TV channels, the publishers only have room for twenty-five words or so to describe the movie. Filmmakers and financiers soon realized that if the movie could not be described in this short space, the program would not be advertised in the TV guide, no one would watch it, the ratings would plummet thereby reducing the value of commercials sold on the show or movie.

The twenty-five words or less, or initial premise line, is the one or two sentences that describes your story. Write yours here:

Some examples:

John, twenty-five and a balding banker, realizes that his boring, well-paid job in the financial district keeps him from finding a better life and getting Mary, the girl of his dreams.

The goal of finding a better life is too vague and too general. We all want a better life. Wouldn't this be better as:

Banker realizes that to win the girl he loves, he must love his job less.

Now this is getting more specific, if a little lame. At least you can see a moment where the hero wins, or loses, his dream. But what about the girl. Perhaps there is more to this. What about:

Young banker realizes he loves a girl more than his job, only to discover that the girl loves his job more than him. And tomorrow is payday.

Now we have a bit of friction. This girl sounds like she might be up to something. It's still pretty lame, but notice how the story shifts balance every time you rewrite the sentence.

Hint It is easy to describe mood atmosphere and setting without actually telling us the story. Make sure you tell the story.

---

3. High concept vs. low concept

The film industry likes stories that can easily be summed up in fewer than twenty-five words. *Panic in Needle Park* was summed up as '*Romeo and Juliet* on Junk'. *The Green Mile* was summed up as '*Forrest Gump* on death row'. *Aliens* as '*Jaws* in space'.

A movie that can be summed up like this is called a high concept movie. Name three other movies that can be summed up in just a few words:

```


```

There are other movies that are more difficult to sum up so readily. These are called low concept films, and usually deal with relationships between the characters in the story. These movies are usually adaptations of novels or short stories. For example, *Thin Blue Line*, *High Fidelity* or *The Shawshank Redemption*.

4. Hero's basic action

The basic action is the main thing that your hero will try to achieve over the movie/story. Your hero might do many different things in the movie, but try to find the one basic action that happens in the middle of the story, or which occurs most.

By focusing on this basic action, you will also be able to see clearly the essential struggle that may ultimately change your hero.

For example, in *Thelma and Louise*, the basic action is that they go on a car journey. And the struggle was the decisions and misfortunes that befell them on their journey.

What is the hero's basic action in your story?

```


```

5. Details of the basic action

By describing the basic action in more detail, you will find additional clues about the forces causing or forcing your hero to change. Look for both good forces and bad forces, positive and negative. Write them down here:

Negative
```

```

Positive
```

```

You will probably come up with words like jealous, indecisive and disloyal under negative qualities, and brave and honest, for positive qualities. Remember that the stronger the qualities, whether negative or positive, the stronger your hero.

6. Psychological and moral weaknesses

A good story shows a character at the beginning with a variety of moral and psychological handicaps.

Hint: The larger the weakness, the stronger the conflict.

List the weaknesses that your hero has at the start of the story:

What are the psychological – strictly personal – flaws that keep your hero from achieving their goal/goals? For example, indecision or fear. Write them here:

What are the moral flaws – having to do with acting properly toward others – that keep your hero from achieving their goal/goals? For example, irresponsibility, insensitivity, recklessnes or greed. Write them here:

figure 2.1
Exercise in Magnification Techniques

Hollywood frequently uses a technique called magnification to add conflict to the story. What are the qualities that are distorted, or magnified for effect in the following films?

Good Will Hunting	
Edward Scissorhands	
The Godfather	
Being John Malkovich	
Copland	

7. Struggle

Look at the basic action and the psychological and moral weaknesses of the hero and answer these questions:

What struggle does your hero have to surmount in order to accomplish the basic action?

```

```

Worst nightmare – what is the one thing that your hero fears most?

```

```

What is the worst thing that your hero could face?

```

```

8. Ghost

All good stories have a ghost. Ghost represents that from the past that the hero fears. Each genre treats ghost in a different way. In horror, of course, the ghost takes a physical embodiment. How often have you seen this movie – the hero pacing in front of a white picket fence. It is night. On the hill is a darkened, haunted house. What does the writer do to our poor hero? Make them go up the hill, to the house, and live in their own worst nightmare.

In detective stories, the ghost is referred to as the personal crime. The detective, hired to solve the murder, is also responsible for a murder, before the story started. An excellent example is the Michael Douglas character in *Basic Instinct*, nicknamed 'Shooter' for his accidental killing of a German tourist.

Name or describe your ghost:

```

```

9. Hero's potential

How can your hero think, or chose, act well, or accomplish at a level higher than at the start of the story?

At the start of your story, your hero has the potential to rise, but has not yet fulfilled this potential for various reasons.

He or she may be unable to rise because of physical flaws, sociological flaws or psychological flaws. They may be overcome by fear of their worst nightmare.

Defining your hero's potential will allow you to take your hero to higher highs and lower lows through the story.

```
┌─────────────────────────────────────────────────────────┐
│                                                           │
└─────────────────────────────────────────────────────────┘
```

10. Final twenty-five words or less

Revise and restate your initial premise if necessary, in the clearest way possible. Your premise may not change, or it may change dramatically. In either case, you are finding and honing your story.

```
┌─────────────────────────────────────────────────────────┐
│                                                           │
│                                                           │
│                                                           │
│                                                           │
└─────────────────────────────────────────────────────────┘
```

The movie quiz

Playing this quiz may give you a clue to the type of story you are telling. The following films are grouped because they share a common characteristic. Can you determine why they are grouped on the right side or the left side?

High Fidelity	*Reservoir Dogs*
Pulp Fiction	*Terminator*
A River Runs Through It	*Being John Malkovich*
The Beach	*There's Something about Mary*
Erin Brokovich	*The Sixth Sense*
Fight Club	*The Blair Witch Project*
The Shawshank Redemption	*Castaway*

The left-hand films are adaptations from novels or true-life stories. The right-hand column is for films made from original screenplays. Right hand movies tend to be hero driven stories where the goal of the hero and whether or not he/she attains the goal is the basis of the story. In left-hand movies, the story is much more about the relationships between the various characters, and the goal of the hero becomes less important to the story.

I call right-hand movies stories in the masculine mode, and left-hand, stories in the feminine mode. Until recently, most Hollywood movies are right-hand stories, although the Oscars give two awards – one for best original screenplay, another for the best adaptation.

Since the mid-nineties, literary agents have been scouring central and eastern Europe for novellas and novels published in the early 1900s that were commercially successful, even if the work was only published in Serb in Yugoslavia. The screenplay rights were purchased by these agents for a few dollars, and then resold to Hollywood. The theory is that if the story was commercially successful, even as a book eighty years ago, then it is more likely to be commercially successful as a movie today!

Jo Blackford

Data Co-ordinator

Elsevier

FREEPOST - SCE5435

Oxford

Oxon

OX2 8BR

As well as conforming to data protection legislation in the way we store your details, Elsevier does n
sell or exchange the email/mail addresses of our subscribers to any other company outside the Reed
Elsevier group.

Return this card today and enter £100 book draw

Select the subjects you'd like to receive information about, enter
your email and mail address and freepost it back to us.

TECHNOLOGY

☐ **Architecture and Design:**
History of architecture ○
Landscape ○
Urban design ○
Sustainable architecture ○
Planning and design ○

☐ **Building and Construction**

☐ **Computing: Professional:**
Communications ○
Data Management ○
Enterprise Computing ○
IT Management ○
Operating Systems ○

☐ **Computing: Beginner:**
Computing ○
Programming ○

☐ **Conservation and
Museology**

☐ **Engineering:**
Aeronautical Engineering ○
Automotive Engineering ○
Chemical Engineering ○

Health & Safety ○
Environmental
Engineering ○
Plant / Maintenance /
Manufacturing ○
Marine Engineering ○
Materials Science &
Engineering ○
Mechanical Engineering ○
Petroleum Engineering ○
Quality ○

☐ **Electronics and Electrical
Engineering:**
Electrical Engineering ○
Electronic Engineering ○
Radio, Audio and TV
Technology ○
Computer Technology ○

☐ **Film, Television, Video &
Audio:**
Audio/Radio ○
Post Production ○
Lighting ○
Theatre Performance ○
Photography/Imaging ○
Radio ○

TV ○
Film/TV/Video
Production ○
Journalism ○
Multimedia ○
Computer Graphics/
Animation ○
Broadcast Management &
Theory ○
Broadcast & Communications
Technology ○

☐ **Security**

MANAGEMENT
☐ Finance and Accounting
☐ Hospitality, Leisure and
Tourism
☐ HR and Training
☐ Pergamon Flexible
Learning
☐ Knowledge Management
☐ Management
☐ Marketing
☐ IT Management

Name:

Email address:

Mail address:

Postcode   Date

Please keep me up to date by ☐ email ☐ post ☐ both

Science & Technology Books, Elsevier Ltd., Registered Office: The Boulevard, Langford Lane, Kidlington, Oxon OX5 1GB. Registered number: 1982084

11. Testing the concept

Why wait until your movie is written, shot, edited and marketed to find out if it is going to be a blockbuster. Try out your twenty-five words on everyone you know now. Every time you meet someone, stranger or acquaintance, you must let him or her know what you are doing. You are trying to get them to ask you 'Can I know more?' You can then tell them your twenty-five words. As you are speaking to them, observe their reactions. It's a good idea to jot them down. If it is a comedy – did they laugh, and if so, how spontaneous was the laughter? If it was a horror story, did your twenty-five words gross them out? Or, did their eyes glaze over with boredom. No matter what the reaction, ask them 'What do you think about that?' or 'Would you like to see a movie like that?' or 'Any way I could make this better?'

You are essentially creating your very own market research campaign coupled with some advance PR about the movie and about yourself. The big advantage is that you can instantly rectify any story flaws, and make certain that you are working on a marketable screenplay. If you share your life with someone, this is a great time to incorporate their suggestions and ideas into your twenty-five words. They will probably welcome the chance to be involved in your project – but be careful that they realize that you are not going to be sharing the script credit!

Everything in the film industry that I have observed comes down to one thing – a script that can attract a reader will find an audience. To attract, a script must be great, not good.

Three Reasons You Won't Write Your Screenplay

1. Lack of confidence

How many times have you moved up to your computer, full of inspiration for your screenplay, turned it on and been faced with a giant blank? This is lack of confidence in your idea. Some people call it writer's block, but it actually is just lack of confidence. Never give in to these feelings – you'll stop writing. You are entering uncharted territory, and writing this script will be challenging, and exciting. Enjoy!

Hint Go back to your basic premise, and work and rework it until you are absolutely satisfied that this idea will work for you.

---

2. Self-destruction

The human race is unique on the animal planet in that each individual homo sapiens has developed a unique and special way to self-destruct. I know you have yours, and I have mine. Let's not go there now!

3. Procrastination

Procrastination is my personal favorite. Ask my editor, Jenny Welham. We had an initial meeting for this book at the idea stage. What an inspiring meeting. I then had to produce an outline and a sample chapter. That wasn't too hard, and I delivered it only a few weeks after the agreed deadline. But then the task of writing the actual book. I vowed I would write every day for an hour, until I had broken the back of the book. Each night, I would turn on the computer and stare at the page. After a few nights, I realized that by 'writing' my book, I now had the cleanest apartment in London – all the odd jobs at home, like repairing blown light bulbs, had been done, and there were no longer any dust bunnies under the bed. I will do anything to avoid writing!

Hint Discipline. A little bit every day is better than nothing. Or do like Hemingway, and leave each day with an unfinished sentence on the page. Those few words will pull you right back to where you left off, and make it easier to keep writing.

Summary

1. Making a plan/premise is your first task and it is the most challenging.

2. Test market your premise on everyone that you can.

3. Revise if necessary. Your next task is to create a structure.

Let's put it all together and become a really good yarn-spinner – we are now ready for tale assembly.

3 Tale Assembly

Tale assembly or story structure is the way that your story unfolds. In this chapter, I will describe the various story structure theories currently on offer from the script doctors and gurus such as Syd Field, Michael Hague, Linda Seger, Robert McKee and so on. I will then attempt to explain story structure in a unique way, and in the next chapter, I will tell you to set everything in this chapter aside and explain structure from the point of view of character and character development.

Story is to film what melody is to music. There is a well-known story of Amadeus Mozart as a teenager that explains this concept best. As a child prodigy, Mozart earned a very respectable income travelling from court to court playing music. One morning, after a particularly late night, Amadeus' mother failed time and time again to rouse him. Imagine her cajoling him with lines like 'If you don't get up now, you won't have time to get your wig on before the coach comes.'

I suppose Amadeus was no different than any of us as teens with our parents threatening us with disinheritance if we were late one more time for school.

In desperation, or so we are told, Mozart's mother went to the piano at the bottom of the stairs leading to Mozart's room and played 'doh-ray-me-fa-so-la-ti…'. Mozart leapt out of bed, raced down the stairs and finished the thought with a resounding 'doh!'

Story is to film what melody is to music, and scene is to story what note/phrase is to melody.

The job of a screenwriter is to create tension and release it. Create new tension and release it. Over and over again until the end of the film.

Story Structure Paradigms – Three-Act Story Structure

There probably isn't a screenwriting book written that does not use the term 'Three-Act Story Structure'. Although I thoroughly disapprove of this term, and the use of this paradigm, I do believe that three-act structure, despite its limiting use, to be useful for novice screenwriters.

The use of three-act structure goes back to classic Greek philosophy with the teachings of Aristotle. He made a revolutionary discovery that all stories, regardless of length, had three distinct parts – the Beginning, the Middle and the End. Furthermore he defined the three elements as follows:

The Ending – that part after which there is nothing. The Beginning – that part before which there is nothing. Therefore, the Middle is the part in between. This seems passé by twenty-first century terms, but was treated as a fabulous discovery by the Greeks of the day.

A few millennia passed, and then in 1974 the American script assessor and author Syd Field published a book called *Screenplay* in which the three-act structure was expanded in detail.

figure 3.1
Syd Field's Three-Act Structure

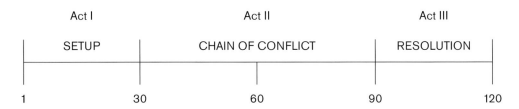

Act I	Act II	Act III
SETUP	CHAIN OF CONFLICT	RESOLUTION

| 1 | 30 | 60 | 90 | 120 |

Three-act structure

Get your hero up a tree, throw stones at him/her, get your hero down.

This too, seems very simplistic in the twenty-first century, but at the time was considered groundbreaking work. All major film and television companies made Field's book, and his subsequent ones, required reading for their script doctors, writers, executives and script development personnel. Again, these books are useful for novice screenwriters.

There are two basic flaws in three-act structure. Firstly, three-act structure is based on theatre, where the curtain falls after each act. There is no curtain in cinema – cinema flows. Secondly, the plot points at pages 30, 60, 90 and 120 are too few and too specific for modern storytelling.

The irony is that when Syd Field was at Raindance in 1995 he told me that his three-act paradigm was outdated, that it was his publisher who kept proposing book ideas based on his now outdated paradigm. Field told me that he preferred a much more fluid, more advanced story structure paradigm, and in that year was studying Mexican cinema which made the most of advanced story structure paradigms.

Nonetheless, three-act structure has merit. Let us take a look at three-act structure. I will analyze each section, or act, tell you what you need to achieve in each section, and then teach you some tools that you can use in order to execute your plans more efficiently.

Beginning

The beginning of your screenplay is the most important. Agents and producers say that they will read the first ten pages. If you don't get them hooked then they will say the dreaded word 'Pass.' Fortunately there are many tools you can use in the beginning of a screenplay that will distinguish your script.

The tasks of beginning

1. Introduce the hero

Tools originate in the mind and become a physical reality to assist with our daily work. Tools described in this book are designed in the mind, and assist in the work of writing of your screenplay.

By hero, I mean the person through whose eyes the movie is told. This character is always introduced early in commercially successful films.

Heroes are introduced in one of three ways:

Running start – where the hero is already in pursuit, or being pursued. Most action adventure films start this way.

Family or community start – where we see the hero with his/her family, flatmates, co-workers and so on. Everything seems right and normal with the hero, but we know that something dreadful is going to happen. The opening scene of *Jaws* is a good example of this.

Slow burn – do not contemplate this method. The less said the better.

2. Tell us the time and the pace of the movie

There is a big difference between the opening of a James Bond film and a Merchant Ivory film. There is no science here, but your reader will know from looking at the first page what sort of pace the movie is. How many scenes on the front page? Are there three or four scenes (fast paced) or is the first page part of a three-page opening scene (soft romance or drama)?

3. Tell us what the movie is really about

I'm talking about the theme of the film. Theme is not the story. Story goes before theme. But theme is the glue that binds the story together and is what your movie is really about. Theme is not story. Anti-pollution is not a theme. But the greed of the factory owner crippled by the love of the money he/she can save by ignoring the cost of cleaning the water before it enters the river is theme, such as *Erin Brockovich*.

Writing theme is one of the most troubling tasks writers face. My advice is don't write it at all – ignore it. Finish the first draft of your screenplay and look at it. Maybe something will pop out, and give you an idea. In order to enhance the idea, perhaps you will think of a line of dialogue or an action that will click the idea into place.

Hint Draw a movie poster of what your movie is about. Don't worry if you can't draw or that your people look like stick men. Often what your movie is really about, the theme, will become obvious through this drawing. Next draw a tableau, a frozen image that encapsulates the theme of your movie.

A common error of new screenwriters is in learning where to start the movie.

For example, in the hands of an inexperienced screen writer, *Gone With The Wind* might start with the birth and early education of Scarlet O'Hara, her passage into adulthood, her first love, her second and so on, until about forty-five minutes into the film we would join up with the original.

It is nearly impossible to teach how to write theme. Perhaps the best advice comes from zenist advice for an archer – you cannot hit a target by aiming at it. You can only hit when you feel it (and for screenwriters) in your heart. If you decide what the theme is too early in the writing process, you will inhibit yourself. For example, you may decide to write a tragic melodramatic piece, which is really a dark comedy trying to get out. If you start with the theme, you may limit your creative process and restrict it to the tragic theme.

Hint A clue to theme, whether in action or dialogue, always appears on page three of commercially successful films. See if you can find the line of dialogue that pertains to theme from the following extract from page three of *Chinatown* (Robert Towne) below.

```
INT. GITTES' OFFICE - GITTES & CURLY

Gittes and Curly stand in front of the desk, Gittes
staring contemptuously at the heavy breathing hulk
towering over him. Gittes takes a handkerchief and
wipes away the plunk of perspiration on his desk.

                    CURLY
                  (crying)
        They don't kill a guy for that.

                    GITTES
        Oh, they don't?

                    CURLY
        Not for your wife. That's the
        unwritten law.

Gittes pounds the photos on the desk, shouting:

                    GITTES
        I'll tell you the unwritten law,
        you dumb son of a bitch, you
        gotta be rich to kill somebody,
        anybody and get away with it.
        You think you got that kind
        of dough, you think you got
        that kind of class?
```

Doesn't this speech really describe what *Chinatown* is all about?

Tools of the beginning

1. Choosing the world of the hero

Creating the world of the hero is one of your first tasks and also one of the most important. Where you site your story will determine to a large extent what type of story you are telling. It will also determine what sort of hero your story has. The four worlds are:

Firstly, the Wilderness – the hero in a story set in the wilderness is the superhero. Most religious stories are set in the wilderness. In stories set in the wilderness, the hero is either travelling alone, or with a band of disciples. Wilderness and the forces of nature surround the hero. The hero is subjected to attack from roving bands of barbarians.

At the climax of these stories, and the element that makes writing them today so difficult, the hero receives a divine revelation that will change forever the way that humans live and think. *The Ten Commandments* is such a story. Of course, today when filmmakers attempt such a story, at the moment the hero receives the divine inspiration, and we lean forward to gain that pearl of wisdom that will change our lives forever. The screen goes a bright white, and the music hits the really high notes, and when the images return, we are none the wiser.

Secondly, the Village – stories set in the village are unique. Village life, once predominant, has declined during the twentieth century and the traditional village life will certainly be extinct this century. This gives stories set in the village a certain sort of nostalgia.

The village is surrounded by wilderness. It is better prepared to withstand the forces of nature, but is still at risk to famine and disease. The village is under constant threat from roving bands of barbarians. The village buildings are all roughly the same height, and it is possible to stand at the edge of a village, look down the high street, and see the last buildings on the other side of the village.

Not only are all the buildings of the same height, but the citizens are roughly the same stature in society – the parson, the innkeeper, the sheriff, and the town's folks are all roughly the same class. Some village stories will have one person who commands the respect of the others, but this person can be contradicted by the other villagers without fear. Most American westerns are set in the village.

The hero in the village story is the classic hero. The classic hero has several distinct traits. Despite the teaching of the screenwriting books in the past that the hero must develop and change, or that your hero must go from A to B, in village stories the hero does not change. The classic hero is usually an outsider who arrives in the village, and is either mistaken as a barbarian, or is hired by the villagers to save them from the barbarians. At the end of a story set in the village, the hero leaves, unchanged by what he/she has seen or done. He rides off into the sunset is a typical ending for a village story.

What has changed over the course of a story in the village are the villagers – they are either better off as a result of the actions of the hero (*Seven Samurai*) or they are exposed for their corruption and evil (*Red Rock West*). The hero in these stories usually reverts to force or martial arts to solve the problems with the opponent. It is hard to imagine John Wayne negotiating with a baddie in a western movie – he usually out-duels or out-muscles the opponent.

Thirdly, the City – in the city there is no wilderness and no barbarians. The buildings have changed from the village. Large skyscrapers, tunnels, bridges and vast buildings take up their place in the city alongside the homes of the city-dwellers.

The people in the city differ from the villagers in an important way. Whereas the villagers are approximately the same in power and strength, city-dwellers are divided by strength and power – the rich and the poor, the strong and the weak, the haves and the have-nots.

The hero is the average hero and when we first meet them they are usually involved with their families, or are at work. We know that something will go wrong soon, even though the hero looks pretty secure. The hero witnesses an injustice, and the story in the city is how the hero tries to bring justice.

Fourthly, the Oppressive City – in the oppressive city, the rules for living have gone haywire. Although there are basic rules in the village, and there are more detailed rules in the city (like parking restrictions), in the oppressive city, the rules have totally taken over. Whereas there are maybe no-smoking zones in the city, in the oppressive city you can be shot dead if caught smoking. The hero is the anti-hero – someone that doesn't fit easily into this society. The anti-hero is often pursued by an oppressor trying to make the hero conform, or is trying to escape from the oppressive city. *Blade Runner* is a good example.

So, what is the setting of *Alien*?

Wilderness, because it is set in space? No.

The Village, because it is set in a vessel? No.

The City – obviously not.

The answer is the Oppressive City, because of the rules imposed on the inhabitants.

2. Who's the hero and what do they want?

Most screenplays fail because the hero does not have clearly defined wants and needs (goal and inner problem). You must make it crystal clear to the reader what the hero wants within the first ten pages of your screenplay, or you will loose the reader and the sale. Ninety-five percent of the screenplays I read during my time as a scriptreader failed because they did not have a hero with clearly defined wants and needs.

3. Create empathy for your characters

The audience (reader) must feel for each and every character in your script. Only then will a reader identify with your story. The reader does not need to like your characters, but has to identify with them.

Tools for creating empathy:

Firstly, put your hero in a predicament.

Nothing draws an audience into your story, and creates empathy for a character, than putting them in a predicament. The audience immediately connects with the character, and done properly, the audience will fidget and squirm with your characters.

Consider the opening of *Rainman*. Tom Cruise is a complete jerk. But we care about what happens to him. He is sitting in a car, he is stuck in traffic, his cell phone brings him news that his business is about to go bankrupt, and his girlfriend is arguing with him. Who hasn't suffered at least one of these calamities?

Secondly, show your hero learning something.

Audiences love to be taught something. How many times have you seen this scene: the assassin in the tiny room overlooking the square. His target, the President, is about to arrive. What does the assassin do? He/she assembles the weapon. We think to ourselves 'So that's how they do it!' – useful information should we ever need to assassinate someone!

Anything that you can do to show your audience something, either by demonstration (as above) or through your characters trying to learn, will create immediate empathy in your audience for that character. It also involves the audience in your story by making it personal to them.

4. Timelock

Timelock is described as 'an event that must occur within a specific prescribed time', or else dire consequences will befall the hero. The ticking bomb is a common example.

When a timelock is used, energy is compressed into a short time space and the drama increases significantly. It also is a device that the audience can relate too through personal experience

Bridge on the River Kwai has an interesting double timelock. The first three-quarters of the movie are – build the bridge, build the bridge and build the bridge. The last quarter of the movie is – blow it up, blow it up and blow it up.

Hint Successful writers not only use these tools, but do so in a fresh, bold, original and dynamic way. Always try to twist the tool.

---

5. The switch

Just when you think something is going to happen, something else does. A switch can be used throughout your script, can be used in small scenes, or in the large plot spine of your story. A switch keeps the audience guessing. A skillfully constructed switch should not show. The switch is used frequently in advertising, usually for humour, and is very satisfying to watch.

This is a script for a one-minute advertisement for the Raindance Film Festival created by the writer/director Jarl Olsen:

```
INT. WOOD SHOP - DAY

SFX. WHIRRR!

A spinning circular saw blade hums to life.

A bleary-eyed WORKER blinks.

Workers POV. A radial arm saw goes in and out of
focus as it cuts through a two-by-four.

                    VO ANNCR
          Now you can stay up for fourteen days
          and nights watching independent films.

The worker yawns. He begins to nod out while still
operating the saw. (THIS DOESN'T LOOK GOOD).

SFX BZZZZZZZZZ!

                    VO ANNCR
          Feature films... (Bzzz) ...Short
          Films (BZZZ)... Documentary films.
          (BZZZ!) New work from the most
          promising talent in Great Britain,
          America and the world. Films no
          lover of the art form can miss...

BZZZ... KLAK-A-KLAK!

The worker looks down - has he cut off his finger?
He yawns, instinctively covering his mouth with his
prosthetic hook. He goes back to sawing wood.

RAINDANCE LOGO UP.

                    VO ANNCR
          Raindance Film Festival.
          You can sleep when it's over.

(SFX:SAW OUT) BZZZ-KLAK! BZZZ-KLAK! BZZ...
```

Notice how few words are used for this screenplay. Were you able to visualize this scene? Could you hear the hum of the saw?

6. Stacking and layering

One problem befalls your hero, then another, and another. Stacking.

Sometimes a writer will have a series of problems, which they scatter throughout the screenplay. Gathering several of these problems together and throwing them at your hero one after the other 'stacks' the problems and gives your hero a greater challenge.

Layering the story in different levels is another way to involve your audience. Different people pick out layers at different times, and when they do, they feel special and unique, and smile to themselves 'wonder if anyone else got that?' How many figured out the ghost layer in *The Sixth Sense* before the ending? If you hadn't, the ending had a powerful resonance due to the 'Bruce Willis is already dead' layer.

Hint Stacking and layering are immensely appealing to an audience.

---

7. Backstory

Tools are an important detail in any story, and not just because they indicate the general time period of the story. Tools represent the ways particular people magnify their power. Which tools the characters use and how the characters use them can have great implications for the story.

Sometimes called the exposition, the backstory is where you provide the reader with the necessary information to explain to them what happened before the movie started. This information will generally assist in explaining to the audience why your hero wants his/her goal so much – the motivation.

A common mistake of new writers is knowing where the true beginning of the story is. In *Castaway*, for example, a new writer might start with the birth of Tom Hanks followed by his school years, first love and then first job, second job and so on until he gets the job with a courier company. By the time we would get to the beginning of *Castaway*, we would probably be on page forty-five.

Hint Backstory is what happened before the movie started and provides information necessary to explain the hero's motivation.

Back story can be done through a montage as in the opening of *Tootsie*; through dialogue, as in the opening of *As Good As It Gets*; or as a visual element as in the opening of *Silence of the Lambs*.

Try to find a new, bold, fresh and imaginative way to state back story.

If you were writing a gangster movie, and had to have a scene where the older, senior members of the mob have to explain to the young Turk the ropes and the ins and outs – what would you write?

The cliché is the restaurant scene with everyone sitting around chewing on Havanas.

But if you simply changed the setting to, say, the sauna, you would be able to compare the bodies of the old and the young as well as comparing their social power as they sit sweating.

8. The plan

We need to see the basic plan of the hero at the beginning of the film. Not at the very beginning, but certainly within the first ten minutes. Your main character will start with a goal, and then put together a plan to accomplish the goal. During the beginning of the film, the hero will assemble the elements necessary to achieve his or her goal. At the moment the hero tries the plan for the first time, it will fail. At this point you are in the middle of the film.

9. Ghost

It is no longer good enough to write a good single genre film. Hollywood does not buy single genre films. Hollywood buys double genre films, for example romantic comedies. Hollywood really seeks double genre films that transcend the genre like *Sixth Sense*.

Ghost is that event from the past that the hero must overcome in order to achieve their goal. Each genre has a different approach to ghost. Horror has a ghost that is so strong that it physically appears. How many times have you seen this movie? A broken down house on the hill, and on the street below, our hero paces nervously back and forth – usually in front of a white picket fence. What does the author of horror do? Make the hero enter the house and live in their own worst nightmare.

In crime and detective stories, the detective is plagued by a personal crime that he or she committed before the movie started. In *Basic Instinct*, Michael Douglas' character mistakenly shot a German tourist. Since that moment, he has always been referred to as 'Shooter' – a nickname he despises.

A common mistake of new writers is that the ghost is overcome too quickly, or that confronting the ghost is not painful to the hero.

10. Nightmare

Ask yourself what is the worst possible thing that could happen to your hero, or what is the single most terrible event or situation that could befall your hero. This is not the same as ghost. Ghost is an actual event or person that your hero fears. The worst nightmare is something that has not happened yet.

Nightmare usually takes one of three forms – physical (as in losing health, or life); social (as in losing one's place in society); or physiological (as in being forced to abandon one's beliefs).

Hint Perhaps the worst nightmare is in fact your own worst nightmare. Have you taken the time to decide what your worst nightmare is? Can you go deeper and find an even worse nightmare that could befall you?

Agents and producers – the first industry people who will read your screenplay – say that they will judge your script on the first ten pages. If they like what they see, they will read the rest. If they don't, they will say the dreaded 'Next!' Creating a good beginning is ninety percent of the battle.

In actual fact, industry readers will rarely read as much as the first ten pages. They will read the first few pages. If you do not have the reader hooked, they will not persevere and read your entire screenplay. There are simply too many scripts in circulation by writers who do know how to hook readers.

The reason why writing an entertaining script is so difficult can be demonstrated by recent market research in the US, which shows how limited the attention span is of the typical US audience.

In America, a worker returns home and heads to the medicine cabinet or fridge to get his/her favorite form of relaxation. They plop down on the couch to surf the hundreds of channels available. The longest a viewer will stay on a channel where they do not have a destination (i.e. the Big Match) is fifteen seconds.

Compared to your script, fifteen seconds is a quarter page, about eight lines. So in the first eight lines, you need to write something that attracts the reader so much that they are willing to commit to a further eight lines. And again, at the bottom quarter you need to write something so amazing that the reader will lift their hand and turn the page!

Try to see if you can give this nightmare a twist and come up with a new nightmare that will integrate with your story to add depth and texture.

11. Foreshadowing

Little things made big. Often a small scene at the beginning of the film foretells the ending of the movie. Or sometimes, a tragedy is foretold moments before it happens. In *Raiders of the Lost Ark*, Satipo says 'But nobody has come out of there alive!' Minutes later, he is dead.

12. Mirroring

Mirroring is when sub-characters act out emotional responses that are too large for the hero to respond to, or cannot respond to. In a scene with a horror element, the hero cannot show fear without losing face. But a sub-character can. The hero's and audience's emotions are expressed through the minor character.

Mirroring can be expressed through physical actions or dialogue. Often a sub-character will mime or imitate the actions of the hero.

The Middle

In the beginning, everything seems right and fine with your hero. They have a goal, and we see them develop their plan. But the plan doesn't work. Not only does the hero have to develop a new plan, but they have to decide whether or not they still want their goal. The hero cannot develop a new goal at this point. If they do, you will be creating a story with a fragmented desire line and your story will fracture.

For example, have you told anyone that you have purchased this book on screenwriting? If you have, did you tell them it was because you wanted to hone your screenwriting skills? Have you told them that you have started reading it? Invariably they will ask how is it? And you respond with terms like interesting, helpful or challenging.

What would this person say if you said 'I found this screenwriting book good, but have decided to study figure skating instead'? Your friend would roll their eyes around and wonder at your commitment to a career. You have fractured the story line in your career.

Screenplays cannot do this either. When the hero's plan does not work, they need to devise a new plan, but keep the same goal.

It is in the middle of a screenplay that the story is played out, where the plot thickens, where the hero's plan is challenged, defeated, revised and challenged again. In the middle we get everything we don't expect. Writing the middle is also the most difficult part to achieve, especially if you have not worked out the entire story properly. If you know where your story is going, this job will be a lot easier.

Tools of the middle

1. Wrinkles and reversal, obstacles and misfortune

The plot thickens. By keeping the audience guessing what will happen next, you will create interest in your story.

Tarantino used this technique in *Pulp Fiction*, only in reverse. When you thought everything was fine, the John Travolta and Samuel Jackson characters would start reciting scripture and then kill someone. Later, they pull out their weapons and as they were about to kill someone, lose interest and walk away.

2. Predictability

I've got a secret

Any time that you withhold information from a character on the screen, or from the audience, you create added suspense and drama with the 'I've got a secret' ploy. You can withhold information from the audience, or from both characters, or from just one character. When the missing person receives the information, it is referred to as a 'reveal' and the drama is over until the next reveal.

When I read a script and criticize it as predictable, I really mean that the script is too predictable, for predictability is one of the most satisfying of dramatic tools. For example, in *Gremlins*, what does the Chinese shopkeeper say, but, don't get water on the little furry creatures. Of course, what happens?

If you have ever lived with a baby, you will remember that babies love to play peek-a-boo. What entertains a baby about peek-a-boo is not that they will make direct eye contact, they just don't know when.

Hint Which is more dramatic, A. You know that the hero is going to be killed by walking through the door, or B. You do not know that the hero is going to be killed by walking through the door? The correct answer is A. Predictability is used often in the movies. How many times have you seen this scene – our hero, usually a woman, walks down a corridor to her apartment (often New York), fumbles with the lock, enters the apartment and is jumped by the villain.

---

3. Coincidence

Coincidence is another useful dramatic device, if used skillfully. Audiences will accept one coincidence in a story, but rarely two. For example, in *E.T.* isn't it a coincidence that the little space guy runs into the garden of the children's house? If he had run into the house next door, the one with the senior citizens, it would have been a completely different story. If multiple coincidences are used, we usually feel that the story is contrived, or stylized to the point of unbelievability.

Using a coincidence successfully means you have asked the audience to suspend their disbelief at a crucial juncture of the movie. If you use a coincidence unsuccessfully, the audience will generally not forgive you, and your movie will be marred with comments like 'It was a great story until that bit about the spaceman in bed with the mother.'

4. Big gloom

The big gloom is the point where your hero is so far from their goal that they want to give up. They can't of course, because that would be the end of the movie. But we believe that they will give up. At this point another character, usually a mentor, or a wise old man, comes by and encourages or inspires the character to continue.

The big gloom is the low of lows. Writers who exclude this scene automatically make the climax (which generally follows this scene) less dramatic. The best way to create a high is to contrast it with a low.

Endings

Short film scripts are totally different. Shorts are often cyclical stories that start and end in the same place. But if after a minute or two in a short you don't know what it is about, trouble ensues. And, with a short, you don't have time to recover.

The task of the ending is to wrap up the story promised on page ten and to tie up all the loose ends.

Often you will see a movie, which was pretty good, but will say after the movie 'That was pretty good, but what happened to the Danny Devito character that disappeared about an hour into the movie?'

In cases like this, the writer has not tied up all the loose ends.

There are just two types of endings.

Firstly, cause and effect – usually in stories in the masculine mode, or right-hand stories.

Or secondly, ambiguous – this type of ending requires the audience to work, making it less popular among industry filmmakers who deem it a financial risk. Did she pull the trigger or not? Did they fall in love or not?

Ambiguous endings seem more popular during periods of civil unrest. The Vietnam War era spawned numerous stories with ambiguous endings. My favorite is *Easy Rider*. In this film, the physical action has a very clear and concise ending. What is unclear is what the film is saying about social values – reflecting perfectly the mood of the time, and explaining this low budget film's popularity.

One's ultimate aim in the ending of a film is to create resonance, similar to the resonance in a music hall as the conductor cuts off the last note of the orchestra. The last chord drifts around and around the hall for a few seconds, creating wonderful resonance. Then the applause starts.

In the movies, resonance is described differently. It is called Buzz. It is the conversation that breaks out following an exceptional movie. Perceptible above the music track over the closing credits, and certainly obvious as the patrons stream past the popcorn stand following a performance, buzz is a highly sought after commodity which signifies commercial success for a movie.

It was the discovery of buzz that led me to my theory of screenplay structure.

My office is about a twelve-minute walk from the large screens in Leicester Square in the heart of London's West End. One of the few advantages of running a film festival is the opportunity to see films on one of the largest screens in Europe. If I have a ticket to a film starting at 6:30pm, I know that I can leave the office at 6:35, walk to the theatre and take my seat, missing the commercials and trailers, just in time for the opening 'pop'.

I hate missing the opening few seconds of a film. I have kicked off so many screenings at the festival. I introduce the filmmaker, listen to the introduction, wait for the applause to stop. I signal to the projectionist to start the show. I turn halfway up the steps to see the first frame of the film hit the screen. I almost hear a 'pfffit pop!' as it hits.

After seeing about a hundred films, I noticed that I always arrived at the cinema needing to go to the toilet. Having squeezed every last second into my workday at the office, it was in considerable physical discomfort that I would arrive at the cinema, thinking I would I have a few seconds to hit the toilets there. But I didn't want to miss the pop. So I would head into the cinema, sit down, and wait for the pop and a suitable break in the action to hit the restrooms.

I noticed that in certain movies I left after a few minutes, others after ten minutes, others a half hour, and in some movies, I would sit in physical agony for the entire two hours. I then compared story structure to this experience and realized that a story, two hours long, needs to be pegged in nine different places, or the story will sag. People will hit the restrooms or the popcorn bar.

Have you ever been in a movie with a friend and decided to excuse yourself? When you come back to your seat a few minutes later, what do you say? Have I missed anything? If they say 'No' it means that the writer hasn't been achieving their goals.

Here are the nine basic steps to story structure. One page of properly typed screenplay equals one minute of screen time. Thus, the numbers below can refer to screen time or page count:

Page 1 – to set the time, the pace and the setting. There is a big difference between the opening page of *Terminator* and the opening page of a Merchant Ivory film.

Page 3 – something that refers directly to the theme of the piece.

Page 10 – by now you must be able to answer the following questions: Who is the hero, what do they want, and how are they going to get it?

Between pages 10 to 30, we see the hero prepare to execute the plan.

On page 30 something happens that throws the story in a 180 degree swing. The hero's plan does not work.

The hero then attempts to come up with a new plan of action. Remember the goal cannot change or you fracture the storyline.

On page 45, the hero's plan fails again, although it may not be as traumatic as the page 30 scene. It is not as traumatic, because the hero has already been disappointed once, and now realizes that the achievement of their goal is going to require a much greater commitment than on page 10.

The page 45 scene is more of a psychologically upsetting scene – a bit like when you returned to your parents house a few weeks after you first moved out. When you went into your room, your clothes and bed are still there, but your father has turned your room into his hobby room, and your mother has taken down all your posters. You are still welcome to return home and live there, if you want. In other words, you can still return to your life as it was on page 10, but doing so would be an admission that you are somehow weak.

Short films

Shorts are to features what sonnets/haiku are to novels. Shorts have a variety of interesting structures.

The page 60 scene is very dramatic. The hero realizes that the new plan doesn't work again, but if they are to achieve their goals, they will have to enter a strange land so far from what they know, that they will not be able to get back to the safety of their life on page 10. This is the point of no return.

The hero takes a huge breath, clenches their fists and heads off with another plan. Suddenly, on page 75 they realize that this new plan won't work either, and now they are isolated and/or lost with little or no hope of succeeding, plus the fact that they stand to lose everything.

I call this the big gloom.

Suddenly in the midst of their despair, a guardian angel, or a kid on a skateboard comes by and finds out what the hero wants. They offer a golden titbit of advice. 'So that's how you do it!' Your hero responds, and leaps forward with new energy and resolve, like Thomas the Tank Engine 'I know I can, I know I can', and your hero heads towards the ultimate test at page 90 – the final battle where he or she will either win everything, or lose everything.

The last pages are the resolution, which can vary from a few lines, as in *North by Northwest*, to several pages, as in *Castaway*.

It is important to remember that these page numbers are guidelines only, and can be moved in a fluid way to suit your story.

The only page numbers that really are firm are pages 1, 3, and 10.

figure 3.2
Elliot Grove's Nine-Step Structure

In order to explain how buzz works, let us look at the three different types of movies, buzz wise – A movies, B movies, C movies

In a C movie, you sit down, and watch the movie. You may leave the cinema several times to make a telephone call or buy popcorn. You may even leave before the final credits start if you feel that you can guess the ending. As you leave the cinema you almost forget that you have seen a movie. When you get home the telephone rings. You answer. It's your best friend in the world asking you what you did today. You reply that you had a difficult day at work, bumped into a colleague on the street, comment on a story you saw on CNN, and oh yes, you almost forgot. You saw a movie. What was it like? I can't remember!

European vs. US scripts

American scripts tend to be 120 minutes/pages long, whereas European scripts are closer to ninety. In a European script, the page 30 scene is usually around page 20 to 24, the point of no return as early as 45 to 50. But the page 1, 3 and 10 are the same in commercially successful scripts.

B movies are different. You probably stayed in the cinema for the entire movie. At the end of the screening, you pause and turn in the aisle to look at the credits for a moment. When you get on the street, you are still pondering one of the penultimate scenes. When you get home, the telephone rings. Your best friend in the world again. The first thing you say is I saw a movie tonight. What was it like? Pretty good. There is this really good scene half the way through. You've go to see it. And oh yes. Danny Devito plays this really interesting cameo role that ends about an hour into the movie.

Have you seen a C movie or a B movie?

An A movie is totally different from a B or a C movie. You are glued to your seat for the entire time, no matter what physical discomfort you are in. At the end of the movie, you yearn to your friend and comment on the movie. Everyone else in the cinema is doing the same. You stay and watch the credits, allowing the least dregs of ambience wash over you. You contemplate the movie the entire way home. When you get home you rush to the telephone and call your best friend in the world. You have got to see this movie! And it is the first thing you are conscious of when you wake up the next morning.

Hint Most screenplays fail because the reader cannot see a hero with a clearly defined goal in the first ten pages.

Planning Your Structure

Structure is easily confusing and baffles many writers.

Structure is the term used to describe the way in which a story unfolds. In real life, structure could be used to describe the way that human beings solve a real life problem.

Fill in the following blanks as a planning tool to assist in plotting the essential elements of your story.

1. Problem/Need

Problem – the predicament your hero is in at the start of the story.

> [ ]

Need – the inner problem which is preventing your hero from having a better life.

> [ ]

2. Goal

A specific goal is when we can see an actual moment when your hero achieves or loses it.

What your hero wants more than anything else and seeks over the course of your story. This cannot change.

> [ ]

3. Motive

Why your hero wants the goal.

> [ ]

Hint Make it personal.

4. Stakes

What happens if your hero fails or succeeds.

> [ ]

Hint The stakes must be high.

5. Opponent

The relationship between the hero and opponent is the single most important relationship in your story. The opponent is the person who is competing with the hero for their goal, and/or is the person who stands in the way of your hero.

Describe how each opponent will attack your hero.

6. Plan

Characterization

Notice how much this section refers to specific elements of character. Really, you should re-read this chapter after the next one on characterization.

The plan is the set of guidelines the hero uses to overcome the opponent and win the goal. Since the opponent is the main obstacle to the hero's goal, we also need to see what the opponent's plan is.

Hero's plan   Opponent's plan

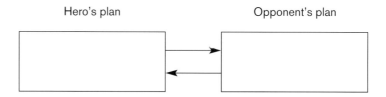

Next, try to list the reaction and action between the hero and opponent as each character tries to achieve their goal.

Hero's counter-plan   Opponent's counter-plan

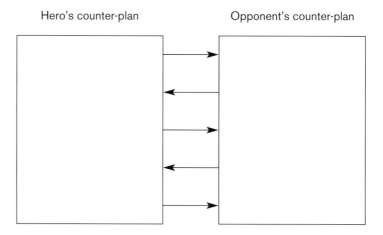

7. Battle

The final battle is where the opponent and hero fight, and the outcome determines who achieves their goal.

List the characters in conflict. You would be surprised how many screenwriters aren't sure who should be in the final battle. This definitely is a sign that the character essays are incomplete.

8. Convergence of space

Refers to the narrow space, or the gauntlet where the final battle takes place. Note how many climax scenes are on a rooftop, a ledge, in an alleyway – anywhere that is small. Squeezing the final battle into a tiny space heightens the emotion and drama of the scene.

Where will your final battle take place?

9. Similarities between hero and opponent

A good battle exists when both the hero and the opponent share attributes. Often the opponent is stronger than the hero. See if you can list these similarities.

10. The Big Gloom

What is the lowest point of the conflict?

> (blank box)

11. Self-revelation

I attended a rehearsal for ballet dancers to watch my daughter rehearse a new dance. The choreographer would ask the pianist to play a short sample of music, about twelve bars long. He would place the dancers in the final position. Listening to the music again, he would place the dancers in their first position. Then he would show them the three or four positions in the middle and let the dancers grow the section together from the ending and the beginning.

I think this is excellent advice for writers. If you really want to know where your story will end up, you have to know where it starts. And often the best way to know where a story starts is by deciding, boldly and firmly, where it is going to end. And then work backward to choose the beginning that best enables you to tell the ending.

What is it that your hero learns about themselves by going through their struggle? Just as in our own lives we learn as we achieve our goals.

Psychological revelation – what the hero learns about their self.

> (blank box)

Moral revelation – what the hero learns about treating others.

> (blank box)

Moral decision – where the hero proves their moral revelation by actually doing the right/wrong thing.

> (blank box)

Summary

1. Find the basic premise of your story.

2. Be prepared for change.

3. When you are stuck, ask yourself what the worst nightmare is.

4. Test market your premise on your friends.

5. Change, revise, rewrite. You are finding your story.

6. Make certain you know your characters inside out.

You are now ready to explore characterization.

4   Characters

Most screenplay books have a slim chapter on character development. These chapters are generally skinny on content because they separate character from structure. These books say that characters must grow and develop and further explain the attributes that qualify this – generally when a character learns to act better towards other people and becomes a so-called better person, or learns a difficult lesson.

Sometimes you will see in a screenwriting book a line drawing which states that a character must go from A to B. Occasionally, a story will show a character in a downward spiral. (*Leaving Las Vegas.*) Talk of structure that ignores characterization is really unhelpful. In fact you could ignore the previous chapter, if you want, because characterization is closely intertwined with structure. If you choose to define structure as character – structure is really the way that your character's plan to achieve his/her goal unfolds.

In other words, at the beginning of a movie we usually see the hero in a predicament. Additionally, we see that the hero has a goal. The hero then develops a plan, based on his or her experience, as the most likely way to achieve the goal. Of course, the plan originally chosen rarely works, and the hero makes new plans based on new information (gained from experience) and tries until this new plan fails too.

We the audience love to watch this story, because we hope to find a new way to solve this problem, too. It is very similar to your plan in life. Let's say your overriding goal is to create an excellent screenplay. All the rest of us aspiring screenwriters are dying to see which techniques and tools you use in order to create a great screenplay. You try this combination of tools and techniques, and we go 'What a great idea!' Ooops! That doesn't work. In our excitement, we just know that this alternative plan will definitely work. But our hero, in his/her naïveté, has chosen this route, a route condemned to failure. But do you know what? It nearly works! And so on until the end of the story. At the very end we either go 'So that's how you write a great screenplay!' (happy ending) or 'I told you that wouldn't work!' (sad ending).

In this case, the way the hero tackles the problem at hand creates the structure for the movie as we follow the hero's ups and downs.

Casting Your Movie

Creating characters

The first step in creating characters is to create a list of the parts in your story. As you work on the basic premise, you will have a list of characters that grows from your work. Start a blank page of paper for each character. Remember that you may end up with some characters that you do not use – almost like an audition. These characters are not wasted. They could shed light on one of the characters in your script.

Character name
Try to make the character's name relate to his/her role. The role played by Clint Eastwood in the Oscar-winning movie *Unforgiven* is William Munny, a reformed assassin. The name integrates with the story.

Resumé
Summarize the character's role in a brief paragraph. Pretend you are placing an ad in a newsletter for auditions that goes out to actors.

Role
Each character can be described as a friend or enemy of the hero – opponent, opponent-ally, sub-plot character.

In order to develop strong characters, describe each character in a series of different ways, use additional paper if necessary:

Traits
List the traits that will make your character unique. For example, Melvin Udall in *As Good As It Gets* has a compulsive obsessive disorder.

Nightmare
What is the very worst thing that can befall your character.

Positive values
What are the qualities that are good about your character.

Negative values
What are the qualities that are bad or weak about your character.

figure 4.1
Characterization Chart

Résumé 1 Character Name

Role

Résumé 2 Character Name

Role

Résumé 3 Character Name

Role

Résumé 4 Character Name

Role

On each blank page write the character description and their name. Then create a free-form essay, either in point form, or as a story, about this character. Push the boundaries of what you know about each character until you know them intimately. A good exercise is to buy a newspaper, open it at random and point to a headline. Would your character have an instant reaction? What would it be?

Now summarize the main attributes of each character in a line or two.

Now go back to the cast list overleaf and try to incorporate this new information as concisely as possible into each character's résumé.

Creating empathy

Show them learning something. Audiences love to watch someone learning a new skill, or learning how to deal with a new situation.

Show them in a predicament. When an on-screen character experiences a situation common to the audience, we empathize with the character. For example, a lover's argument, or a rude parking attendant.

Hint Even if your character is the vilest and most despicable character in the entire world, the audience must identify with them in order to connect to the screen.

Avoiding stereotypes

Stereotypical characters are the result of typecasting in Hollywood. Major actors have control over the types of characters that they will agree to play. Hollywood has a whole school of writers who create stories simply for these actors.

Sometimes your story may include a stereotypical character such as a fat banker, dishonest politician, or homeless person. These stereotypes will weaken your script and tension will drain from your story. The tool to use to combat this is character traits.

Give each character a trait we wouldn't expect.

Fat banker – love of acid jazz.

Homeless person – a working knowledge of medieval painting.

Dishonest politician – an expert in judging sporting matches.

Try to make a square peg fit into a round hole. Exaggerate for effect.

Hint Not only are stereotypical characters boring, they promote prejudice. The stereotypical characterization of black people in Hollywood took two generations to live down, and still is a problem. Similarly, the stupid, cheating, fat, brutal analogies associated with people of different races is simply wrong.

Tools for Creating Character Development

Stories are really very simple. E.T. fell to earth and has to get home. Character development makes your story complex. How your characters grow will depend on their goal and the plan they develop to achieve their goal. It will also depend on how they learn to cope with the changing demands of their conquest, and by their ability to adapt to the challenges from those that oppose them.

When a character learns something, they often say 'Oh! So that's how you do it.' A light bulb goes on as your character has a self-revelation.

1. Goal

Your hero must have a clearly defined goal. You must be able to see a moment where your hero achieves (or loses) that which they aspire to. A common flaw of new writers is to have a goal such as 'I want a better life', or 'I want to move from the city', or 'I want a better job'. These are all too general. Besides, we all want a better life.

A story with this type of goal means that the hero is involved in a lot of internal thought, making this story suitable for a novel.

A different tack would be to find another hook that you can hang your storyline on, that would give you a chance to explain why you think your hero wants or needs a better life.

Remember that your hero's goal cannot change. If your hero's goal does change you will fracture the storyline.

2. Inner need

Try and personalize your story. Try to give your hero a second problem to solve at the same time as they are trying to achieve their main goal. Doing this will add a human dimension to your story and give your story an emotional base.

The strangest thing about writing is that you may not realize what true emotional need, what inner problem, your hero has. To find a really powerful inner problem see if you can look at your own life and see what your own inner problem is. Thus through writing your script you may identify and solve your own inner problem. Surely a result worthy of the effort to conceive and finish a screenplay in its own right.

If you do not know what your inner problem is, or fail to identify a strong inner problem for your hero, an experienced reader will pick this up on reading your script.

One of the first scripts I read was a story set on a mythical island in the Caribbean. The story was based on the American invasion of Grenada. The General and his wife were sent to quell the rebellion, and were accommodated in a five star hotel. Once you accepted this fact, I noticed that whenever the General and his wife were in the suite, they had no physical contact. When the General had to leave in the morning to go downstairs to battle, he would bend over and peck his wife good-bye with a very tenuous kiss. I called the writer (a forty-something male from a small city in the North of England) up and told him that he had to resolve the sexual relationship between the husband and wife. At this point he broke down into tears and told me that after sixteen years of married life, he had told his wife that he was gay, and they had just split up. Now if the writer had included a gay element in this military story, it would have had much more power. And the story would have been timely. It was written around the time of Bill Clinton's inauguration and the gay controversy sweeping the military at the time.

Audiences love to learn details from the screen that they can incorporate in their own lives. Writers have something to give an audience. Basing our script on our own life makes it personal and invaluable.

Another interesting point is that the hero will not be able to achieve their outer goal until they resolve or deal with their inner need. The best way to illustrate this is to look at your own life. You will not achieve your own outer goals, will not realize your ambitions until you resolve your own inner problems. I am the perfect example.

Much has been made of the fact that I started Raindance Film Festival on my own with a hundred dollars. The festival grew to a certain size, but my goal was to make it the best independent film festival in Britain, if not Europe and the world. But my progress ground to a halt five years ago. I just couldn't make it work any better. My goal was thwarted, not by an opponent, but my own inner problem. And I didn't even know what my inner problem was until I switched the lights on one Monday morning, and by some miracle was able to see the Raindance office in a new light. Papers were stacked to the ceiling. Desks were overflowing with files, unpaid bills, paid bills and scraps of memo pads with important telephone numbers. I picked up the mail and in it was a nasty letter from the taxman. Then it hit me. I had to get organized. My inner problem was that I didn't make myself do the one thing I hate – paperwork. I went to work. Hired an accountant. Registered the company, and cleared up the office. I actually threw out sixty black bags of garbage on that day. And since then, Raindance has flourished to the extent where I can see it approaching my outer goal.

Hint Your hero will only achieve their outer goal when they are able to conquer their inner problem.

---

3. The plan

Your hero will have a clearly defined goal – 'I want to…' – and this has to be specific. The most common error a new screenwriter makes is to create a hero without a clearly defined goal. As in real life, any screen character without a clear goal is uninteresting to the reader/audience. Make the plan as precise as possible.

The plan can be physical like the map in the opening of *Raiders of the Lost Ark*. He has a map of the location of the cave with the idol. The plan could be the physical object that needs to be delivered, such as the Fedex package in *Castaway*.

The plan can be social. Dustin Hoffman needs acting work in *Tootsie*.

The plan can be psychological, as in a love story.

The plan can either work or not work. If the plan works, then the drama in the story comes from the hero trying to find out how to make it work.

If the plan does not work, then the hero is challenged to find a new plan. In the process the hero discovers that the goal is even more difficult to achieve than he or she first thought and has to commit further to the quest for the goal, or abandon the goal. By choosing to commit further, by trying to find a better plan, the hero has to expose him/herself to risk.

4. Motivation and desire

Why your hero wants something is important too. Try to find out the motivation for your hero. There is an outer motivation, as in *Witness* where Samuel Lapp witnesses a murder. It is the motivation to discover the villain that propels the story along.

There is an inner motivation to action too. Sometimes your hero will react to a situation based on his or her inner problems. This can be because of a fear, or a deep-seated belief of what is right and wrong.

5. Characters on the brink

Building characters that matter to an audience is made easier if you show the characters on the brink. It is also a great tool to use in order to create empathy for your characters. List the brink scenes in your own life – childbirth, marriage, divorce, homelessness, bankruptcy, windfall, illness, death, redundancy, addiction and so on. A story has more power if the characters are on the brink at the start of the picture.

For example, in *Ghostbusters* the three main characters have just been made redundant. In *Star Wars* the Death Star threatens civilization.

Relationships of the Hero

One of the biggest mistakes writers make is seeing their hero alone with no relationship with the other characters. This results in a weak hero, cardboard opponents and minor characters. In many ways, a character is defined by who she or he is not, which could lead the writer into the trap of passive characters. (More suitable for novels.) That's why the single most important step in creating great characters is to compare all characters to the hero. For added contrast, intensity, conflict and excitement make sure that the entire cast of your movie is as different as possible from each other.

Every time the audience sees your hero compared to, or relating to, another character, they see the hero in new ways – which adds dimension and texture to your story. It is the same as in true life. The reason offices organize parties is so the heroes of the workplace can be seen in an informal atmosphere with their loved ones – shedding another ray of light on their character. By doing so, the secondary characters are also forced to become complete human beings – as complex and as interesting as your hero.

1. The hero and the opponent

The most important relationship in your movie is the relationship between your hero and his/her main opponent. How these two characters interact with each other determines the drama of the story.

Many new writers curiously ignore this relationship. Another common flaw is choosing the wrong character as the opponent. This is the result of not exploring the entire cast list through the characterization essays.

2. Creating a good opponent

A good opponent is a double of the hero. Which means that the opponent is human too – human with weaknesses, failings and strong points, just like the hero.

The opponent will have moral weaknesses, preventing him/her to act properly towards others.

The opponent will have an inner need, based on the moral weakness, as does the hero.

The opponent will have a goal, hopefully similar to that of the hero.

The opponent will be stronger, smarter, more cunning, better looking (depending on your story) than your hero. This allows the opponent to pressure the hero, and in turn forces the hero to stretch beyond their normal ability. For example, I would not be a suitable opponent for Stallone in *Rocky*, because the outcome of the story would be a foregone conclusion.

3. Values

We all live life according to certain values. Your hero and opponent do as well. Each of your characters bases their actions on a certain set of values, which they believe is right, even if these values contradict your own personal values, or the values of society and the culture we live in.

Good stories set up the values of the hero with the values of the opponent. We watch the movie transfixed to see which set of values are superior within the confines of the story. Thus we can watch a movie like *True Romance* and cheer for Christian Slater, a bank robber.

4. Moral argument

Stories with an evil opponent are rarely as compelling as a story with an opponent with good and bad qualities. Evil opponents operate in a mechanical and inhuman way that alienates us. Again, true life serves us well. There is rarely a situation with clearly defined good and evil, right and wrong. Good stories show characters that believe they are right and can argue their case to each other, and to the audience. They justify the values of the opponent in detail, even if they are wrong.

5. Achilles heel

The opponent should be the one person best able to attack the hero. The opponent should know the hero and their weaknesses so well, that when they attack, the hero either has to overcome their weakness or be destroyed. Often the hero knows a good opponent.

Furthermore, the hero often is not aware of their weakness until the opponent reveals them.

Hint The hero learns from the opponent.

Think of drama as a football match. If the best football team in the world is playing a bunch of high school dropouts, then the best team will score every time they get the ball and the audience will be bored. If, on the other hand, the best team in the world is playing the second best team in the world, each team will have to play their best game ever, and the audience will go wild. Similarly, in drama, the hero and the opponent should drive each other to greatness.

6. Creating contrast with the hero

If two runners are told to deliver a package to an address, which is more interesting? By different routes, or the same route? If they follow the same route, it becomes a race against time, with all the drama and excitement of a competition.

Similarly, in a good story, the hero and opponent will share many of the same qualities and attributes. We then can compare the hero and opponent trying to achieve the same thing, and can see which method works best. The Bible has a marvelous tale about Moses. Moses needed to get some soldiers together to fight the enemy. When he asked for volunteers, he was flooded with applicants. Not knowing what to do, he took the men to the river and asked them to drink. The men drank from the river in different styles – some lapping, some scooping water in their hands. He chose the men who stood and scooped the water because they kept an eye out for danger – and they became his élite.

The contrast between hero and opponent is powerful only when both characters have strong similarities. Each then presents a slightly different approach to the same life problem. In the similarities do the crucial differences, the instructive differences, become most clear?

Another advantage of making your hero and opponent similar, is you keep the hero from being a totally good guy, and the opponent from being totally bad. This allows greater audience identification.

Characterization resources can be found in the unlikeliest places – newspapers and magazines like *Hello, OK!, The National Enquirer* are full of true life stories that document character traits of heroes and opponents.

As screenwriters, we are sometimes baffled about our colleagues who become successful. Sometimes the writers with no more talent than we have become successful at gaining the commission we want, and in so doing become competitors for the same job – a practical illustration about the dramatic strength of having a hero with the same qualities as the opponent.

Hint The conflict between the hero and the opponent is not about good and evil. It is about two well-meaning characters who have strengths and weaknesses.

---

7. Geography

It's pretty hard to hate someone on another continent, or in a different state. Believe it or not, I have read a number of scripts where the opponent is plotting his counter-attack from across the ocean. Long distance relationships will not work.

In real life, you would tend to get as far away as possible from someone you really dislike. But this is a movie. Try to create togetherness for your hero and opponent. Squeeze them together. Make them occupy the same space. Force them to cohabit. The energy that creates will make your film glow.

Hint Good stories show the values of the opponent conflicting with the values of the hero.

Conflict

A compelling story contains more than one main conflict between a hero and an opponent. It contains a series of conflicts between the hero and a variety of other characters, and the values they stand for. A successful writer understands what the conflicts and values are, and learns how to map these out over the course of the story.

Simple stories show the hero attacked by one opponent. Although the value structures between these two characters can be simply and powerfully stated, these stories can lack the depth and texture demanded by a sophisticated audience. It is by the interaction of the different characters that your story will become more complex and challenging to your audience.

In the best stories, the hero is assailed by a range of opponents – the main opponent, and two or three sub-opponents – creating a powerful series of attacks and counter-attacks. This collection of characters allows the writer to show the hero attacked in a variety of ways. This adds the possibility of layering your story in a series of subtle and complex ways that add depth and texture to your story.

The characters also form a society, in which the writer can examine more complex beliefs. The trick to making a story dense with conflict is to have each character attack each other as well. In doing so, each character becomes important to the story, and has a reason for existing, other than to merely attack the hero.

You can also repeat this structure on other levels in your story – the family, the workplace, or society. Each level gives you another opportunity to state your beliefs, your theme and the underlying values of your story. Writing a screenplay is your chance to firmly state your values.

You can choose to layer your conflict in one of two ways.

1. Lateral conflict

Two characters of approximately equal power or ability will fight for the same goal. The writer with this structure is able to explore how these two opposing values create conflict.

Sometimes, both of the main characters will discover something about themselves and their values will blend together. The blend consists of the positive aspects of both sets of values, allowing the writer to state what they think the best rules for living are.

figure 4.2
Power Structure Chart A

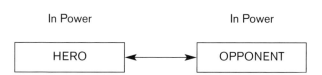

2. Perpendicular conflict

Perpendicular conflict suits stories that examine power structures within the society of your film. Adding a perpendicular layer increases the conflict exponentially and gives your story a rich and deep texture. Perpendicular conflict has to do with the opposition between those in power versus those who are out of power. A story with a horizontal and vertical opposition of characters and values might look like this:

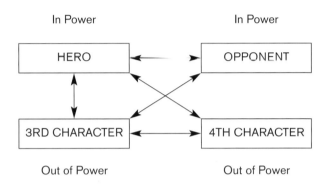

The conflict among the various characters and the values they represent tend to happen in two ways – horizontally and vertically.

Hint The world must come from the hero. In other words who your hero is will define where the story is set.

The Staging

To create the world of your story, you must first place the story on a stage. The stage is the basic space of drama. It is a single, unified place surrounded by a set. Everything on the stage is part of the story. Everything outside the stage is not.

Hint If you cut from the stage of your story, the drama will dissipate.

The challenge is to find a stage that will grow and develop along with your story, and enable you to provide a strong visual element that will also be able to provide clues to the story. In a sense, good staging is really a subplot. Good staging will add substance to your story. Look for staging that will enable you to tell the story you want to tell.

The seasons

When you need to show a passage of time and a certain pace, consider using the seasons. The development of the seasons gives the audience a physical reminder of time against which to measure the decay or growth of the hero.

Classic literature uses seasons with certain probable meanings that you can either go with, or go against. Casting across type immediately adds another dimension to your tale.

Classic season staging goes like this:

Summer – your hero exists in a predicament, or lives in a world of freedom that is vulnerable to attack.

Fall – the characters begin to decline.

Winter – the characters reach their lowest point.

Spring – the season of rebirth and rejuvenation.

Writing against type would show a character at their lowest point in the summer, and at their highest in the depths of winter. This change to the natural order would help keep an audience from knowing what to expect next, adding suspense to your story automatically.

Frame your story

A builder would never build a house without putting up a frame. A writer must put up a frame, too, before starting to build the story. The easiest way to frame your story is to determine exactly where your story will end. Then decide when and where you want your story to start. With these two firm points, it is much easier to spin your tale.

Holidays and rituals

Using universal holidays and rituals helps establish the mood of your story quickly. This means that the writer can set up the wedding, or a Christmas story, or the baptism, with a minimal amount of preparation.

Rituals and holidays themselves have their own rhythm and drama that can add to your story and allow you another way to express emotion. If the holiday expands to a national level, then it becomes political as well as personal, giving yet another layer to the story. The more layers in your story, the more complex. If handled well, these layers enhance your tale.

Hint Understand the philosophy of the ritual you want to use and decide whether or not you agree with it. This will enable you to attack or defend the holiday. This plus the season it is in will enable you to maximize the stage setting.

Nature

Choosing a natural setting should be done after you evaluate the meanings embedded in each setting. The forest, the ocean, mountains or the wilderness all have different meanings. Try to find the one that suits the story you want to tell. Perhaps you can choose a natural setting that cuts across the grain of your story.

Weather

Story telling has long used the weather to create a powerful visual representation of the inner turmoil of the hero. Like setting, you can use weather in its current context, or twist it making your story ironic or cynical. It is no accident that rain, lightning and thunder precede events most foul in Shakespearean drama. Similarly, the weather can be used to add drama to your story, and provide the stage for your characters. Some classic associations of weather are:

Lightning and thunder – passion, terror, and death.

Rain – sadness, loneliness, boredom, and coziness.

Wind – destruction, desolation.

Fog – confusion, mystery.

Sun – happiness, freedom, or corruption hidden below a warm exterior.

Snow – sleep, serenity, death.

Symbol

A symbol is something that represents something other than itself. Symbols in your movie take on new meanings in addition to the meaning they had to the audience before the movie started. A symbol can be an object that already has a meaning, like a cross or flag, or it can be a new object that you have introduced to the script like, for example, the lipstick in *Thelma and Louise*.

Society

Placing your story in a society gives your story more definition. The simplest way to do this is to say 'London, 1880'. Every story has a definition such as this. This particular definition gives us more information about the characters, but has the weakness of relying on the reader's preconceived ideas of Victorian London. A more precise way is to define the culture of the time. But defining all the nuances of Victorian England is simply too difficult. It would be like asking Michaelangelo to carve David with a toothpick. And of course, your audience would be bored.

Institutions

Placing your story in an institution has many advantages. Institutions like the corporation, the hospital, the mob, the factory each represent society in microcosm. Find an institution that suits your story.

Hint Great writers twist an existing symbol to give it new meaning.

Community

Since a screenplay is such a pared down art form, simply placing your characters in a society, or even institution, is still daunting. The only way to make this work would be to write pages and pages of description to explain the staging to your audience (not a good idea), or narrowing down the structure of your stage even further will enable you to get more information to the audience visually.

The trick is to look for a means to organize your setting in a way that allows the audience to jump to the right conclusions for your story.

Being John Malkovich is an example of a unique setting. The simple act of setting the story inside someone's head transformed the entire story.

Many writers use the metaphor of the city as jungle – a terrifying place, where danger, even death, lurks at every corner. Your characters can be attacked from above, from below, and from the side. No one can be trusted. Populated by 'animals' and filled with hunters and the hunted, this city is not a fun place.

The challenge to modern screenwriters is to discover a new metaphor, as yet unused, as a way to tell the story.

Hint Elevate your story by creating a unique metaphor for your setting.

Social Stage

Social stage is the point at which the society of your hero has developed. All societies evolve through distinct social stages. Choosing a specific social stage allows you to communicate a great deal without resorting to dialogue.

For example, if you see a character alone in the desert, you immediately know that his or her immediate overwhelming concern is to find water, and to survive.

Without turning this book into a dissertation of cultural development over the millennia, let's simply put the social stages into four unique areas – each with a unique type of hero, a unique kind of opponent, special concerns and particular values:

Wilderness and the super-hero

There are no buildings in the wilderness, and the hero travels alone or with a band of disciples. Nature is vast and all-powerful, threatening the existence of everyone. The hero is a super-hero because they are the only characters capable of fighting the forces of nature and surviving. Death comes early and quickly to the weak. The people's main concern is to survive, reproduce and be in harmony with nature, using the knowledge and strength of the super-hero.

Village and the classic hero

Society has evolved to the point where man has created basic shelter that will survive the seasons. The social structures of the village are young and developing. The village is surrounded by wilderness and is prone to attack by barbarians. The villagers mistrust anything from the wilderness, to the point that anyone they do not understand, or who is different to them, is considered to be barbarians too. The barbarians want the village destroyed, because the village represents the new, and it encroaches on their freedom to roam. The barbarians do not understand the change in the society that has created the village.

Into the world of the village comes the 'classic' hero. Larger and physically stronger than the villagers, almost barbarian-like, the classic hero relies on martial arts to survive. The villagers see in the classic hero their only person capable in defeating the barbarians.

The classic hero will use his talents as a warrior to help the fragile community deal with the savage forces they cannot physically or morally handle themselves. Society has not reached the point where discussion and verbal argument are tools for dissipating problems. The village does not have a court house, and will usually have a very simple gaol.

Have you ever been driving in the countryside and stopped for a meal or drink in a local establishment off the beaten path? Do you notice how the locals look at you when you enter? You are a barbarian bringing a new way of doing things to the village.

Village stories share a sense of good and evil, black and white. Although the values of the villagers and the classic hero may not be correct, according to our principles, basically everyone in the town is good, and everyone outside of the town is a barbarian or savage for whom destruction is the only option.

By warring with other characters from his own social stage, the classic hero is a doomed figure. He (classic heroes are predominately male) is used by the villagers to destroy the barbarians in order to allow the village to grow and prosper. The classic hero has no place in the village, and once his task is done, leaves, or is forced to leave.

Examples of the classic hero include the pioneer, the westerner, the super-cop (who lives in a city filled with barbarians) and the samurai.

City and the average hero

As the village grows and spreads out, at some point it reaches a physical boundary, and can no longer spread horizontally. It must now spread vertically. The village develops into the city. Contrasting with the social stage of the village, the city is a place of hierarchy, rank, privilege, vast differences of wealth and organization.

This is the world of the average hero, of everyman or everywoman who is ordinary in every way – no stronger, brighter, dumber, or wealthier than anyone else in the city.

The average hero is concerned with the nesting instinct (creating a place in society, to providing a home, to raising a family). He or she is concerned with equality and justice (making sure that everyone follows the same rules for living). He or she is probably also concerned with avoiding the slavery of bureaucracy and government.

Some examples of the average hero can be found in Michael Dorsey in *Tootsie*; Karen Blixen in *Out of Africa*; Frank Galvin in *The Verdict*; and Dorothy in *The Wizard of Oz*.

Oppressive city and the anti-hero

When the city grows so dense, so tight, so technological and bureaucratic, it becomes a place of enslavement. Where it once was intended as a place of nourishment, where its citizens could expect to have a decent job and a decent life, a place where the arts and community flourished, it has decayed to the point where it is no longer able to help its citizens. Instead, it uses its citizens to further itself, devouring individuals in its thirst to sustain its bulk.

Stories set in this stage feature the anti-hero. The anti-hero can have two distinct traits.

He could be a person who will not be beaten down by the oppressive city and who is therefore sent into exile. *Cool Hand Luke* is an example.

Or he could be the person who stays and is beaten down – the incompetent, the bumbler, a character who is unsocial or anti-social.

Examples of the anti-hero include Chauncey Gardner in *Being There*; early Woody Allen characters; Ratzo Rizzo in *Midnight Cowboy*; and Travis Bickle in *Taxi Driver* as well as Jim Carrey characters in *Me, Myself and Irene* and *Pet Detective*.

The next development of society is for it to crumble under its own weight, and the citizens (those who survive) are returned to the wilderness – for example, *Lord of the Flies*.

Hint As society gets larger, nature and the hero get smaller.

A huge challenge for screenwriters is to explain how it is possible for nature, society, and the individual to coexist and prevent the evolutionary cycle from repeating.

Hint Usually the most effective way of marking time and placing the hero within a society is to place him/her in a particular social stage. People living in the wilderness tend to create main characters who are gods or super-heroes. In the village world, the hero is the 'classic' hero. Stories set in the city world use the average hero, the everyman or everywoman. The main character in stories set in the oppressive city is the anti-hero.

While writing this chapter, the British newspapers were full of stories of hospitals that stockpiled parts of dead babies to be used for research or transplants – a perfectly good cause. The difficulty was that the parents had not been told, and in a bizarre case straight from the oppressive city, a mother was photographed leaving the hospital with the body of her child in two dozen lab bottles.

Social Metaphors

When writing for a pared down form, such as screenplay, it is always useful to draw upon universal experience in order to quickly create the setting. This enables your audience to see your story within the context of something that they already understand.

The family

When writing a short film, or a film using a very limited budget, creating a metaphor that is instantly recognizable is crucial, i.e. the wedding, the funeral, graduation day, the Hen party. Your audience will then be able to see your story clearly, and be able to understand the details you bring to this setting.

Everyone in the world is part of a family. The family is the basic unit of drama and of human life itself. The family provides the first relationships for the hero. The relationships that the hero forms with parents and siblings will powerfully shape the story. Through these relationships we will see and judge the hero's ability to grow and develop.

Hierarchy

You must consider the power structure of the family – who is in charge, who has the most influence, who uses this power and who abuses it. Then you place your hero somewhere in this power structure and the audience will observe how the hero's position changes relative to the power over the course of the story.

Municipality

As in real life, where you or your characters live can have great impact on your audience. If you live in a luxurious flat overlooking Buckingham Palace, the audience will read one lifestyle. If your hero lives in a cardboard box outside Buckingham Palace, the audience reads a completely different lifestyle.

Homes range from the very small and humble, to the huge and grandiose. Each home will help to express the character. And you can also cut against type.

Obviously, each social stage has different types of buildings, and the audience will understand the social stage in part by the types of buildings you show them.

Wilderness/Village

As village life is threatened by extinction, stories set in the village will become increasingly nostalgic.

The wilderness and the village are almost always shown in relation to one another in a story since it is the contrast between the two that emphasizes the change of the hero. In the village we only see essential buildings, because the village represents a society at its most basic state – the livery stable, the jail, the saloon, the dry goods store, the schoolhouse and the church. Some of the buildings should be unfinished to accentuate the growth and the forces of change that are continually overcoming the wilderness. Villages often feature wooden fences that separate the village from the wilderness. Made of wood, fences represent the fragile barrier between the old and the new, and suggest visually the vulnerability to attack.

Town

As villages become larger and more successful, the social order starts to change and diversify. This is represented by the buildings, which are taller and denser than the buildings of the village.

Three-storied buildings are common in the town. The layers suggest a society that is becoming established, with the social layers not present in the village.

A strong sense of community is a feature of town life. Although the buildings can be multi-story, they are still small enough so someone on the street can talk to someone leaning out of the upstairs window.

Nature is interspersed through the town. The society has not become so artificial that nature is driven out. The characters in the town live in harmony with nature, and respect it for its power.

City

The city is organized vertically. Everyone living in the city is classed by how high up they are – either in the physical structures, or where they are in terms of personal power or wealth. The contrast between the dizzying heights and the subterranean passages is extreme.

As most of us live in the city, see if you can find a way to bend or distort this setting to add impact to your story.

The classic way of demonstrating the difference between power and wealth is to place the rich and powerful in penthouses at the top of sky-scrapers, the middle classes in the middle floors, the poor and the vanquished on the street, and the criminals in underground lairs.

Thus every time you see Batman's opponent, you are led to a powerful room deep in the bowels of the city. Audiences identify with the subter-ranean room, and the writer is able create texture for the story without having to resort to more than the actual description of the set.

The buildings of the city are divided into compartments. Buildings in the village tend to be one large room, where all the action takes place. Town buildings, although multi-layered, tend to focus on a single room as well. But stories in the city divide buildings up into a series of com-partments or rooms. Rooms function not only to allow people to congregate, but are also used to divide and isolate one from another. Thus, while stories in the city deal with positive values like creating love, nest building and justice, they can also range through the negative val-ues of intrigue, secrecy and injustice.

Unlike the village or the town, there are no communal bonds in the city. People communicate using messages, and move from place to place. It is highly impersonal.

Summary

1. Structure is the way your character's plan unfolds.

2. Make certain that your hero has an outer goal and an inner problem.

3. Choose a social stage that fits the character of the story you tell.

4. Never forget the instinctive storyteller lurking inside you. If you find anything in this chapter that confuses you, set it aside and return later.

You are now ready to start piecing your screenplay together.

5   Scene Writing

A screenplay has two parts – the dialogue and the descriptive passages. The descriptive passages in a screenplay are called the *black stuff* referring to the amount of space they take up on the page. Dialogue margins are much narrower.

Script readers frequently reject scripts because they contain too much black stuff. A script with a high percentage of black stuff appears verbose and ponderous.

But script writing is a visual medium and your script will probably have more description than dialogue.

The irony is that in the trade they say that agents and producers (hopefully the first two people to read your script) will never read the black stuff. Instead they read the dialogue, and when they don't understand what is happening through the dialogue, they push their eyes up the page and through the descriptive passages until they understand what is going on, and then they drop back down the page to the dialogue.

It would be a little bit like going into a cinema and requesting a screening of, say, *Gone With The Wind*, and asking the projectionist to put a board in front of the lens, and turn a magic switch and play you the entire movie without the pictures, the sound effects track or the movie track. When the story is not carried by the dialogue alone, then you would go to the projectionist, rewind a minute (page) or two and replay with the pictures until the dialogue made sense.

Script readers always approach a script with the three 'ums'.

When they pick up a new script, the first um is when they check the length of the script. The next um is as they open the script at random to see if it is properly and professionally typed. The last um, they flick through the pages for an idea of the amount of black stuff to dialogue.

There is no science to this, but by fanning the pages one can get a rough idea of whether or not the script is a talking heads movie, or a descriptive piece.

We do this ourselves when we browse through a bookstore. You probably did this when you first saw this book. Did you not pick it up, and flick through it to see how dense the type was, how long it was, and how many illustrations it contained? Maybe you started to read a chapter to judge the writing style and quality of the ideas.

The next irony is that screenplay is a very sparse, honed down art form and you are denied any of the literary tools used by novelists, lyricists and poets. Simile, alliteration, metaphors and rhymes have little or no place in a screenplay.

The Basic Rules

You can only write what you physically can see on the screen

You cannot write: `Elliot is depressed.`

Think about how you can show that Elliot is depressed. You could say:

`A tear splats at Elliot's feet.`

Hint If your screenplay has too many internal thoughts, you are writing a story better suited to the novel form.

A writer's job is to describe all the action on the screen

I often get the following line of descriptive action:

`They make wild passionate love.`

Remember that a page of screenplay is a minute of screen time. The writer assumes that this love scene will take a minute or two, yet it occupies a single line, making it last a few seconds. I always ask the writer for more detail: Who is on top, what are their hands doing, where are their lips? I also want to see the choreography of the scene – any trick pelvis moves – who knows, I may learn how to improve my sex life!

With your minute, or page of screentime, you now have to decide how long you are going to take to describe this love scene, or car chase. How long is it going to last in your mind's eye of the movie? A minute is a very long time. And if your car chase or love scene is two minutes long, you now have two minutes/pages in which to show us a chase scene from hell or the poke of the century. Don't wimp out. Show us every visual idea you have. Inspire us, titillate us.

Hint When you start writing a new scene, sit back and try to imagine yourself sitting in a cinema in front of a blank screen. What would you like to see?

Beware of overwriting

A common mistake new writers often make is to overwrite the descriptive passages.

I recently read a script as a favour for a friend. If you had an extra $25,000 to spend on a venture, would you write a cheque for this:

```
Elliot sits on the stool, his left leg crossed and
supported on the rung. He reaches for a coffee in a
shiny blue mug with the word HOLLYWOOD in gold sit-
ting on the shelf to his left. He brings the coffee
forward to his lips. He suddenly passes the coffee
from his left hand (elbow bent) to his right as the
telephone RINGS...
```

Not only is description such as this overwritten, it is confusing to follow and gives the actors too much detail. It is also dry and boring, and fails in the writer's first task – to inspire everyone on the shoot.

I rewrote the passage as:

```
ELLIOT fidgets on a stool.
Coffee splashes from his cup.
The phone RINGS.
```

Structure of a scene

A scene must have its own structure, similar to the whole movie – beginning, middle and end.

The plot devices discussed in Chapter 3 also pertain to scene writing – reversal, stacking, the switch.

Developing a strong personal style

The knack of writing descriptive passages distinctively is acquired through practice, and through reading scripts of commercially successful movies that you admire. Once you have achieved the ability of writing compelling descriptive passages, your career as a writer will develop rapidly. Remember too, that you are at all times writing for the reader – the person with a cheque book. It is this person that you must inspire first.

This scene doesn't appear for nearly a minute (a page), and when it does it is cross cut with the courtroom scene. But it is the opening of the screenplay.

Let's consider the following example of an excellent descriptive passage. It is the opening of *Shawshank Redemption* written by Frank Durabont from the novella by Stephen King:

```
A dark empty room.
```

```
The door bursts open. A MAN and WOMAN enter, drunk
and horny as hell. No sooner is the door shut than
they're all over each other, ripping at clothes,
pawing at flesh, mouths locked together.
```

There are four movies that are created during the filmmaking process:

– the one you write
– the one the director makes
– the one the actors create
– the one the editor makes

He gropes for a lamp, tries to turn it on, knocks it over instead. Hell with it. He's got more important things to do, like getting her blouse open and his hands on her breasts. She arches, moaning, fumbling with his fly. He slams her against the wall, ripping her skirt. We hear fabric tear.

Now imagine again you have a spare twenty-five grand to invest in a movie. Can you see the difference from the example above? Did this scene turn you on? Did you get images of the setting, the action in the scene? Most importantly, would you like to read more?

The method of scene writing

This is a plan I have developed for writing a scene. It involves getting a piece of paper for each scene and drawing a chart.

figure 5.1
Scene Writing Chart

Scene no.	12
Previous endpoint	Bob hits the bottle in the local bar
Cast members in scene	Bob, Mary
Point of Scene	Mary and Bob break up
Goal of main character	Bob goes to Mary's office to propose
Endpoint	Mary tells Bob that it's over
Conflict	Mary is tired of waiting for Bob to propose
Twist	Bob shows Mary a ring

Write the scene, what happens, without dialogue

Write the scene from start to finish. Remember we are not writing dialogue yet. If you have an idea for dialogue, note it on the back of a piece of paper, or write it in the margins.

Do this for the entire script. You then pass over the script and ask yourself of each scene – is there a briefer, faster, fresher way that I can say the same thing?

Make the necessary revisions until the entire script flows.

You may want to use the action flow chart.

Action flow chart

Which hurts more: banging your head on a corner of a cupboard, or being zapped by a raygun? Obviously, the laser blast. But what exactly does that feel like? Have you ever been hit by a raygun blast? On the other hand, how many times have you banged your head? When you see an actor bang their head you go 'ouch'. If you see an actor being melted by a raygun, you have no connection with the pain.

Always try to write personal pain. A good example is in *Die Hard* when John MacLean played by Bruce Willis steps on broken glass.

Your story is not just about one character trying to reach their goals. It is about numerous characters all trying to achieve their goals, sometimes working together, and sometimes working against each other.

This chart is a visual aid that can assist you in keeping track of the actions of the different characters.

List actions that the reader or audience cannot see, so that you can fully flesh out each character. Each character must be fully motivated and active throughout the story. You can also tag scenes to keep track of how many violent scenes/loves scenes you have, for example. The result is a story with multiple lines of action perfectly choreographed with well-defined characters.

Make up a chart with the following headings:

Tag
The type of scene: conflict, love, violence etc.

Scene
A short description of the scene.

Hero
The actions the hero takes to reach their goal.

Four character columns
The actions of the main opponent and other key characters.

Three open columns
For tracking the actions or objects of any character or story element.

Symbol
List up to three symbols that can be found in that scene.

See figure 5.2 over the page.

figure 5.2 Action Flow Chart

	Tag	Scene	Hero	Character	Character	Character	Character	1	2	3	Symbol
10	Tears	Bob spills his guts to Joe, the bartender and gets very drunk	Bob to get drunk		Joe to be a friend to Bob				Bar		
11	Fight	Bob goes to Mary's office to propose	Bob to give Mary the ring	Mary to break up with Bob				Office			Ring
12											

The Eighteen Tricks and Traps of Successful Description

1. Write action, not description

Don't think of writing description, think of writing action – movement. Describing an inanimate object is boring to write and boring to read. And especially boring to a reader with a chequebook!

Remember, your job is to inspire the entire cast and crew. One of the key people on the crew who has to visualize your script is the Production Designer. It is the Production Designer's job to create the actual sets you have described. Sometimes the log line of the scene will do it:

```
INT. RAINDANCE OFFICE - DAY
```

Most screenplays are static and the scenes do not flow. Writing movement into a scene makes your script more interesting to read, immediately distinguishing it from ninety-five percent of all the other screenplays in circulation.

From this simple line, the Production Designer will know to create a room with desks, telephones, and computers. The Props Master will add further details, like the clutter and knick-knacks. Here is where you, as a writer with the biblical quote, can use your creativity to inspire.

It is not your job to describe the clutter, the furniture and knick-knacks, unless required by the plot.

If the slugline says `INT. RAINDANCE OFFICE - DAY` the reader will imagine desks and office furniture. You do not need to mention them.

If the slug line doesn't convey all of the information necessary, then you need to add some simple description.

```
INT. RAINDANCE OFFICE - DAY.

A puddle of water is growing in the middle of the
floor.
```

Now we start to get a more detailed picture of the set, but it is still ambiguous enough to allow for the collaboration of the Production Designer and Props Master.

Once you have all the necessary description of the scene you move on to action. You are still writing description, but you are creating pictures with movement in them – your characters and objects moving in their world. By creating movement you will also enable the reader to visualize the scene. Achieving visualization in your reader will enable them to watch your movie.

You aren't describing things, you are describing things happening. When we use our words to paint pictures, we are painting moving pictures – and that is interesting to a reader. Which means that you have a better chance of selling your script.

Hint Action is the element between patches of dialogue.

---

2. Attention to details

There are times when INT. RAINDANCE OFFICE – DAY is too generic. The reader needs additional information. The trick is not to bore the reader by completely describing the setting. This could lead you to an overwritten scene – one of the fatal flaws of scenewriting (see overwriting below). Instead, find the one (or two) details which give us clues, and let the reader's imagination fill in the rest.

```
INT. RAINDANCE OFFICE - DAY

Files and half empty coffee cups litter the room.
```

or

```
INT. RAINDANCE OFFICE - DAY

A lonely paperclip partners a vase of flowers on the
boardroom table.
```

These are two very different offices. How is the first office different from the second? Imagine yourself as a Production Designer. What sort of table lamp would you use in the first office? How would that differ from a lamp in the second office? The carpet is different, the curtains are different, the pictures thumb tacked to the wall in the first are very different from the lithos and expensively framed posters in the second.

Hint Carefully select a detail which implies other details. Try to distil the entire situation. Then you can sum up an entire room in one short sentence which also explains character as well. Notice how there are two very different Elliots in the following two scenes.

---

3. Paint movement

If you describe people and objects as moving pictures, you can hide the descriptive passages within action, within movement.

Instead of a boring, static still life, you give the reader the excitement of action. You can hide the description within the action.

```
INT. RAINDANCE OFFICE - DAY

ELLIOT slumps amongst the cluttered files and trash.
```

The reader is focusing on Elliot, and doesn't even notice you write the description of the office. No static words in this scene – just movement.

Hint Good descriptive writing does three things at once – it shows things happening, describes the location, and illuminates character.

---

4. High school English

Readers in the industry are accustomed to an easy read. The language used is of the same level as a high school English essay. Avoid complicated words and convoluted descriptive passages.

5. Maximize your vocabulary

The key to economical and dynamic writing is word choice.

During your first draft, you may write a dozen words to explain a situation. Later, you may hone it down to one or two words which explain exactly what you mean. You have hit two birds with one stone – you create quick, easy-to-read sentences coupled with greater impact than your puffed-out original.

6. Avoid wimpy verbs

```
Elliot walks into the room.
```

Walks is not specific. *Walks* is too general. How many words can you think of for the word *walk*? Does Elliot limp in, stride in, jump in, sneak in, jog in, slide in?

If Elliot saunters in, strides in, struts in, strolls in, marches in, paces in, or bounces in, not only does this give us a specific type of walk, but adds to the action and character while removing clichéd words from your script.

7. Classified ad

Screenwriting is a very pared down and sparse art form. The challenge for a writer is to create the greatest possible impact with the fewest possible words. A novelist can spend pages and chapters describing the minutest of details. A screenwriter has just ninety to one hundred and twenty pages to get a complete story across.

Hint Economy is the creative challenge.

Economy is not only the most important part of a screenwriter's job, it is the most difficult to learn.

How do you learn lean, compact and dynamic writing?

One of my tasks at Raindance is to write copy for the various ads we use to promote the film festival. As you know, newspapers charge by the word. A good trick when you start to write a scene is to imagine that you are writing a classified ad for a newspaper, and you only have a limited budget – say $10. This particular newspaper charges 0.75 per word. Try to see if you can describe the scene and leave yourself enough change to buy yourself a coffee! While writing or rewriting, I will take apart every single sentence and try to find a bolder, fresher, quicker way of saying the same thing. In a first draft, I might have six or seven words that end up being replaced by one. I try to recognize every time I have used unnecessary words or beat around the bush. You will learn how to get directly to the point.

Try to write scene description like you are writing a classified ad.

Hint Scenewriting is like writing haiku where you have a very limited number of words. Try to use words that imply other words.

---

8. Find the emotion

Don't describe how something looks, but how it feels. The Production Designer will decide how the set looks, the Casting Director decides on how each character will look.

The writer describes the attitude of the scene, the feel, the emotion.

One of my favourite writers, William C. Martell, writes dynamic description that seeps with emotion. Consider the opening of *Hard Return*:

EXT. URBAN JUNGLE, 2019 AD - EVENING

The wreckage of civilization. Crumbled buildings, burned out cars, streets pockmarked by war. Downed power lines arc and spark on the street.

This place makes Hell look like Beverly Hills...

Except the battered twisted metal sign reads BEVERLY HILLS.

Night is falling. Fingers of shadow reaching out to grab anyone foolish enough to be in this part of town.

The only time the future is mentioned is in the slug line. Every other word in this scene describes how the future, this scene, feels: frightening, ugly, dangerous.

Did your skin on the back of your head crawl when you read this? Did you get a visual image of the scene? If you were the Production Designer, how many different possibilities would you have in order to recreate this scene?

Suppose you were an actor who had to walk down the street? How would you do it?

Hint Well-written descriptive passages describe the scene's emotion.

---

9. Avoid poetry

Too much imagery, alliteration, homonyms and other forms of word play can make your script more interesting. But overuse these tools and your script will end up looking cutesy.

Avoid asides to the reader. Your job is to involve the reader in the story, not impress them with your verbal dexterity.

Good screenwriting is both interesting and invisible. Word play should service the script, not show what a good education you have.

10. The four-line rule

If you want to *whiten* your script, a good rule is the four-line rule. No passage of action should last longer than four lines.

If you have a big action scene which lasts a page or more, break it up with spaces. Every four lines, put in a blank line. This instantly adds more *white stuff* to your script!

Another quick trick for long action passages is to have at least one line of dialogue on every page… even if it's just a character yelling 'Watch out!' This breaks up the page, and gives the reader a break from reading actions described.

11. Style on the page

Try to make each page look attractive and easy to read. Develop your own personal style of writing descriptive passages.

Experiment. After a few scripts, you will develop your own style and your own *voice* in descriptions. Developing a voice is an important step in taking command of the page (more on that, later).

12. Character

Do you think you could completely describe a character in three words? John Dahl managed that amazing feat in his script for *Buffalo Girls*, made as *The Last Seduction*.

This is a wonderful example of clear, succinct writing.

`BRIDGET GREGORY, bitch-ringmaster-goddess.`

He manages to convey Bridget's occupation and attitude, which allows us to imagine details about everything from the number of tattoos to hair length, personal grooming and wardrobe in a mere three words.

13. Active verbs

Use active verbs. Elliot doesn't *try* to sit on the chair, he *sits* on the chair. Better yet, he *crashes* into the chair. *Try* is an energy-sapping

---

There are two ways to make a character's quest for global destruction personal:

1. Make sure your hero has a stake in the outcome, and make sure the audience's identification with your hero is very strong. For example, in *Ransom*, the hero loses his child; in *Patriot Games* and *Gladiator*, the hero loses his family.

2. Have the villain's plan threaten the audience. Buying a cinema ticket allows you to sit in a cinema. You are minding your own business when suddenly you see that a deadly virus has been spawned, and is rapidly spreading throughout the civilized world (i.e. the USA). The villain, usually a British actor like Alan Rickman, demonstrates how quickly the virus will spread in an hour, a day, two days! Suddenly, sitting in the audience munching your popcorn, you see that your own existence could be threatened unless someone (Arnold Schwarzenegger) stops the virus. The story has become personal. If the hero does not stop the virus, we will perish! Successful films that operate this way include *Deep Impact*, *Twelve Monkeys*, *Jaws*, *Terminator* and *Star Wars*.

At the time of writing, foot and mouth is ravaging the UK. For a movie about this to work, one needs to find a personal story around which the impending doom of foot and mouth could be told.

verb: it saps power from the active verb. Other pitfalls to avoid are *starts to*, *begins to* and *…ing* – *walks* is stronger than *walking*.

14. Avoid widows

Typesetters call the last word of a sentence that carries over onto a new line of print a *widow*. A single word which takes up an entire line of space. In the rewrite process, kill all the widows. Rework the sentence until it fits entirely on one line. You should aim for a widow-free script. Another benefit is that this discipline will force you into choosing the correct words and eliminate any unnecessary words. As a result, your widow-free script will look cleaner on the page.

15. No ands or buts

In real life, pain hurts. Screen writers merit the attention of an audience by making an emotional connection with them. By making an emotional connection with the audience, you allow them to participate in your story.

And and *but* are almost always unnecessary. You can almost always delete them.

16. Confidence

An experienced writer knows exactly what each page has to say, and knows how to say it. Write strong sentences with strong visual images, and remember that the page belongs to you. Write with such clarity that anyone can open your script at random, read a passage and know exactly what is going on. Don't fill your pages with energy-sapping verbs in long, run-on sentences. It's your script. It's your idea. You are the writer. Write with confidence.

Hint Remember the three reasons you won't write a screenplay: lack of Confidence is number one!

---

17. Page turners

View each page as its own unique drama. At the end of each page, you must have built up enough suspense that the reader is actually willing to exert the energy to raise his or her hand, grab a hold of the page and turn it.

Build a page turner into each page of your script.

Add extra spaces or trim entire lines just to end a page on a moment of suspense. If there's a moment where the hero is about to be killed but saves himself, put the 'about to be killed' at the end of one page so you have to turn the page and keep reading to get to the saves himself part.

William C. Martell even adds artificial suspense to the end of a page to keep those pages turning. One of his thriller scripts has a scene where the hero comes home, and his girlfriend suggests they go out to dinner.

Boring! The hero enters his apartment on the second to last line on the page. So he added:

```
Hands reach out from behind the door and grab him!
```

At the top of the next page, we find out it's his girlfriend. Lines like this not only turn your script into a page turner, they add suspense, reversal, and excitement.

18. Editing

If you think your description is a little overwritten and could use some trimming, be brutal. Kick out every word that is not earning its space.

Design the page so the eye is drawn down, and make sure that you have a page turner at the end of each page.

Exercise for Writing Descriptive Passages

This simple exercise is one you can use in a variety of situations, and will enable you to hone your descriptive passage writing skills.

1. Take a careful look around the room you are in at the moment and describe everything and everyone in it, including yourself.

2. List the movement in the room. If there is no movement, try to recall how you entered the room.

3. See if you can include some of the objects in the room in the description of movement.

4. What is the emotion of the room?

```
┌─────────────────────────────────────────────────────────┐
│                                                           │
│                                                           │
│                                                           │
│                                                           │
│                                                           │
└─────────────────────────────────────────────────────────┘
```

5. Imagine you are sitting in front of a blank cinema screen. What must you tell the production designer to achieve the look of the room?

```
┌─────────────────────────────────────────────────────────┐
│                                                           │
│                                                           │
│                                                           │
│                                                           │
│                                                           │
└─────────────────────────────────────────────────────────┘
```

6. See if you can sum everything up in four lines – the look, the movement and the feel of the room, including any character description.

```
┌─────────────────────────────────────────────────────────┐
│                                                           │
│                                                           │
│                                                           │
│                                                           │
│                                                           │
│                                                           │
└─────────────────────────────────────────────────────────┘
```

Summary

1. Organise yourself. Know which scene comes when, and what the source of conflict is. Use the charts provided, if they improve clarity.

2. Write out the action and keep it as brief and dynamic as possible.

3. Develop your own individual style.

4. Never forget to draw on your instinctive storytelling ability.

We are ready to write dialogue.

6 Dialogue

Creating dialogue is the last step in the screenwriting process. Dialogue writing should not be attempted until the story outline, and the character studies have been thoroughly completed.

Writers who attempt dialogue before the story has been planned in detail usually find that the act of writing dialogue is so much fun that they forget that the story is the major issue, and find that the characters take over the story and dictate their terms of play to the writer.

It is easy to spot this in a script – the writer finds themselves boxed into a corner by their unruly characters, and in order to compensate for their behaviour, the writer simply adds a new character, usually about page thirty, in a desperate attempt to drag the story back on course.

This never works, and the script is ultimately doomed to oblivion (assuming the writer has the fortitude to complete it).

Writing instructors and screenwriting books are filled with ironies when discussing dialogue. All screenwriting books call for minimal dialogue.

Agents and producers, the first two people who will read your script, don't read the descriptive passages (black stuff) they just read the dialogue. They pass their eyes down the middle of the page reading the dialogue, and if something confuses them, or doesn't make sense, they back up the page until they come to a descriptive passage, and then proceed.

A picture is worth a thousand words. Think of it. By reason, the best dialogue would be no dialogue at all. Movies are a series of pictures. But to see a movie with just dialogue, like an agent or producer, would mean asking the projectionist to place a card over the lens and just play the sound track.

The next irony is the common adage 'Don't talk about doing something, do it'; or 'Actions speak louder than words'. Again, no dialogue seems to be the way to go.

People love to watch a story. A story consists of a person with a plan. It doesn't need to be a good or clever plan, but audiences love to watch and see if they can learn something by watching how a plan unfolds.

These are just a few examples of the paradoxes facing a screenwriter embarking on writing dialogue.

When approaching a scene in preparation for dialogue writing, you should have the following available to you:

- The character studies for each of the characters in your head. If the characters cannot speak to you, outside of the scene, or if you cannot ask them a question and actually hear (or feel) their response, then you have not adequately got to know your characters.

- A scene outline along with clear in and out points (Chapter 5).

- Any twist or reversal that you might have.

- A list of which characters are in the scene.

At this point, try to see if there might be a better way to tell the story or make the point of the scene. Often a new idea will spring to mind, or you may recast the scene with different characters from your cast list (don't make up a new character!).

Dialogue Tracks

When you are ready to proceed, imagine yourself in a music recording studio. You will write dialogue as if you are in a recording studio – by laying down tracks. Write dialogue for the entire script, once for each track. Take your time to create clear story and moral tracks. You may not have key words or moral argument in each scene. Later, when your dialogue writing session is complete, you will be able to mix (edit) the tracks to create powerful and satisfying dialogue.

Write these tracks – story dialogue; moral dialogue; key words.

1. Story dialogue

The talk about what is happening in a scene:

>   SWEET-FACED WOMAN
>   I'm just going to get some flowers,
>   dear. I'll be back in twenty minutes.
>   It's tulip season today. I'm so happy.

(Mark Andrus and James L. Brooks, *As Good As It Gets*.)

It may be helpful to construct a simple chart to track the following:

Goal
Figure out which character's goal is driving the scene. Someone must want something more than anyone else in the scene, and that character's goal will be the spine of the scene.

Conflict
Who opposes the character's goal?

Plan
The character with the goal now comes up with the plan which may be either direct or indirect. The plan refers to how the character will reach the plan within the scene, not within the story.

Twist
Scenes with twists are more exciting than scenes without.

Endpoint
A firm statement or a completed action to a surprising revelation.

figure 6.1
Story Dialogue Chart

Scene no.	
Goal	
Conflict	
Plan	
Twist	
Endpoint	

Write the scene, what happens, with dialogue

2. Moral dialogue

The discussion about what is and what is not valuable in life, and right and wrong, provides depth, texture and scope to the scene.

Values

Let your characters express their values and what they like or dislike. This allows you to compare different versions of how to live.

> LOUISE
> Just for the future, when a woman's crying like that, she's not having any fun.

(Callie Khouri, *Thelma and Louise*.)

Moral argument

Two or more characters come into conflict about what is right or wrong on the grounds that a particular course of action will hurt someone.

> MELVIN
> (to Simon)
> What I know is that as long as you keep your work zipped up around me, I don't give a fuck what or where you shove your show. Are we done being neighbors for now?

> SIMON
> (to Frank)
> Do you still think I was exaggerating?

Frank can only smile

> FRANK
> Definitely a package you don't want to open or touch.

> MELVIN
> Hope you find him. I love that dog.

Simon, terminally non-confrontational, still finds himself compelled to turn back toward Melvin.

> SIMON
> (directly)
> You don't love anything Mr. Udall

Simon closes his door leaving Melvin alone.

> MELVIN
> I love throwing your dog down the garbage chute.

(Mark Andrus and James L. Brooks, *As Good As It Gets*.)

3. Key words

Words which carry certain meaning which may mean something else to the audience and give a different meaning. When embedded in a story, key words provide crackle, zap and pop. You may want to repeat this word several times in different situations creating juxtapositions that give different shadings to the words.

Famous key words include 'Show me the money'; 'A man's gotta do what a man's gotta do'; 'Make my day, punk'; 'Yada Yada Yada'.

4. The final mix

Now it is a simple matter of taking the three tracks that you have created, and mixing them in the same way a sound recording engineer mixes the different tracks. Many scenes will rely on story dialogue,and you will spice it up with dashes of moral argument and the odd spike of key words.

The Fifteen Tricks and Traps of Dialogue

1. Keep it simple

Writing dialogue becomes fun and simple when you know your characters really well – through your character essays. When you achieve this, your characters will actually 'speak' to you.

No confusing words or difficult names. If your script has an African character name or is a sci-fi picture with technical jargon, remember that your script is being written for the reader. Try to keep it simple. A good screenplay is written in high school essay style and vocabulary.

2. Keep it short

Economy is the creative challenge. Ask yourself if there is a better way, a shorter way, a more direct way to express your thoughts in each and every scene.

There is a marvelous moment in *Escape from Alcatraz* when the child psychologist, a fellow prisoner of Clint Eastwood asks how his childhood was. 'Short', was the terse reply. No one actually speaks like this, but in this moment, we find volumes about Clint Eastwood's character.

3. Make each character speak with an individual voice

Each character should have their own individual way of speaking. Often a writer, so accustomed to writing each character as they themselves would speak, forgets that each individual in the world speaks a little differently. Each of the characters will say the same sort of thing in reaction to the main event of the scene.

This flaw is actually the easiest, and the most fun to correct. Deciding the individual voices of the characters, and then doing a dialogue rewrite is amusing and entertaining.

4. Forget dialect

A script written in a dialect will be considered a script by a rank amateur first timer. If you write such a script – you will be considered, at best, a talented amateur.

I had to read a script written in a heavy West Yorkshire accent. It was almost impossible to understand the colloquialisms. I even asked some vintage Brits in the office to translate, and they found it difficult. Remember that dialects are difficult to understand.

When *Trainspotting* played in Scottish in America, it was subtitled. Even my British friends find the thick Glaswegian accent difficult to understand.

Scripts are written in basic English. The choice of words will tell the reader if the character is slanted towards cockney, street urchin or southerner.

Casting directors will also dislike your script if it is written in dialect. Simply by writing your female lead as a cockney means that you have limited the choice of actress to those who can pull off a cockney accent. You have encumbered your script.

On the set, your cockney accent further eliminates the possibility of collaboration with the actors – the dialect is preset.

If you want your character to speak in French your choices are:

```
                    ELLIOT
                  (in French)
        It's 10 a.m. I'm still drunk.
```

or

```
                    ELLIOT
        Dix heures du matin. J'suis toujours bourré.
        (It's 10 a.m. I'm still drunk.)
```

5. No difficult words

You have to be easy on the reader. Any time you drop in a difficult word, or a word that you have invented (to explain some new age technical concept) you slow down the reader. The reader has to either look the word up, call someone, or skip over it in the troubling knowledge that they don't really get what it is you are saying.

6. Don't underline

Have you ever, in a speech of dialogue, in order to emphasize a word, underlined it? Don't do it. You look like a rank amateur first timer, and you have eliminated the possibility of collaboration with the actors. You are also directing from the typewriter, which is not your job.

Well-written dialogue should speak for itself. Pauses and key moments should be obvious.

Only underline a word if you think that the reader and the actor who reads your script is so stupid that they won't otherwise get it.

7. No '...'

Have you ever, in a speech of dialogue, in order to denote a pause, used '...'? Again you are directing from a typewriter, eliminating the possibility of collaboration with the actors, and making yourself look like a rank amateur first timer. There are exceptions to this rule.

Firstly, only use '...' if you feel that the plot hinges on this specific point, and/or you think the reader or actor won't be clever enough to get it.

Maybe you should limit yourself to five '...'s per script.

The second exception is the interrupted speech:

JOANNE
How old is Elliot? I'll bet he's...

BERNICE
...thirty-six.

You can use this as often as you like in your script.

8. No parenthetical directions

Do you put in actor's directions such as 'whispered', 'angrily', or 'shouted' under the character name?

ELLIOT
(angrily)

The exception to this rule is when you want to show an interrupted speech by another actor.

JOANNE
(to Ben)
How old is Elliot? I'll bet he's...

BERNICE
...thirty-six.

Again you are directing from the typewriter. Well-written dialogue will show how it is to be spoken.

If a professional actor receives your script with parentheticals, they will cross them out with a heavy black pen. If you put these directions in, you are eliminating the possibility of their creative input to the script.

I once worked as a touch-up artist on a film where a huge, Rambo-shaped man was arguing with his petite wife. Instead of hitting her, the script, with parentheticals, called for him to go to the kitchen door and smash it so hard that it would splinter. We rigged a stunt door, and during the rehearsals, the actor pretended to hit the door. We rehearsed the scene over and over again until we were ready.

At the moment of the take, the actor went to the door, on cue, with his massive arms knotted for a killer blow, whereupon he sighed and gently stroked the door.

The response from the crew was spontaneous. At the end of the take we all applauded. The power and energy of the actor, and the fact that he could have easily demolished the entire house, if not the door, with his bare hands, yet was rendered powerless by the emotion of the scene, was memorable for its intensity.

Although we later did a take with the actor physically smashing the door (as per the parentheticals) it was the first take the director kept.

9. Musical beat

People naturally speak with individual rhythms. By speeding up, slowing down, and emphasizing key words, people speak with a natural beat. Even though you have edited and honed your dialogue into lean lines, you must make certain that your dialogue sounds like real speech. To do that, you must restore the musical beat.

10. No long speeches

Try and remember the four-line rule. It applies to dialogue as well as descriptive passages. Certain masters of the screenplay write dialogue that goes on for pages. Tarantino opens *True Romance* with a monologue that is three-and-a-half pages long.

Writing dialogue like Tarantino on your first script will earn you derision. When you are at a level like Tarantino, you can write what you want.

There are times, however, when you will want to write a speech longer than four lines. You could double space after a few lines:

> QUINTO
> You used to laugh at me and my
> little jingle – Got a problem?
> Someone not treating you right?
>
> Owed a bit of cash? Call Quinto.
> The professional prick. Here I am,
> couple of years down the road.
> What do I find? You.

(Elliot Grove, *Table 5*.)

Or you could add stage directions to break up the dialogue:

> LARRY
> I'm trying to get the cash. Everything
> I do these days has to do with cash.
>
> Ramona flings the script to the floor.
>
> LARRY (cont'd)
> And the weather doesn't help, either.

(Elliot Grove, *Table 5*.)

11. No funny punctuation

Screenplays are written in a standard screenplay format (see Chapter 16). The correct way to use punctuation is standard English punctuation. In my days as a script reader I used to read screenplays submitted in a whole series of punctuation styles, such as the triple exclamation mark! Using punctuation such as this makes your script look like a comic book. Avoid.

12. No on-the-nose dialogue

By on-the-nose dialogue, read obvious dialogue, which telegraphs the action, for example:

```
Elliot reaches for a glass of Perrier.

                    ELLIOT
        I am thirsty. I think I'll get a drink.
```

On-the-nose dialogue is story dialogue track without sound editing. Most of what you write in your first 'track' will be on-the-nose.

13. Start late, end early

Ask yourself 'Is there a briefer, fresher, quicker, more dynamic way to say the same thing', of each and every single line of dialogue.

14. Avoid reality

New writers are tempted to include the humming and hawing of real speech in their dialogue. Such additions ignite the 'first time amateur' lightbulb above your head. Experienced actors are trained to know where the 'you knows', and 'mmms' are to be included in the dialogue. Leave them out! You are precluding collaboration with the actors, and you wouldn't want to do that, would you!

15. Start on page three

As a script reader, I read a script, sometimes two, every single day for nearly six years. Most scripts submitted to me came as a 'T'.

figure 6.2
The T Script

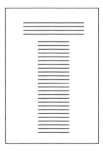

About one in ten came as an 'I'.

figure 6.3
The I Script

You can imagine the drama at my home a few seconds after the thud of the mail on the front steps. I could hear the footsteps of my partner racing to the door, and listen for the telling rip of the envelope.

'What have you got?'

'A *T*.'

'An *I*.'

Wow. Such drama.

It would seem that one of the easiest ways to distinguish oneself in a fiercely competitive market is to start your dialogue on page three.

Certainly, agents and producers would be forced to read the black stuff for the first few pages. But how good are you? Could you manage to write three pages of compelling action? That's just three minutes of screen time? If you manage this, remember, you will catapult yourself into the top one percent of screenplays written in the English language this year!

Hint Great dialogue should move either the story, or reveal something about the character. The best dialogue is no dialogue. A picture is worth a thousand words.

Writer's Block

Do you suffer from writer's block?

Writer's block has absolutely nothing to do with lack of creativity. It has everything to do with lack of confidence. Look at your life and try to identify any recent situation which may have undermined your confidence and then ignore it. Believe in yourself. You are at your own page seventy-five. You will feel much better and write better dialogue.

Dialogue Diagnostic Tool

Organise a table reading with friends or actors so you can hear what your dialogue sounds like in voices other than your own.

Organizing a table reading

There are many ways of conducting and organizing a table reading of your script. The first time you do this, you may find the whole process somewhat scary. The basic trick is to create an environment where you and the readers feel comfortable and safe.

Finding actors

Do you have trouble writing dialogue? Pull out your character essays. The chances are that you have still not fully researched your characters.

Remember to write the tracks. If you still have problems, try writing the story track only and then organize a table reading. Chances are the actors will have valuable suggestions on how the dialogue can be made more life-like.

Actors are usually receptive to table readings. They are informal, they can meet other actors and writers, and they get an opportunity to practice their craft. Ultimately, the actors might be considered for the role. Actors can be organized by placing notices in the backstage entrances of theatres, in acting schools, and on the Internet.

Setting a time and place

Evenings are a good time, especially early in the week. Setting a table reading for a Friday night when everyone is either exhausted or in a party mood is usually unwise. A neutral venue, like a rehearsal room or church hall, is great if you can afford it. If not, have people into your home. It is also advisable to let everyone know what the timing is. If the reading is to start at seven and finish at nine, write that in all your notices, so participants know what the time demands are. And make sure you start and end on time.

The ground rules

Please be aware that in our day and age people are very suspicious of meetings with strangers. Do whatever it takes to make everyone comfortable with you, and never take advantage of anyone!

Styles of reading

You can cast the script with actors, and have them just read the dialogue scene by scene. Some actors will put in basic gestures and follow stage directions if asked. I feel it is most useful to hear the dialogue only at this stage. It is also a useful reference to tape record the dialogue for later. Make sure you have the actors' permission.

Another type of table reading is the round circle – especially useful if you do not have enough actors for all the character parts. Simply start off reading the first paragraph of descriptive passage until a line of dialogue, all of which are read in turn around the table. This technique is useful because you hear the dialogue for each character read by several different voices.

Saying thank you

Actors do not expect to be paid, but it is polite to offer them some form of refreshment. It doesn't need to be fancy or expensive, just thoughtful.

A day or two after the reading, put a simple 'Thank you' card with a considered note in the mail to each participant. You will be amazed how readily they will agree to working with you again!

Afterwards – the rewrite. Collate all the notes from all the table readings and incorporate the suggestions and ideas into another rewrite.

Summary

1. Write minimal dialogue.

2. Preserve the musical beat, and make it sound like people talking.

3. Write three dialogue tracks – story, moral argument and key words.

That's the theory! Let's put it all together in the writer's blueprint.

7   The Writer's Blueprint

So much for the theory and the discussion of screenwriting technique. The time has come to start putting it all together. Where I grew up the saying was 'Time to stop chatting, roll up your sleeves, and get your hands dirty!'

I have purposefully skipped over formatting and typing rules. These are discussed thoroughly in Chapter 16. Many writers get to this point and then fail to actually write because they are afraid that their lack of knowledge about the finer points of formatting will interfere with their creative process. I get calls all the time from talented writers who want to chat. After I discern that they are healthy physically and mentally, I ask them how their latest script project is going. They always hesitate, draw a deep breath and wonder aloud if they can ask me a deeply personal question, like is 'gunshot' capitalized or not?

Hint Worries about formatting are one of the devices used by writers to procrastinate and put off writing their script. Procrastination is the third reason you will not write your script.

But here we are facing the excitement of writing a screenplay.

I have developed a step-by-step system over the years at the Writers Lab which I believe works. It certainly works for me. If you follow these steps, in order, you will end up with a well-structured screenplay. I have devised this system as a complement to your own intuitive storytelling ability. If these steps do not work for you, you have my permission to disregard them. I would appreciate any of your comments on how to make them better.

Here we go! Do you have an idea for a movie? Terrific. I thought so. Everybody has an idea for a movie. The problem is, it is in your head. The journey from your head to a piece of paper is just eighteen inches, but may as well be a million miles. In fact, mankind in general probably finds it easier to land a man on the moon than get an idea those eighteen terrible inches to a piece of paper.

The Seven Steps to a Successful Screenplay

Step One – Ideas

Ideas are the bricks and timber of a screenplay. An astute writer will carefully create a stockpile of ideas, and organize them in a way that will make retrieval easy. We are each different, and ideas come to us in different ways. Some excellent idea generation techniques are discussed in Chapter 15.

Remember to write ideas down. If you don't write them down, you are a dreamer, and you will never write a screenplay. They say in the film business that writers write, joggers jog and thinkers think. If you get paid for thinking, let me know.

Idea storage is an important consideration. Like any organization system, retrieval is the key. Just because you have every Welsh newspaper published since 1933 doesn't mean you have anything of value. It is only of value if you can effortlessly retrieve the newspapers published exactly one week before JFK's assassination, if that is the story you are working on. That has value.

This is how you store ideas – you must always jot them down. To carry an idea around in your head is dangerous and unhealthy.

Dangerous because you may lose it. Unhealthy, because an idea in your head will create stress that will lead to a cancerous feeling that will gnaw away at your self-confidence. An idea in your head is merely a thought. Once it is written down and stored properly, it can be retrieved at will, reassessed, juxtaposed with other ideas, and developed.

I recommend jotting the idea down on a recipe card, or on a page in a small, pocket-sized notebook. You should attempt to write the idea down in as few words as possible – three to eight words. The words should be just enough to jolt you back to the state you were in when you thought of the idea. You will then enter the mental state you were in when you thought of it – playful, sad, happy or whatever. At this later moment, you will be able to work on the idea further.

Once you have decided on a specific idea that you would like to develop for a film, then the ideas might be collated as to where they might fit in the movie. Of course, the beauty of this approach is when you have a handful of ideas, stored on index cards, you can stand the cards up on a table, flip them down one after the other, and see your entire movie from beginning to end. It is also dead simple to reorder/edit the scenes.

Step Two – The basic premise

Create the basic premise. For full details see Chapter 2. Ideas are the bricks and timber, the building materials of a screenplay. Your next step is to create an architect's sketch of what the finished building/ screenplay will look like. This is an idea boiled down into a few lines. This will become your road map, to which you constantly refer, to make sure you are on course. Write them here:

```




```

Hint The paragraph should read as – This story is about [describe, do not name] the hero, who [what they want more than anything else in the world] but [allude to the main obstacle] and [tease us with the ending].

Step Three – Characters

So far you have a big pile of building materials (ideas) and a road map. But undertaking a huge project on your own is daunting. Characters are the people who will help you.

But you need to get to know each of the characters helping you as if you were working on a long construction project. After all, you are going to get tired together, some of you may get injured, or damaged emotionally. Some of your team of characters may try to bully, or cheat. You need to understand each character as intimately as if they were living in real life.

Get going on character research. Write those character essays. See if you can combine traits from one character with traits to create a fascinating and compelling character for the screen.

Character Name

```


```

Trait(s)

```




```

Description

When you have finished the character essays, give yourself this quiz. You should be able to answer the following questions in one minute.

1. How old is your character?

2. Where were they born?

3. Where did they go to school?

4. What grades did they get?

5. What does their father do?

6. Who is their closest friend?

7. Which is their favorite TV programme?

8. If they were a magazine, which title would they be?

9. What would they wear to go out to the theatre?

10. What is their favorite music?

11. If they were to buy their lover a spontaneous gift, it would be

```
┌─────────────────────────────────────────────────────────┐
│                                                           │
│                                                           │
└─────────────────────────────────────────────────────────┘
```

You should know the characters in your movie so well that you can answer these questions immediately. If you take longer than sixty seconds to answer these questions, it would probably indicate that you do not know your characters well enough.

Go back to your character essays and write some more! The writing part is fun, because it is in this stage that you are meeting new people.

Here are the first few lines of my ten-page character essay:

```
Larry Raine is tired of hearing everybody saying
'What a loser' everytime he steps out of his office.
Out of money, but not out of his dream, Larry is
determined to get his movie 'The Big One' made.
```

The plan

This section may look deceptively simple. And it isn't simple at all. If you figure this section out, you are pretty much finished. I have devised a few questions, which I hope will make your journey easier. Only use my ideas if they help. Remember the instinctive storyteller inside you.

What is your hero's goal?

```
┌─────────────────────────────────────────────────────────┐
│                                                           │
│                                                           │
└─────────────────────────────────────────────────────────┘
```

Hint A goal is something that we can see when the hero achieves it, or fails to achieve it. A goal must be specific.

How does your hero plan to achieve the goal?

```
┌─────────────────────────────────────────────────────────┐
│                                                           │
│                                                           │
└─────────────────────────────────────────────────────────┘
```

Hint A plan is not a goal. The plan is the method by which your hero believes he or she will achieve the goal.

Who opposes the plan?

```
┌─────────────────────────────────────────────────────────┐
│                                                           │
│                                                           │
└─────────────────────────────────────────────────────────┘
```

How does your hero protect himself or herself?

How does the opponent counter the hero's plan?

How does your hero protect himself or herself?

Copyright

The next chapter deals with copyright. In case copyright issues bore you, here are the main points:

1. You own the copyright of your screenplay as soon as it is created.

2. Copyright disputes are about whether or not you can prove the creation of your screenplay.

3. Before you send your script out to any one, you must lodge a copy in order to get a birth certificate for your screenplay.

How does the opponent counter the hero's plan?

The plan is the set of guidelines the hero uses to overcome the opponent and win the goal. Since the opponent is the main obstacle to the hero's goal, we also need to see what the opponent's plan is.

Hero's plan   Opponent's plan

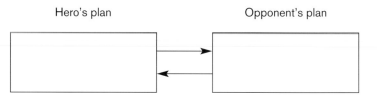

Next, try to list the reaction and action between the hero and opponent as each character tries to achieve their goal.

Hero's counter-plan   Opponent's counter-plan

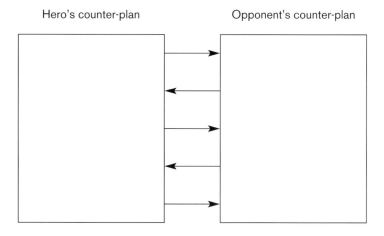

Step Four – Scene outline (structure)

With your cards in order, you can now use the best no-budget filmmaking process in the world – your own inner projector. Simply get comfortable, and look at each card, a scene at a time, and you will 'see' your movie. Be brutal. Edit and re-edit until your movie 'looks' fantastic.

figure 7.1
Index Card

Structure is the way your hero's plan unfolds. It is an organic process, and not one that fits easily into the traditional three-act story paradigm.

You may find it helpful to use the nine-point paradigm I outlined on page 37. Only use a paradigm if you find it helpful.

Some writers use index cards and write their ideas for each scene on a card. Others elaborate this by using a variety of color coded cards – blue for the opening (and emotionally less tense) through yellow and pink for the emotionally charged climax.

If you are writing on a script program like Final Draft, it will allow you to write the scenes on a computer, and then print them out as index cards, which you can then use to make notes, rearrange the order etc.

Point of Scene	Scene No.	

Remember that you do not write dialogue at this point! If you think of a line of dialogue, write it on the back of the card so you can come back to it later. Try to keep your initial thoughts to a few words. Later, when you start writing the scene, you will find these words jog you back to the moment when you first thought of the scene. Another advantage of writing cards is the ease that you can reshuffle scenes.

Step Five – Scene writing

Use a scene analysis sheet to plan each scene.

figure 7.2
Scene Writing Chart

Scene no.	
Previous endpoint	
Cast members in scene	
Point of scene	
Goal of main character	
Endpoint	
Conflict	
Twist	

Write the scene, what happens, without dialogue

Using a visual organizational tool may assist you in plotting your movie.

figure 7.3 Action Flow Chart

No.	Tag	Scene	Hero	Character	Character	Character	Character	1	2	3	Symbol

Step Six – Dialogue

Write the three tracks of dialogue – story, moral argument, and key-words. Then balance them. Do a table reading and rewrite.

When you have got your screenplay as good as you can, you are ready to market your script. But before you do that, who is going to try to rip you off, and how can you prevent it?

Step Seven – Troubleshooting

Chapter 17 is a useful troubleshooting guide which may assist you in analyzing your script. When you look at this guide, try to see if anything leaps out as a possible problem with your script.

Most difficulties in the script can be found in the first few pages. If the movie starts at the right place, it usually flows from there.

To get the right start, go to the ending. How do you want your movie to end? Did she really die? Did he kill him? They robbed the bank and got away? Pick your ending, then go to the beginning. Then have a close look at Chapter 17.

This is also the day that you should start writing your next screenplay.

Summary

1. Know your basic premise inside out.

2. Know your characters inside out.

3. Play and replay your movie at card stage, before you start writing. When you have your scenes and scene order completely firm, write the screenplay.

Who's going to rip you off, and how to prevent it? Copyright is the next consideration.

8   **10,000 Monkeys – Copyright**

Copyright law around the world is based on a simple premise – surrounding the planet earth there is a cloud of spirituality, of ideas. Any two people at the same time can pull down the same idea. And ideas are free.

What is copyrightable is the expression of the idea, be it as a poem, sculpture, libretto, novel or script. Sometimes, the difference between what is an expression of an idea and what is an idea can become complicated. Lawyers love the billings they make for cases such as this.

Basically, two screenwriters can come up with the same storyline for a movie. They write two very different screenplays, but the storyline idea (which cannot be copyright protected) cannot be disputed.

I have taught enough screenwriters in enough countries to know that if you are reading this, you are getting pretty paranoid by now. Please force yourself to finish reading this chapter, so you can develop a positive mental attitude towards copyright.

Many writers and artists labour under the misconception that they must fill out an official form, and write the letter '©' in order to assert their claim for ownership of the copyright. In fact, all countries recognize that the artist owns copyright from the moment it is created.

The difficulty arises in proving that ownership in a court of law.

Protecting Your Screenplay

1. Protecting the idea

You cannot protect an idea. This is the whole point of copyright law. Your first task after coming up with a great idea for a movie is to write as detailed an account of your idea as possible. Generally, a page or two is not sufficient. A judge may be unable to distinguish your ideas from competitors. Three pages are better, but I recommend ten. After all, you have an idea for a movie that will end up being ninety to a hundred-and-twenty pages long. Surely you can outline the key points in ten pages.

Hint Keep your idea strictly to yourself until you have written it down.

---

2. Ownership

If you have a great idea for a movie, you cannot tell anyone about it until you have registered the idea for copyright. Tell a shrewd producer that you have a great idea and he/she will ask you 'Have you written the script? A treatment?' If the answer is 'No' to either of these questions, you have just gifted them with your idea. And there is nothing immoral, sleazy or dishonest about this. It is just the way that copyright works.

You own the copyright of your script or treatment the moment it is created. Suppose you are in your ivory tower, typing your hundred-page screenplay. You are on a complete roll, when suddenly, near the bottom of page ninety-nine you hear the two most dreaded words a screenwriter will ever hear bouncing up the walls of your ivory tower – 'Honey! Dinner!' You race down for dinner, storm through your food, and race back to your typewriter only to discover that an erstwhile copyright thief has taken the ninety-nine page manuscript from you, and typed a new page hundred and is now claiming ownership of the script. The question of ownership would be defeated in court in this example. You created the screenplay (minus page hundred) and you own the copyright. The only way that you would lose the copyright is by assigning the title of the screenplay to someone else, presumably for a wad of cash. The difficulty is in proving that you own the copyright.

3. Creating the birth certificate

Screenwriters can apply to have their scripts registered upon completion, in a similar way that parents apply for a birth certificate for their newborns. It is called a Certificate of Registration, and is available from the Writers Guild of America at www.wga.org

At the time of writing, the fee is a modest $20.00. Send a copy of the final version of the screenplay. For your money, you will receive a letter with the date your script was received along with a serial number (to assist in file retrieval). Keep this number confidential.

Other writers register their scripts with the United States Copyright Office. You can check the current fees from www.loc.gov/copyright or call (202) 707 3000.

Other arts organizations in the UK, the trade union BECTU and also Raindance provide the service free to its members.

Now you can promote and market your script to your heart's content knowing that you are able to prove the date of creation.

4. Proving ownership

However, there is an additional piece of administrative detail, which you must attend to in order to back up the birth certificate. Should you ever go to court in a copyright dispute with another writer, or with a producer who you suspect of using your script without permission, you need to prove that you are the one who registered the screenplay. In property transactions, this is called chain of title, where your solicitor will look at the deeds of the house you are buying and trace all the previous owners back in time to make sure that the title has no unpaid mortgages, liens for city taxes and so on. Screenplays are classed as intellectual property, and the laws governing the trading of intellectual property are similar to those governing real estate transactions.

Screenwriters also need to prove chain of title, although it is less formal than in property dealing. You have to keep a formal record of everyone you speak to about your screenplay.

Each time you meet someone and discuss your screenplay, make sure you obtain their business card or contact details and send them the following letter:

The reason for explaining copyright is to demystify the issue of who can rip you off. In order to sell your script you have to be able to tell everyone about your script. If you don't, nobody will know you've written it until after you're dead and gone!

Elliot Grove
Raindance
81 Berwick Street
London W1F 8TW

dd/mm/yy

Dear Elliot,

It was a pleasure meeting you at the cinema last night, and I enjoyed discussing with you my forthcoming screenplay 'Top Title'.

I look forward to working with you.

Yours sincerely,

Your name

Mail a copy to the person you met. That person will probably toss your letter into the bin whilst muttering 'Nutbar… I never agreed to work with that writer!'

But what you have established is the start of a written contract with that person. By their silence, they have given tacit approval to your letter, and the start of a written contract is born. Later, if you discover that this person is making a movie without you, then you can get your attorney or solicitor to write them a letter stating in effect:

Elliot Grove
Raindance
81 Berwick Street
London W1F 8TW

dd/mm/yy

Dear Elliot,

After my client spoke to you on dd/mm/yy, I am surprised to hear that you are making a film based on their idea without them

I look forward to hearing from you.

Yours sincerely,

Your attorney's name

A producer or director faced with a letter like this will have to immediately deal with your claim to ownership or risk losing their investors with the threat of expensive litigation.

Sometimes, in situations like this, you will get a response like 'Isn't it amazing about the common currency of ideas in circulation? Our idea is similar, but not identical to yours. Please go away.' Or 'Pass!'

Now you are going totally paranoid. I know it! Persons known to you have somehow stolen your idea and are ripping you off *before* they have seen your screenplay.

Writers must be prepared for this, and it is not as outlandish as it seems. The film executive who tells you this has probably heard a thousand pitches. Even if he or she can't quite remember whether they have heard your pitch before, they will pass even if they think it sounds like another idea they have heard. They do this because they are very concerned about litigious writers pressing a claim for ownership. Life is too short to contemplate litigation.

As I mentioned above, the entire world's copyright laws are based on the concept that ideas are free and can be accessed by anyone. Indeed, copyright law contemplates the likelihood that more than one person can have the same idea at the same time.

Hint Remember, it is the expression of the idea that is copyrightable.

---

5. Ten thousand monkeys

American scientists proved the theory of 'Isn't it amazing about the common currency of ideas in circulation' with an experiment in the South Pacific. There they found six islands, on which lived a unique species of monkey, totalling ten thousand. On five of the islands grew sweet potatoes, a very good food for monkeys – but none of the monkeys ate sweet potatoes. Approximately six hundred monkeys lived on the sixth island – the one without sweet potatoes. The scientists introduced sweet potatoes, trained a few monkeys to dig up the potatoes, take them to the ocean and wash them, and then eat them. A very strange thing happened when approximately a hundred of the six hundred monkeys were digging up the sweet potatoes, taking them to the ocean and washing them and eating them. Suddenly, the monkeys on the other islands started to dig up sweet potatoes, take them to the ocean to wash them and eat them.

Isn't it amazing about the common currency of ideas in circulation?

When I moved to London from Toronto in 1986, I was used to being a Lone Ranger. In Toronto, if I had an idea for literally anything, I would be isolated by all my acquaintances (I didn't really have 'friends') because they thought me, with my crazy ideas, quite weird. But when I moved to London, not fully appreciating the difference in size, and the broad depth of this cosmopolitan and multi-cultural city, I suddenly felt at one with a huge number of unseen friends. And whenever I have an idea I would read about it in the newspaper the very next day – pretty scary for a writer.

Remember that whatever your idea for a movie is, I can guarantee you that at least a dozen other people in the world right now have exactly the same idea. The only difference is that you are reading this book and attempting to discover a better way to get it out onto paper. Remember that all ideas are basically sound. What makes an ordinary idea exciting is the way you bend, reshape and state the idea. The expression of the idea is yours, and yours alone. The bolder and fresher you can be, the more valuable your idea will be in the market place.

Hint Don't let the common currency of ideas discourage you.

---

6. Misfortune

What if you have a great idea for a movie, register it for copyright, and voilà – someone else is making the movie? What would you do? Sue? Commit suicide? Give up writing?

Misfortune is a weird and dangerous thing. Consider this true story of a writing friend of mine in London. She came up with a concept for a television show based on the true-life experiences of people living alone, but sharing accommodation. In order to secure stories, she placed ads in London's famous *Time Out* magazine advertising for people to write in with their stories. She prepared a questionnaire for potential participants which she returned to each person who responded to the ad. This process took place over an extensive period of time. Just as she was approaching her goal of getting the right mix of people for her series of shows, she was summoned to New York on an urgent family matter. While there she picked up a *Village Voice*, where to her amazement saw an ad that was worded identically to hers. She responded and received a questionnaire exactly like the one she had prepared in London, some eighteen months earlier. Back in London, she conferred with an entertainment attorney, another good friend of mine. He told her that she had a case for copyright infringement, which he was willing to pursue for nothing, as a favour. Hard costs would be from $5,000 to $10,000. As she didn't happen to have that much cash lying around for a speculative enterprise as this, he advised her to pass. Even if she won her case she would still have to prove that she had suffered financial damages. As it was difficult to see how a classified ad in New York could possibly infringe on a television show destined for the United Kingdom, she decided to let go. A few months later, the trades announced the production start of a movie I cannot name for legal reasons, but roughly the story of single Caucasian females.

My friend had a great attitude to this misfortune. She shrugged her shoulders and simply said that it proved that her ideas were commercially viable, and she moved on.

Hint Misfortune happens. Don't take it personally. Learn to move on.

---

7. Waiver letters and submission releases

Sometimes when you submit a script to a production company, they will send your script back with a letter that they want you to sign. The letter basically states that they want you to cast aside your legal right to sue them for copyright infringement if they ever make a film resembling in any way your screenplay.

My advice is simple. If you don't feel comfortable with the letter don't sign it. The film company will not read your script. Go find someone else. Of course, I believe that astute writers understand that these writers are designed by film companies, not to make it easier to plunder screenplays, but to defend them from dishonest screenwriters. Either way you look at it, don't do anything until you feel comfortable.

A submission release looks like this:

Person
Company
Town
Code

Re: [Title of material submitted], Number of pages

Dear Sir or Madam

Enclosed I am submitting to you literary works/screenplay [insert title] for your consideration under the following express understanding and conditions.

1. I hereby confirm that I am submitting the enclosed material voluntarily. I hereby agree that you are under no obligation to me regarding this material unless you and I have signed a written agreement which will then become the only contract between us.

2. I hereby confirm that any discussions, whether oral or written, between us regarding the enclosed material shall not be construed to form an agreement regarding the purchase of said material.

3. I hereby confirm that should the enclosed material not be new or original, or if you have already received material similar to [insert title] from others, or from your employees, then I agree that you will in no way be liable to me for use of this material and I do not expect to be paid for such.

4. I hereby confirm that if you produce or distribute a television show(s) or movie(s) based on the same general themes, ideas, situations, geographical settings, period of history or characters as those presented to you today then I agree that you will in no way be liable to me for use of this material and I do not expect to be paid for such.

I hereby confirm that but for my agreement to the above terms and conditions, you would not agree to accept and consider the material [insert title] submitted to you today.

Yours faithfully,

[insert name and signature
of writer, date, address and
contact telephone]

8. Non-disclosure agreements

When you go to a pitch meeting with a film company, you may be asked to pitch ideas to them. Of course, ideas are free and cannot be copyrighted. Some writers know this beforehand, and only reveal ideas they have already written down and have registered. Other writers feel constrained by this, and like to 'pitch from the hip' – firing off any idea that pops into their head. In order to protect yourself, it is wise to ask the executives to read and sign a simple letter acknowledging that A. you were present at their offices on the specific date; B. that you pitched them several ideas; C. if they use any of the ideas you expect to be paid; and D. all parties agree to enter into a formal agreement at a mutually agreed time in the near future.

This letter, when signed, affords the writer some protection against a shrewd, but a sly film producer, trying to wheedle an idea for the next *Blair Witch Project* out of you for nothing, unless you have a really hot script. Then, every producer you speak to will sign your agreement.

Re: [Title of your project(s) or screenplay(s)]

Dear Sir or Madam,

This letter confirms that I am presenting to you ideas today, and delivering to you certain manuscripts, storyboards and documents for your consideration under the following terms and conditions:

1 Authorized use: The Prospective Purchaser may review the enclosed documents and the project to determine the suitability and desirability of entering into an agreement with [your name] and [company name]. Before Prospective Purchaser, an employee or any representative of the Prospective Purchaser shall view the Documents the Prospective Purchaser shall require each individual who will review the documents to read this agreement and sign an agreement identical to this.

2. The Prospective Purchaser agrees that no one shall receive copies of the documents, or shall be verbally told of the documents unless that person too signs this agreement.

3. Time limits: If the Prospective Purchaser decides not to enter into an agreement by [insert date], then the prospective purchaser agrees to return the enclosed documents and all copies made by registered express delivery to:[insert your name and address] within 24 hours

4. Damages: Since the concepts, characters and documents relating to the project are valuable to [insert your name and company] if the Prospective Purchaser discloses breaches this agreement then the Prospective Purchaser shall pay to [insert your name and company name] the amount of [insert the value of your project].

5. Should the Prospective Purchaser agree to proceed with a deal based on the Documents, then both parties agree to signing a long form contract at a time mutually convenient.

[Signature/Date/Witnessed by/Date]

---

9. Acquiring rights to a true life story

Writers will often become aware of a true life story based on a newspaper account or television news piece. In order to acquire the screenplay rights to a person's true life story, you need to approach the individual directly and secure their written permission to base a screenplay on their life.

Probably the easiest way to contact this person is through the journalist who originally created the story. Through this contact, approach the individual directly and see if you can persuade them to allow you to write the story of their life.

There are certain laws governing the stories of criminals. Most countries will not allow a criminal to profit from any story about their crime, through the American 'Son of Sam' laws or similar. If you are contacting a criminal, make sure you engage the services of an entertainment attorney who can offer expert advice.

Here is a sample letter you can use when contacting someone:

Person
Company

dd/mm/yy

Re: [Title of your project(s) or screenplay(s)]

Dear Sir or Madam,

I write to inquire whether the theatrical and film rights to your story are available.

I was able to get your contact details from [name of reporter or journalist].

Your powerful and unique story touched me greatly and feel deeply that your story should be shared with others.

I would appreciate it if you could contact me at your earliest convenience at [telephone number]. Please feel free to reverse the charges.

Yours sincerely,

[Your name]

Summary

1. Take the time to understand the structure of copyright.

2. Never tell anyone an idea until you have written it down as completely as possible and registered it.

3. Be professional. Keep track, by letter, of everyone you have discussed your screenplay with.

4. Make absolutely certain that you have the necessary permission before you start writing.

Now it's time to market your screenplay.

9   **Marketing Your Script**

Just as writing your screenplay requires a method plus creative thought, so too does the task of marketing your screenplay. Try to market your screenplay without a plan, and plan to be confused. So see if you can follow the marketing plan.

Preparation

There are two things that writers hate – writers hate writing and writers really hate selling.

Unless you master the art of selling, you will never be a professional screenwriter – no one will pay you for your work. And selling your work need not be a painful and dreaded experience. In fact, it can be a lot of fun, if you have a plan of attack.

These next chapters are designed to help writers who hate selling, sell their script. But you have to follow my little system. Let's assume you have finished your script and are asking 'Now what?'

1. Let it rest

Put your screenplay aside for at least two weeks. I like to let mine rest for a month. You want to leave it long enough so you forget it – so it seems fresh when you see it again.

Perhaps you will start working on your next project, or simply try to catch up on seeing as many films as you can. This is a sweet moment. You have actually written your screenplay. You still don't want to show it to anyone, but at least you can announce that you are finished.

Leonardo da Vinci used to view his paintings through a mirror from a great distance in order to see the work in its entirety. He believed that weaknesses would be more obvious from a distance, and reversed through a mirror.

Time is your distance. When you return to your script, pick it up and read it for pleasure. You will find some gaping holes in your script so huge and obvious that you won't believe you didn't notice them before. Fix them!

You will also see some things you are really proud of. Congratulations. You will feel a warm wash of self-satisfaction sweep over you. You have succeeded, in part, in your quest to master the craft of screenwriting.

It might also be a good time to pull out the troubleshooting guide in Chapter 17 and have another look with fresh eyes.

Hint Rewriting is a crucial part of the writing process, but is often approached incorrectly.

The myth about rewriting is that it's a cure-all. Many writers think that they can fix their errors in subsequent drafts. They start the first draft before the planning process is complete and thereby create a draft that has fatal flaws.

If you have done your homework and made a detailed plan, your first draft will be built on a solid foundation. Then determine exactly what the theme of the piece is. Make sure all scenes focus toward the theme. Ask yourself if there is a bolder, fresher, quicker way to say the same thing. Cut, cut, cut. Fix the dialogue last.

2. Character rewrite

Go through the script with a fine tooth comb and set aside anything that does not directly pertain to the goal of the main character.

When you read the script again, you will be amazed at how much energy it has. Look at your script and see if there is anything new you can add to the script, or perhaps you can retrieve and recycle some of the material you set aside earlier. Maybe that scene you thought was a great set-up to the page forty-five scene would work better as the page seventy-five scene, and so on.

3. Table reading – the dialogue rewrite

When you have got the script as good as you can on your own, try a table reading.

A table reading with actors (from a local theatre group, or acting school) is a great way for your piece to come to life. Actors would not normally expect to be paid, although it is polite to offer some refreshments, or help with transportation costs.

Spend some time and cast the script as close to the characters you had in mind. Then gather everyone around a table and read the piece. You may have the actors read it as a stage play – dialogue only. Or you may have the actors alternate in reading the black stuff as well.

Tape-record the performance. Actors are trained to read dialogue. There may be phrases that just are hard for an actor to say, or others which do not make sense. Often the actors will make suggestions about the phrasing, or question the purpose of a particular line.

Writers experiencing a table reading of their work for the first time marvel at the experience. The sound of actors' voices helps them visualize their work for the first time, and gives them a huge boost of confidence. It is the first stage in making a screenplay become real.

Make the appropriate notes, and consider them in your next revision.

You are probably so tired of your script now that you might not be able to make it any better. There is probably a little voice inside you nagging away and what you really want to know is what someone else thinks about your script.

Now you are ready for feedback.

4. Your first reader

Who, exactly, do I send my screenplay to?

The first rule of marketing your screenplay is that you never ever send your script to someone unless they ask for it. Film companies are paranoid about litigation and will only accept submissions from people they know and trust – agents, established producers and entertainment solicitors. The trick is to get someone to ask for your script when you don't yet have an agent.

Make ten copies of your script and give it to nine acquaintances. Tell them to read the script and to scribble down any comments, observations, and even flattery, in the margins. Tell them you want their honest reaction. I always give the tenth script to my mother, because I know she won't lie.

Your first observation should be in noting how long it takes each person to read and return your screenplay. If they call you back the very next morning and say what a terrific screenplay you have – that is good. They have taken it home that evening, and opened the first page, started to read it and became so absorbed that they couldn't put it down. And they couldn't wait to tell you about it.

If you bump into them on the street a few days later and ask them 'How are you?' and they say 'Fine, oh yes, almost forgot to tell you – I started reading your screenplay last night and got about a quarter of the way through.' That is bad. They have started reading your script and you failed totally to grab their attention.

A good script is always a page-turner and will never take more than forty-five minutes to read.

Once all the scripts and comments are back, tabulate the results of the readers' comments and see if there are any worthwhile comments you can incorporate into your next revision. If everyone is saying 'I don't get it' – then you must have a fundamental flaw with the storyline. Fix it.

5. Professional reader's report

Certain individuals and organizations provide a script reading service. The quality of the reports vary, but at least you know that the person who has read your script has read quite a few, and their comments will be measured against other scripts currently in circulation.

Fees for this service are about £40 in the UK and $75 in the US. Expect to get four to five pages of written notes on plot, structure, characterization, dialogue, visual appeal and commercial viability.

Experts, such as Michael Hague, Syd Field and John Truby, charge up to $5,000 to read your screenplay. You are buying their considerable experience when you pay this kind of money, and personally, knowing Michael and John as I do, would save the cost of this level of critique for the production company to bear.

Again, incorporate the appropriate comments into your next revision.

At this point, when you feel you are satisfied with the script, you are ready to start the direct marketing of this script.

Curiously, an embittered screenwriter started a story circulating in London recently.

To prove that readers were incompetent of recognizing his great script, he rewrote *Chinatown* word for word, changing nothing but the characters' names and the title of the movie. Coverage returned to him used comments like 'shallow and superficial characterization', 'ruins the story' and so on.

And don't forget! The day after you finish your first script is the day that you start working on your second. Your second script will be much easier, because you will have a system to follow. You are learning how to run your screenwriting business.

Hint If you were a reader for Miramax and read my script and thought it was good, would you recommend it? What would make you recommend a script? If I were reading for Miramax, I would only recommend a script if I thought it made me look good – because I would be looking for a promotion. Thus I would never recommend a good script. I would only recommend a great screenplay – I want to be known as the reader who recommended the next *Chinatown* or the next *Crying Game*.

Professional readers are your first barrier into the film industry. But you need to understand the structure of how readers operate. Readers cannot approve or say yes to your script. What they do say is the word no.

Of the readers I know, about seventy-five percent are female, ninety-five percent Caucasian. The one thing they share is that they are recent graduates of a recent university liberal arts program. In other words, they are people on whose education their parents have wasted a huge amount of money. And they know absolutely nothing about the movies. Which is why they are hired.

There is a saying in Hollywood – 'If it ain't on the page, it ain't on the stage.' To get a job as a reader, the production company gives you a script that has already been assessed. You are asked to read it and comment on it. The company then reads your reviews to see if you picked up the same flaws as they did. Film producers value the opinion of the readers precisely because it is so neutral, and because they have no technical expertise. The minute a script reader becomes an expert, they are no longer useful as readers, although they have a valuable role as story consultants.

Hint Write for the reader. Make sure that your script can entertain at this level. After all, it is the entertainment industry.

---

6. Join a writers' group

Marketing a screenplay can be a lonely business. Joining a writers' group can help. Look at the local library or call the nearest film organization to see if they can give you name of the nearest writers' group.

Each writers' group is organized differently. Some are intended as purely social occasions for the members. Others arrange screenings and talks by agents and producers, and others combine these activities by providing feedback on each other's work.

If you cannot find a writers' group near you, why not start one yourself? Consider the following tips:

Venue
Find a venue. It could be a church basement, an upstairs room in a pub, or someone's living room. It doesn't really matter where it is as long as you have a venue.

Advertise
Flyers or leaflets explaining what you are doing, along with the date, time and place of the first meeting, can be printed cheaply. Distribute the leaflets to film schools, libraries, actors' groups, theatres and art house cinemas. It is really helpful to have a telephone number on the leaflet so potential attendees can satisfy themselves that you are legitimate and not an axe murderer.

Refreshments
At the first meeting it's a good idea to appoint someone to be responsible for refreshments, and someone to volunteer to be the chairperson with the task of being on the telephone. This is useful for last minute changes to the schedule or for adding an event. These positions can also rotate. Meetings can be held weekly, or monthly – whatever seems right for your group.

Small is beautiful
If you have fifteen people respond to your advertising blitz, don't be surprised if only five or six become regulars. Don't allow the small number of writers in your group alarm you – small is beautiful, and you can get excellent feedback from half a dozen people, especially if you can share your common experiences as writers.

Minutes
One way to sustain interest is to write up simple minutes of each meeting. You can email, fax or post these to everyone. People who have missed a meeting will then feel a part of the group, and will free to contribute to the meeting they missed.

Longevity
Don't expect a writer's group to last forever. People change jobs, refocus on their career perspectives and move. Creating pressure on participants to commit to a group forever and ever is really the kiss of death. Your writers' group will exist as long as it needs to help you!

7. Pedigree

This is the most important part of your marketing preparation: building pedigree for your script.

A screenplay can command a very high price. A film production company, regardless of the size, considers the purchase of a script to be a significant investment. Before a company buys a screenplay, it has to be certain of its pedigree.

Usually, established writers sell their screenplays through literary agents, established producers or entertainment attorneys. Each of these people represents a filter that is trusted by a film production company, thereby enhancing the pedigree of the script. In your own life, you probably act in the same way. If a trusted friend calls you and says 'I have just heard a fantastic song by this new artist. You must get their CD.' The next time you are in a music store, you will probably search out this CD, perhaps even buy it.

However, it is very difficult for a new writer to attract the services of an agent, producer or entertainment attorney. So the Catch-22 is how to market your screenplay to a production company on your own.

Building the Pedigree for Your Screenplay

The receptionist theory

It costs money for a film company to accept delivery of your screenplay. Once it is inside their internal system, your screenplay has to be entered in the database, the actual script stored, possibly duplicated, and reader's fees and development executives' evaluation fees must be paid. To get a screenplay into a company, have it read once, a simple rejection letter typed and returned with your screenplay costs at least £200/$300.

Try to get someone in the industry, even a receptionist, to read your script. If they will write you a short letter telling you what they think, even better. You are really hoping that this lowly employee will brag about having read a really fantastic screenplay, and being overheard by one of the moguls next to the coffee machine. The receptionist theory is that this person can refer your script higher up the food chain. Make sure you say thank you properly to any receptionist that helps you.

Film organizations

Get someone from a film organization to read and recommend your screenplay. Organizations like the IFP in America and Raindance in the UK are respected by the industry. If you can get a letter of reference from an employee about your script, give yourself a treat. If you can persuade them to call up the head of development at a film company and recommend your screenplay – fantastic. If you succeed in this, the production company will read your script.

Some film production companies have close ties with organizations. In the UK, Working Title, FilmFour, BBC Films and Pathé are a few of the production companies with close links to Raindance. In America, Fine Line, NextWave and Sony Pictures Classics have ties with the IFP. A film organisation will only recommend your script if they really like it.

Stars

Get a star to read and recommend your script – even if they are unable or unwilling to play one of the parts. Another approach would be to persuade a star physically unsuitable for the part to read and recommend your script with the line 'if only I had stumbled across this screenplay in 1955 when I was younger – it would have been perfect'. Based on this recommendation, you search out a production company with access to an actor similar to the aged one.

Business or community leaders

Script competitions

You have now finished the preparation process for marketing your screenplay. In effect you have already started to market your script. Many of the people you are approaching could purchase your screenplay. By not asking them to buy your script, you are in effect taking the financial pressure off them and if your script is good enough, they will be happy to see you succeed and either recommend it to someone else, or they may buy the script themselves.

Do you think you could get Richard Branson or Bill Gates to read your script and like it? This would almost certainly guarantee a positive reaction from any number of film production companies. Which community or business leaders do you know? Perhaps your local car dealer, local councillor, pastor, sheik, bank manager, could read your script and write you a reference – remember that they really have to like your script. Film companies have a secret weapon on their desk that they use to suss out referees: it's called a telephone!

Producer

Find a producer who has made a film, even if it's not a very good one, and get them to read and comment on your script. They have already succeeded in financing one film and they know how the business works. If they read and like your script then people in the industry will take notice that your pedigree is just a little bit better than average.

Financiers

Any financier, but especially a film financier, has the potential to make your script have impeccable pedigree if they love your screenplay. So start bombarding your local credit controller with your screenplay. If you know anyone who works for one of the film financing banks, or the insurance bond guarantee companies, so much the better. If they read and love your script, and will agree to be quoted, your script starts to take on the pedigree of old leather top desks, waistcoats and Earl Grey tea. This helps make your script bankable.

Readers' reports

If you have had a professional reader's report (i.e. one that you have paid for) that is positive, either mention this in a covering letter, or include the report with your script. It shows that someone (albeit partial to you) had a positive reaction to your script. My experience is that a production company will often request a copy of your coverage, especially if your reader has pedigree. They will then assess the coverage, and make a decision as to whether or not they are interested.

The following chart will help you track the progress of your projects:

figure 9.1
Project Tracking Chart

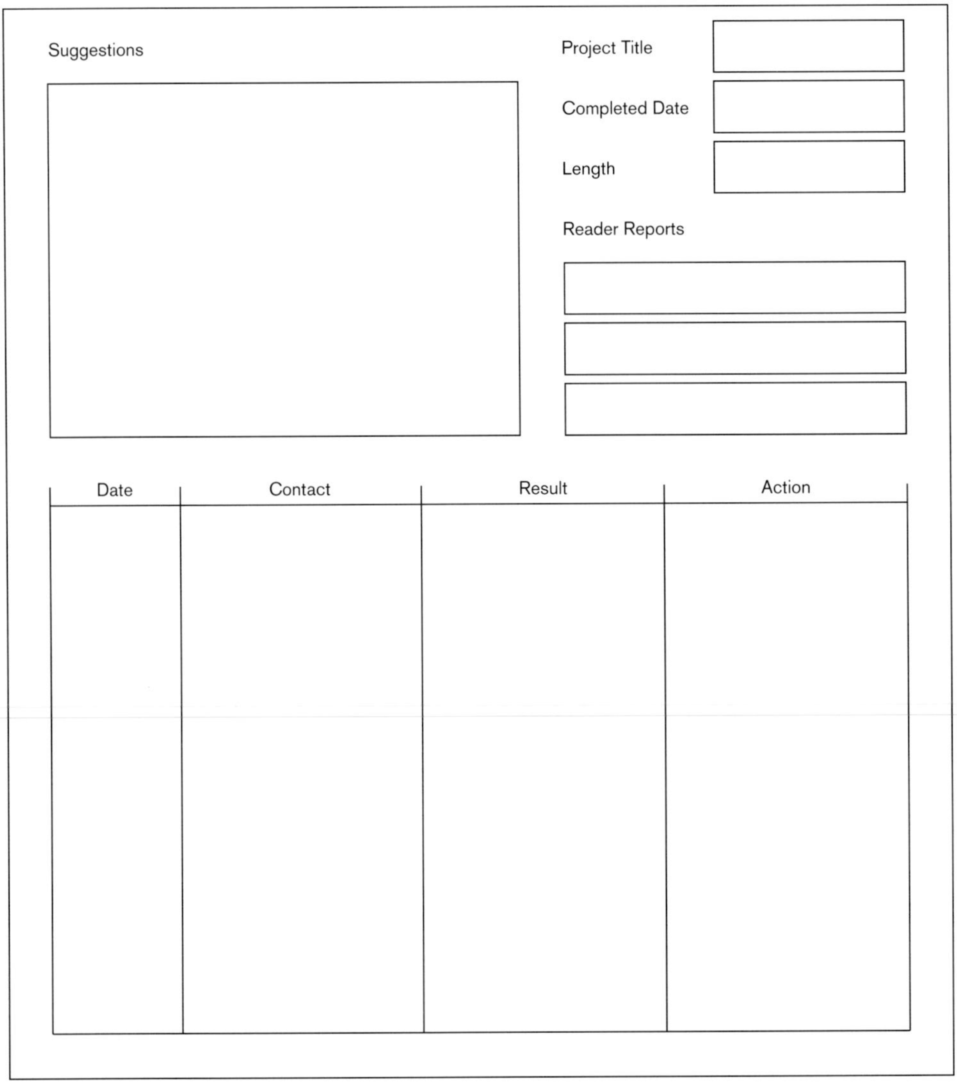

Suggestions		Project Title	
		Completed Date	
		Length	
		Reader Reports	

Date	Contact	Result	Action

Summary

1. Good feedback is bad feedback. The only good feedback is a check.

2. Scripts aren't written they are rewritten.

Next, we need to find out who is purchasing screenplays. And to do that, we have to play the movie game.

10   The Movie Game

In order to illustrate the possibilities of potential sales for your script, it is useful to play the movie game – useful because it visualizes a complicated concept. It is a board game, and it has spaces that you can land on with your script – your playing piece.

figure 10.1
The Movie Game

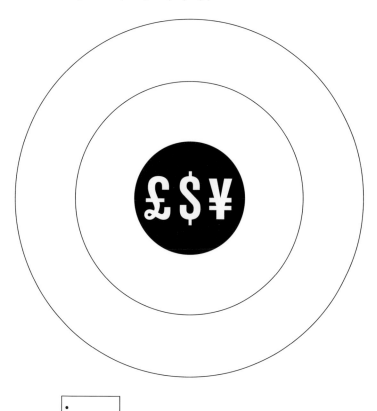

The second ring represents the areas inside the British film industry where screenplays can be sold, and the outer ring represents those areas outside the British film industry.

Hint The object of the game is to sell your screenplay (to get the deal) without any outside creative interference. As a writer, you do not ever want to hear the word 'rewrite'.

The Second Ring

The second ring can be subdivided into three areas:

1. BBC, FilmFour and BSkyB

These companies make films by first time filmmakers on a regular basis. In the case of the BBC and FilmFour, they usually rely on a writer's past performance as a writer of short films, Shane Meadows for example, or of radio drama as in the case of Richard Curtis before snapping up a script for a feature film production.

Until recently, both FilmFour and the BBC accepted unsolicited scripts, but no longer do so. At the time of writing, BSkyB still does. In theory, you can submit your film to BSkyB and if they like it, they will purchase the script and start pre-production. Reality dictates otherwise. It is very useful, when trying to sell your script to put yourself behind the desk of the person you are pursuing.

Hint The golden rule is that water runs downhill – make it easy for them to say *Yes*. Don't expect water to run uphill.

The first task of FilmFour, or in fact, any production company in the world, is to find a director for that wonderful screenplay of yours that they have just purchased. Their second job is to find a producer. Then, of course, the casting process follows.

Make it easy.

Obviously, the more people you can convince to work with you on your script then the easier it will be to sell. The different people – actors, directors and producer(s) you convince are called 'elements'. The fact that they have agreed to work with you on your script is called 'attached'. For example, Michael Winterbottom is attached to the script means he has agreed in writing that he will direct your script.

This is building the pedigree of your script.

The first job a writer has, then, is to attract elements to your script. Probably the single most important person a writer needs to associate with is a producer – and a good producer is very difficult to find. In fact, it is much more difficult to find a good producer than it is an agent. A good producer is someone who is sensitive to your creative needs and vision, but at the same time can fight all the commercial battles in getting your screenplay financed or sold.

A close friend of mine wrote an excellent screenplay and partnered with a producer. My friend was hired to direct his screenplay – for some, a dream come true. Unfortunately, this producer was a novice, and found himself being bullied by the financiers and senior creative staff on the picture to the point where he committed the writer/director's post-production budget to the scene builders instead. My friend realized that the soundtrack played an integral part in the picture – it was a horror picture – and without a music budget, his vision, his script would flounder. It took an Oscar-winning showdown with my friend threatening to

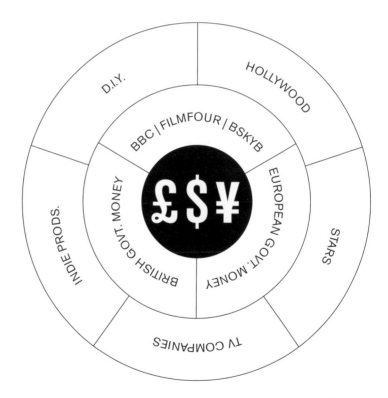

figure 10.2
The Movie Game Played

- ORIGINAL SCRIPT

- SCREENPLAY RIGHTS – NOVEL

- SCREENPLAY RIGHTS – TRUE LIFE STORY

quit the picture and take the script with him that forced the producer to wake up. The point is that you do not want to have to resort to performances such as this in order to get your script made or sold.

If you ever find a producer who is part business head, part artist and who is someone you like to work with, treat him or her like gold.

Hint Build your pedigree as much as possible by packaging the elements of your script together before you present your project.

How to find a producer
Let's be blunt about this. It is the film business, after all, right? You want to hang out with winners, I assume. So if you want a producer, you want someone who is already successful. Wouldn't it make sense to try to find someone who has already done it?

Shingling
In America they use the term 'shingling'. This refers to the shop signs, or shingles that hung out down Main Street. The theory behind this method is that you find a successful producer known to the main funding sources in your country, and ask them to present your script to the funders on your behalf. In exchange, you will agree to pay a percentage, and do ninety-nine point nine percent of the work.

Networking
It's a people business. It's not what you know, it's who you know. So just grab every single contact you have, and see if you can find someone to produce, i.e. haggle, bargain and cajole on your behalf.

Hint Treat a producer like a star. A good producer is essential to your career. But never forget that the producer needs you, too.

---

2. European government money

Through the auspices of an EEC program called MEDIA 2, the European Community dispenses Euro tax money to filmmakers under nineteen different programs. Each program is domiciled in a different European member state, and the program that directly relates to screenwriting is called the European Media Development Agency, or EMDA for short.

EMDA is based in London at 39c Highbury Place, London N5 1QP. Tel +44 20 7226 9903 or fax +44 20 7354 2706.

The beauty of selling a screenplay is that you get to do something physical with immediate, tangible results. Call and get the relevant literature and application forms if you feel that this particular program is going to be of benefit to you.

3. British government money

The Film Council has been launched by the Labour government as a fuel-and-resource-efficient quango. Under the auspices of the Film Council will lie all of the government agencies which existed prior to 1999 including the British Film Institute, British Screen, the Arts Council (lottery funding) and the numerous regional arts boards and other national organizations such as the Scottish Film Council, the Glasgow Film Fund and so on. It is too soon to determine whether or not this policy will succeed. Call and see what script development programs exist. Request the relevant literature and application forms if you feel that this particular program is of benefit to you.

The Outer Ring

The outer ring represents areas by category, where you can attempt to sell your screenplay outside the British film industry.

1. Hollywood

By Hollywood, of course, is meant the professional film and television community centered in Los Angeles. It still is the largest in the world. In fact, there are as many 35mm film crews and equipment available in LA as in all of Europe. Remember that there are many smaller companies in LA as well. Elisar Cabrerra went to Los Angeles with his script determined to raise the finance so he could direct his screenplay. He came back to London with a check for $1,500 and shot the film on video. The rushes were sent back to LA where the film was edited. So, by Hollywood, as I said in the introduction, I also mean the smaller companies around the world, where films are made. London actually is now the second largest centre of English speaking production in the world, and there are many excellent companies operating in the UK who seek a variety of different types of scripts to satisfy their marketing policies.

Hint Knowledge is power. Research a variety of film companies and ascertain what types of films they make.

---

2. Stars

All stars share one thing in common – they have their own production company. They create a production company and hire a head of development to do one thing – find a script (starring vehicle) for the owner of the company.

It is possible that you will have a project, which may interest a specific star. You might feel that you have the perfect vehicle/script for Hugh

Beware of what a star is. In the UK many writers feel they have a star interested in their script, when in fact the 'star' is a cast member from daytime British television. This actor, away from this dull, damp, dark, island is totally unknown. A true star is someone recognized in every country in the world.

Grant. If you can elicit the interest of the head of production at Hugh Grant's production company, and if Hugh Grant likes it, they will purchase the screenplay from you.

Hint If a star buys a script from you, they will usually sever all relations with you and hire their own writer, whom they know and trust to rewrite the screenplay for them.

Here's what will happen when you submit your script to the production company of a star, or any production company:

figure 10.3
Film Production Company Structure

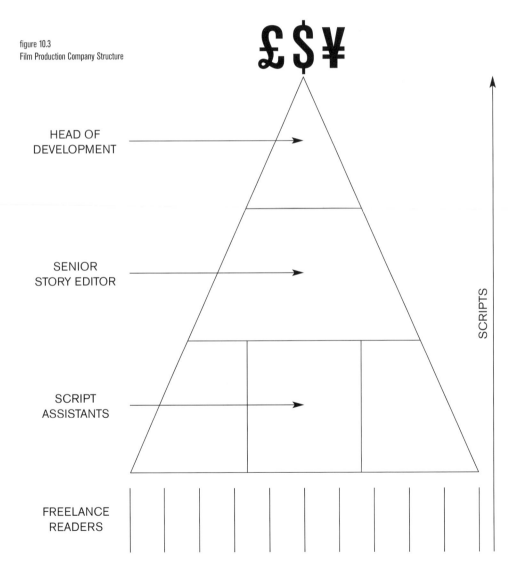

There are really only two types of screenplay. Firstly, there is the great script that is so good, the producer is ordering film stock, and the director is lining up auditions. Secondly, there is the ghastly script. The great script, if it is a comedy, is so funny when you read it, that not only do you laugh out loud, but you pick up the nearest telephone and call your best friend in the world, and say 'Can I tell you a joke?' If it is a horror script, you are afraid to turn the page, if it is a love story, the descriptive passages arouse you. These are signs of an excellent screenplay.

What happens to your script when it gets to a production company?

First of all, let us consider a typical film production company. The personnel are arranged, pyramid style, with the final decision maker, at the top. In a company like FilmFour, the head of production is Paul Webster. His assistant, titled senior story editor, is Jim Wilson. Underneath are several assistant story editors. FilmFour receives between sixty and eighty submissions per week. It is physically impossible for these five or six people at FilmFour to read all of these scripts. So, they don't read any. All of the new script submissions follow the reader route.

When your script arrives, the envelope is opened, usually by an intern, and the script's title is hand-written in magic marker on the spine or on the end of the script, depending which way the particular office's shelving is designed. Your script and your details are then logged onto a database, and your script assigned to a reader. FilmFour currently employs about a dozen freelance readers. The readers are given between four and eight scripts per week, and paid between £25 ($35) and £40 ($60) for their reports on each script. For an unpublished manuscript of a novel, readers are paid as much as £85 ($125) per report.

The reader's report is called coverage. All coverage is structured in the same way, although format varies from company to company. See figure 10.4 over the page, for an example of typical coverage

Let's suppose that in a typical week at FilmFour, ten readers each read five scripts and recommend one each. Then ten scripts would pass up to the next level, where they would be read in-house. Let's say that of these ten scripts, three are recommended to Jim Wilson, and in turn once a week he recommends one to Paul Webster.

FilmFour produces twenty to twenty-five films per year, out of four to five thousand submissions. Inexperienced writers might be forgiven for thinking that this is *bummer*. In fact, it is amazing that FilmFour does twenty to twenty-five deals with feature filmwriters a year, many of whom are first time writers!

Hint Readers exist not because there are so many good scripts out there, but because there are so many diabolical scripts in the system. Readers cannot say yes, but they can and will say no.

Title: OUT OF BOUNDS	Date: 6/9/00
Author: Tony Kayden	Form: Screenplay/119pp
Locale: New York, Los Angeles	Analyst:
Type: Action	Source:
Date & Draft Number: 4/3/00	Revised First Draft

Theme: Alec Cage arrives in L.A. for a peaceful summer vacation, but soon finds himself being chased by drug smugglers and the police.

ALEC CAGE, 18, arrives in Los Angeles to spend the summer with his Aunt and Uncle. At the airport baggage claim, he mistakenly takes the wrong duffle bag. When he wakes up the next morning, he discovers that the bag is filled with heroin. He goes downstairs to notify his relatives and to his horror, finds that they've been brutally shot to death. A neighbor enters and assumes that Alec is the killer. When the neighbor lunges at Alec, Alec accidentally shoots him. Startled and frightened, Alec bolts from the house, fearing that the police will accuse him of the murders.

Helpless and alone, Alec seeks refuge with the only person he knows in LA, a girl he met on the plane named JAMIE. Jamie helps Alec disguise his appearance; she dresses him up in chic new wave clothing. Alec wants to find the owner of the heroin, so Jamie takes him to the local drug hangouts, where they make contact with all sorts of seedy drug types.

Meanwhile, GADDIS, the vicious killer and owner of the heroin, is searching for Alec. Alec contacts the police to try to straighten things out, but the police still think that Alec is the real killer. Alec arranges a midnight rendezvous on an abandoned shipping dock between himself, Gaddis and the police. The rendezvous backfires; several officers are shot and Gaddis gets away. Alec escapes with the police still thinking that he's the guilty one.

Alec goes to Jamie's apartment to discover that it's been ransacked by Gaddis. Jamie's pet bird and cat have been brutally slaughtered. Fortunately, Jamie has escaped. Alec finds her at a local hotel. With the cops hot on their tail, they hide out in an abandoned building where they also make love for the first time. Their brief respite is interrupted by Gaddis, who grabs Jamie and holds her at gunpoint. Jamie and Alec are saved by HURLEY and YOUNGBLOOD, two shadowy figures who have been following them for a while. When Hurley and Youngblood reveal themselves as federal narcs, Alec becomes enraged. He is angry that he's been used as bait for Gaddis. He refuses to cooperate and goes off to confront Gaddis on his own. In a final showdown, Alec blows Gaddis away with a .357 Python.

```
OUT OF BOUNDS
Tony Kayden

Comments:

While the premise of this screenplay is potentially interesting, it
is executed in an unconvincing and uninteresting manner. The first
problem is that Alec's character is not believable. He begins as a
naive teenager from White Plains, New York. But within a few days,
he's acting like Clint Eastwood — commandeering buses, careening
through roadblocks, kicking down doors with a .357 Python, and
delivering lines such as 'Out with your pieces!' and 'I'll give his
asshole a twin brother!' Quite simply, I never believe that an 18
year old kid is capable of this behavior. Because I never believe in
Alec's character, I don't care what happens to him and I don't get
caught up in the story.

Another major problem with the script is the excessive use of
violence, particularly on the part of Gaddis. Examples of gratuitous
violence include the skinned cat, the plucked parrot, and the
shooting of an innocent pawnshop owner. None of these are necessary;
we already know that Gaddis is evil and vicious. It seems that the
main function of the violence is to titillate the audience.

This script has a lot of chase sequences and none of them are
especially original or interesting. Like all the other action
sequences in the script, they seem to have been distilled from TV
cop shows.

While the premise might have made for an interesting movie, this
script fails to engage the reader's interest.


NOT RECOMMENDED.
```

figure 10.4
Example of Coverage

Script reading is an entry level job into the industry, and is poorly paid. Why does anyone do it? To try to get a permanent salaried job at the next tier, it follows that the only way a reader will recommend a screenplay, is if it makes them look good. And how great is your script? If it is merely good, the reader will pass, because their career will not be enhanced by their recommendation of your script. Everyone is trying to move up the ladder.

Readers are the first barrier to your script. A reader, no matter how senior, or respected, cannot approve the purchase of your screenplay. They can only 'recommend' it. Readers can and do say 'Pass' to screenplays.

There is an old Hollywood maxim – *If it ain't on the page, it ain't on the stage*. And no movie can ever be made from a screenplay that the reader cannot see on the page.

The film industry is fiercely competitive. Readers' reports, like those at Scala Productions, are created under adverse conditions, not out of lack of respect for your script, but out of sheer economic necessity. Imagine a hapless intern reading your script with the phone ringing off the hook. You want your script to be so engrossing that they don't hear the phone, even with someone screaming *Get the phone!*

When that happens, the entire office knows they have found a hot script.

figure 10.5
Instructions for Readers

Now, go back to your descriptive passages. Do they really flow? Will they create visual images? Does your dialogue contain the three tracks? Is your script written in basic high school English essay style?

Hint Do not send out your screenplay until it is absolutely the very best you can get it. The readers will not read it a second time.

What happens when a reader gets your script?

Firstly, readers will have guidelines on how to read the script. Guidelines vary from company to company. Some companies have a very pared down reader system. The legendary British producer Nik Powell has a unique strategy at his Scala Productions – interns form his reader base. They are asked to answer the telephone and read your screenplay at the same time. Their reader report consists of two page numbers – the first page where they got interested, and a line why, and the first page where they got bored, and a line why.

Here are some guidelines that were handed out to script readers at a major Hollywood studio. It is somewhat scary that your script is read by someone with little or no script training, who is asked to follow these guidelines while assessing your script.

Checklist For Reading And Evaluating Screenplays

CONCEPT/PLOT

1. High concept; big canvas for films; intimate drama for TV.

2. Imagine the trailer. Is the concept marketable?

3. Is it compelling? Screenplay should deal with the most important event in these particular characters' lives.

4. What's at stake? Life and death situations are the most dramatic. Potential for characters' lives to be changed.

5. Screenplay should create constant questions: Will he make it? Did he do it? Hook an audience with a 'need to know', and they will watch the rest of the film.

6. Original. Please, no more screenplays that start with a character waking up in the morning, so we can see what kind of person he is by the junk he has in his room and his walls. No more genre parodies.

7. Is there a goal? Is there pacing? Does it build?

8. Begin with a punch, end with a flurry.

9. What are the obstacles? Is there a challenge for the heroes?

10. What is the screenplay trying to say, and is it worth it?

11. Audience wants to see people who care, not two hours of gimmicks.

12. One scene where the emotional conflict of the main character comes to a crisis point.

13. Hero must have a choice, the ability to affect the outcome.

14. Non-predictable; reversals within major plot and within individual scenes.

15. Once reality parameters are built, do not violate. Limitations call for interesting solutions.

16. A decisive, inevitable, set-up ending that is completely unexpected. Best example, of course, is 'Body Heat.'

17. Action and comedy emanate from character, not from off stage.

18. Is it believable? Realistic?

19. Happy ending or at least a definite resolution one way or other.

20. Castable parts. Roles that stars want to play.

21. Young characters. Older audiences can relate to young people, because they were young once, and young audiences can relate too. But young audiences have trouble relating to older characters.

22. Heart. Good screenplays have strong emotions at their center. An almost subliminal quality; need to read between the lines. Films with heart – 'The World According To Garp', 'Diner', 'Local Hero', 'American Graffiti', 'Terms Of Endearment', etc., and, of course, 'It's a Wonderful Life'. Heart can be negative emotions: 'Body Heat', 'Chinatown'. Avoid mean-spirited films.

TECHNICAL

1. Story construction and structure; three acts, two plot points.

2. No scenes off the spine of the story; no matter how good they are, they will simply die, and destroy the momentum of the film.

3. Screenplay should direct the reader's eye, not the camera.

4. Begin screenplay as far into the story as possible.

5. Begin a scene as late as possible, end it as early as possible. A screenplay is like a piece of string that you can cut up and tie together — the trick is to tell the entire story using as little string as possible. No shots of cars driving up to houses, people getting out and walking to the door. Use cuts.

6. Visual, Aural, Verbal — in that order. The expression of someone who has just been shot is best; the sound of the gun going off is second best; the person saying 'I've been shot' is only third best.

7. The Hook; inciting incident. You've got ten pages (or ten minutes) to grab an audience.

8. Triple repetition of key points: get through the story as quickly as possible, but for the audience's sake, work on the essential points two or even three times.

9. Echoes. Audience looks for repetition. Useful for tagging characters: 'Annie Hall' ('La De Dah'); 'Indiana Jones' ('I hate snakes'); In 'Body Heat,' Lowenstein's dance steps. Dangerous element; if it's not done right, it looks real stupid.

10. Not all scenes have to run five pages of dialog or action. In a good screenplay, there are lots of two-inch scenes.

11. Repetition of locale — mark of a well-structured screenplay. Helps atmosphere; allows audience to get comfortable. Saves money.

12. Small details add reality. Research.

13. No false plot points; no backtracking.

14. Silent solution; tell with pictures. Reference: the last seven seconds of 'North by Northwest'.

CHARACTERS

1. Character entrance should be indicative of character traits. first impression of people is most important. Great entrances: Rebecca De Mornay's character in 'Risky Business', strolling into the house, posing in front of the open window; Indiana Jones in 'Raiders', leading the way through the jungle, using his whip to snap the gun from a traitor's hand.

2. Root for characters; sympathetic. Recent example of this: Karen Allen's character in 'Starman'. Screenplay opens with her watching a home movie of her dead husband. From that point on, it is no contest; the audience is hopelessly sympathetic and on her side — all in less than a minute of screen time.

3. Dramatic need — what are the characters wants and needs? Should be strong, definite; clear to audience.

4. What does audience want for the characters? Are we for or against this character, or could we care less one way or the other?

5. Character action — what a person is is what he does, and not what he says.

6. Character faults; characters should be 'this but also that'; complex. No black and whites, please. Characters with doubts and faults are more believable.

7. Characters can be understood in terms of 'what is their greatest fear?' Gittes, in 'Chinatown' was afraid of being played for the fool. In 'Splash', the Tom Hanks character was afraid he couldn't fall in love. In 'Body Heat' Racine was afraid he'd never make the big time.

8. Character traits independent of character role. A banker who fiddles with his gold watch is memorable, but clichéd; a banker who has a hacking cough and chainsmokes is still memorable, and more realistic.

9. Conflicts, both internal and external. Characters struggle with themselves, and with others.

10. Character 'points of view' distinctive within an individual screenplay. Characters should not all think the same. Each character needs to have a definite point of view, in order to act, and not just react.

11. Run each character through as many emotions as possible — love, hate, laugh, cry, revenge.

12. Characters must change.

When readers meet socially, they invariably ask each other if they have read anything good. More often than not, readers will say they haven't read a good script in weeks — and they mean it! Script reading lousy script after lousy script can be very tiring. But when a reader reads a good script, they will usually say 'I had a really easy read.'

When a script reader opens your script to the first page and starts reading they are really hoping to find the best screenplay ever written. Again, they want to get noticed higher up the ladder. When script readers fail to get this feeling of anticipation before they start reading a script, they usually give up reading.

3. Television companies

TV companies in America started making cheaply produced films directly for TV to compete with the competition from *Monday Night Football* – a three hour program.

Market researchers discovered during this period, that American households typically had at least two televisions, and that men and women were polarized during the football game. Furthermore, they noticed that men and women preferred different sorts of entertainment – men prefer sex and violence, women a story. In order to satisfy the demands of women, American TV companies began to develop stories about women, for the female audience. Nicknamed Womjeps (Women in Jeopardy) films, or Movie of the Week (MOWs) these films were story driven and usually starred a woman.

Later, presumably after running out of stories about women who hate men, or who have had terrible things happen to them, these television companies produced other stories: typically stories based on news items like *The Tonia Harding Story* and *Princess in Love* (about Diana).

TV movies made from news related articles and stories are created very quickly.

4. Independent producers (indie prods)

An independent producer is defined as a producer working on his or her own seeking financing from within and outside the film industry.

An independent producer is often the first source of financing, or of a script sale. There are literally hundreds of indie prods working throughout the movie business.

The secret to a successful sale following this route is to ascertain which film, currently in production, most closely resembles your story. Contact the producer through his or her production company and see if you can get them to read your script.

An indie prod likes to have one film in production, a second out being sold, and a third in pre-production. Since the pre-production process is long, tangled and twisted, a good producer will have several scripts in pre-production, waiting to see which one gets financed first.

Independent producers can be sourced by reading the trade papers *Screen International*, *Hollywood Reporter*, *Variety* or visiting the e-zines filmthreat.com and indiewire.com

You could also source by capturing title credits from movies similar in style to your script as well as by word of mouth and through networking at filmmakers' groups like the IFP and NPA.

5. DIY

El Mariachi rekindled a trend to super-cheap moviemaking. In 1999 *The Blair Witch Project* demonstrated that it is possible to make and market a movie yourself.

The other encouraging development for filmmakers and screenwriters is the advent of new, cheap technology, which makes the cost-of-entry to filmmaking practically nothing.

Even if you, as a writer, have no intention of making the movie for no money, it is a useful exercise to film a few actors reading your scene in order to highlight successes and failures within the scene.

However, all writers should be aware of the pitfalls of making their own script – the rush to fulfill your ambition of filming your script and launching your career with the next *Blair Witch Project* may cause you to lose your sense of judgement about your screenplay. There is nothing worse than watching a film made with passion by a writer/filmmaker/director or producer, which is based on a flawed script. It is embarrassing. I should know. I rushed the script of the movie I made, *Table 5*, and the film is so inept in places, I can't even believe I shot it.

The scary thing is that during the filmmaking process, I thought those bits were pretty good!

Playing Piece

The movie game is a board game. You can see by the layout of the board that there are hundreds of performers with their own production companies, perhaps twenty television companies making movies of the week, literally thousands of independent producers, and so on. The total number of squares you can land on to sell your script, numbers in the thousands in the movie game.

Onanist and Onanism are used in the context of self-gratification in this book.

Onanism is a term based on the second biblical reference that screenwriters need to be aware of – not the least because it refers to terrible trap that writers can fall into:

And it came to pass that Onan spilled his seed upon the ground. The thing which he did displeased the Lord: wherefore he slew him also. Genesis ch. 38, vs. 9 to 10

Curiously, the Japanese language has the word *onani*, and French has *onanisme*. Both words refer to the practice of 'self-gratification'.

However, the movie game is a board game, and in order to play any board game, you need a playing piece. If you try to play the movie game without a playing piece, you are an onanist.

The playing piece is, of course, the script. There are three things that count as a screenplay.

1. An original screenplay

An original screenplay that you have created yourself, to which you own the copyright and which you can prove that you own the copyright.

2. The screenplay rights in writing, to a novel or short story

The hot game in the film industry in the late nineties was to travel to Central or Eastern Europe and acquire the screenplay rights to popular novels and short stories and resell them to Hollywood. The theory was that if the story worked and was commercially successful in another medium, then it was more likely to succeed as a movie as well.

To obtain the rights to make a movie from a novel or short story use the following procedure:

Inside the front cover of the book the publisher is listed. Contact them and ask who controls the screenplay rights for the particular title. They will give you the details of that party, be it the author, their estate (if deceased), or other company holding the screenplay rights. Simply contact that party and begin negotiation.

As always in the film industry, water runs downhill. Ask yourself what the author is going to be most concerned about. Is it not that you are capable of writing the screenplay to the book? And you have the contacts to get it made by a reputable company with recognizable stars.

If you do source a hot manuscript, and acquire the screenplay rights to this, producers eager to buy out your position will pursue you. Sadly, yes, they have their own pet writers to complete the project. The trick in this sort of market is to try to get two or more producers bidding against each other in order to drive the price up.

In this sort of market, you as writer/talent scout become an entrepreneur – some would say golddigger. And this is not for everyone.

I can hardly imagine J.K. Rowling agreeing to let a little known short story she wrote before the Harry Potter craze be made by a group of students with a wind-up film camera. She did, however, assign the screenplay rights to her next four novels for the down payment on a modest cottage in 1995. Imagine if you had discovered her then!

The more you can bring to the table, the stronger your position will be.

If the writer is little known, you should be able to form a partnership with them, with you contributing the screenplay, and the writer contributing the source material. You would then need to attract the interest of a producer, and a producer capable of raising the production budget of your film plus your writing fees.

3. The screen rights to a living person's true life story

To acquire the rights to a person's true life story, contact the person through directory enquiries, or through the newspapers, radio or television programme where you first heard of the story. Again, the price you will pay depends on the publicity surrounding the case.

Another tack, is to take the true life story of someone who was involved with a major personality, for example, Princess Diana, and tell story of Princess Diana through the eyes of a press officer, chauffeur, chambermaid and so forth. Unfortunately, many employees in this position are asked to sign non-disclosure clauses to protect their employers from this sort of exploitation.

If you find a true life story for a person now living, you must seek their written permission to create a script based on their life. If you are unable to get their permission, you can still write a script on their life if you base the entire script on the public record – radio and TV interviews, or newspaper publications. If you want to use a biography, then you would need to get the permission of that writer. I once owned the screenplay rights to the life story of the notorious British gangster Mad Frankie Fraser. Reputed to have terminated the lives of over three dozen people with his bare hands, Frankie had just returned from Her Majesty's displeasure, having served over forty years for torture. He was eager to have his life story put on the silver screen.

Unfortunately, Frankie failed to develop a strong career arc in crime, and instead of committing one truly memorable crime, he had broken his career arc by committing dozens of lesser crimes, and no film company was interested. After interviewing him, I realized that the true story of Frankie was not in his adult life of violence, but in the reasons he turned violent.

Born to a homeless street urchin before the Second World War, Frankie's early memories are of being led over Charing Cross bridge to forage for food behind the luxury hotels on the Strand and often returning hungry. When the war broke out, he was sent up north to a borstal for young boys. Because of the water shortage he was forced to take a bath in an inch of water. After a few weeks he noticed that the prison governor was masturbating while the boys were bathing, and one week, Frankie was raped by this man. Being small but extremely strong, Frankie nearly drowned the hapless paedophile in the bath and for his efforts was sent to prison. After the war Frankie returned to London where his career as the minder for gangsters like the Krays blossomed.

One Sunday he decided to look up his long-lost mother, whom he heard was living alone in London's docklands. He arrived to find the house empty. A few weeks later, he returned on one of the coldest days on record. He pushed open the door only to discover his mother dead from the cold, slumped in an armchair and holding his birth certificate. From then on, Frankie became extremely violent.

The Onanist's Rash

If you do not have a playing piece, a screenplay, then the players looking for scripts playing the movie game will class you as an onanist. And always remember – everybody in the film industry is very insecure. If you meet them, it will take them about five seconds to ascertain that you do not have a screenplay. From being insecure, they won't be rude or tell you to leave – they will say charming things to you like 'Just send it in when it's finished and I'll look at it right away!'

In your naïveté, you will get home and announce to the people you share your life with that you have had a great meeting. What really happened was that you were politely fobbed off, and what you didn't notice was the person's hand easing under their desk and itching over the 'eject' button. What is more, the minute you finally left their office, they took the page in their filofax with your personal details between their thumb and forefinger and in a quick and efficient flick of the wrist, discarded your contact details forever.

Worse yet, when you attempt to play the movie game without a script, you will develop the 'onanist's rash' – a hideous facial deformity which is very difficult to eradicate. At the time of writing, this affliction had no medical cure. It is also very prevalent in cappuccino bars, particularly in Central London near to my office.

It works like this – the onanist's rash is invisible to the victim. It is caused by the stress on your mental state when you lie. The rash itself is caused by a chemical reaction between the foam on cappuccino and exhaled breath. Recent scientific experiments have shown that chemical changes in the body occur when people lie, thereby altering the atomic composition of the air we exhale.

Cappuccino bars are normally occupied by writers and filmmakers sitting around, nursing cappuccinos and whining about their failed prospects. Whenever a producer asks a writer how his/her script is progressing they raise a coffee to their lips to try to conceal their guilt and say 'Great'. The lying air reacts with the foam and causes a rash to appear on the upper lip. The strange thing about this rash (it is an itchy rash) is that you can't see it. In fact, look in the mirror, especially after a meeting with a producer who sussed that you didn't have a script, and the rash isn't visible at all. But you know you have it. And it really flames up when someone asks you about your script, and you raise the cappuccino to your lips, and try to hide what is going on, by covering the rash with your hand and mumbling something incomprehensible.

Summary

1. There are really only a few different areas you can sell your script to. But each area contains dozens of individuals who could buy your script.

2. Research your market place by reading the trades.

3. Build the pedigree of your script before you submit it.

How do you keep track of everybody without getting confused? Create a power file.

11   The Power File

Accumulating information on potential buyers is one thing, organizing it into meaningful data is another. In this chapter you will learn how to create and use a power file.

First of all, construct a page in your notebook/computer like this:

figure 11.1
The Power File

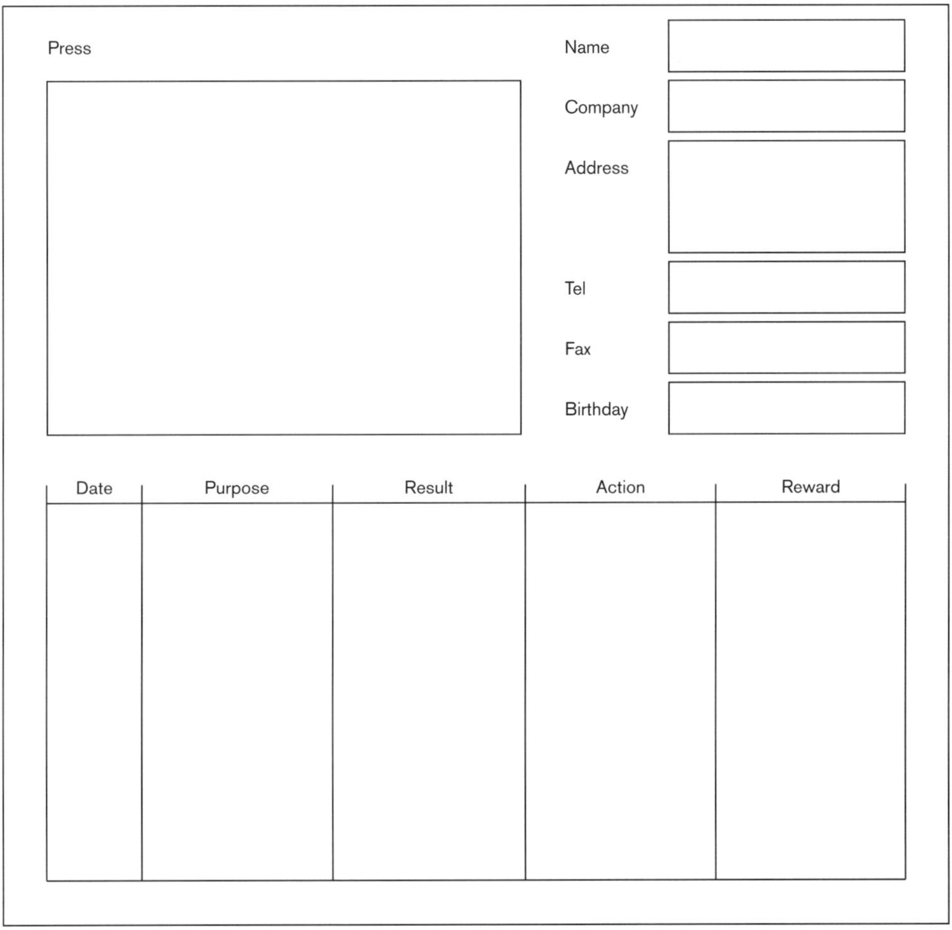

Press		Name	
		Company	
		Address	
		Tel	
		Fax	
		Birthday	

Date	Purpose	Result	Action	Reward

Let us analyze this:

Note that the name of the person you are pursuing appears in the top right-hand corner. Never put a company name there. The film industry is a people industry, and it is not what you know but who you know that counts. People in the industry often move jobs frequently. Eighteen months is a very long time in the film industry to be at one job. People move from company to company, and it is people that you build relationships with.

This isn't so different to when you move house within a city and keep the same doctor, dentist, decorator and plumber.

On the left-hand side, under Press, list the press notices, radio and television appearances or interviews for the person you are pursuing.

Under the person's name, list their contact details, including their birth date. You find out what their birth date so you can send them a birthday card. The film industry is fiercely competitive, and you want to do anything you can to distinguish yourself. If you send someone a birthday card you are flattering him or her and are appealing to their ego.

Everyone in the film industry is very insecure. Anyone who has a successful niche or position in the industry knows that there are at least a hundred others waiting for them to fail or weaken in order to push them off their perch. They know that, because that is how they got to where they are going.

How do you find out their birth date? Of course there are *Who's Who*, websites, and other directories. But what if you are really impatient? Wouldn't you just call up the person's office? And you know who answers the telephone at film companies the world over – interns!

Telephone reception is an entry-level position, but suddenly the person answering the telephone at the office of the person you are pursuing becomes the single most important person in the world – because they control direct personal access to the person you are pursuing. They decide whether or not you are going to be put through.

I call these people threshold guardians, and threshold guardians always deserve their own page in the power file. So start one and treat them as if they are the most important people in the world.

Back to the birthday card. If you live in the UK and are pursuing someone in the UK, it is rather mundane to receive a card from someone in the UK. Isn't it more exotic to get a card from someone from another nation, especially an exotic nation. How about Tibet, China or Kosovo? Maybe you have a friend or relative in such a far-flung place. If you do, you can purchase an international postal order to the value of one airmail stamp back to your home nation. Put the coupon into an envelope along with the addressed birthday card and ask your friend or relative to kindly post the envelope. Time the journey so the card arrives on the target's birthday, and voilà! You will be noticed.

What do you write in the card? If you are pursuing Bob Hoskins, write:

---

dd/mm/yy

Dear Bob,

While in Chechnya researching my latest movie, 'Top Title', I remembered
it was your birthday. I'll look you up when I get back to London.

Regards,

Your name

I'll bet you're asking how to prevent Bob Hoskins from thinking you are
a stalker? Remember, we are marketing your script. The person you are
pursuing has been selected because you think, as a result of your
research, they are likely to purchase your script. You don't have an
agent, the film world is ruthlessly competitive, and you are starting a
communication, which you hope will end up with a one-on-one meeting
with this person. Modify your letter:

---

dd/mm/yy

Dear Bob,

I met you at the Cannes Film Festival last year. While in Chechnya
researching my latest movie, 'Top Title', I remembered it was your
birthday. I'll look you up when I get back to London.

Regards,

Your name

All film people go to Cannes at least once in their careers. Some go every year, others go every other year.

When I go to Cannes, I go with business cards – it is the only way that you can get accreditation. Around thirty-five thousand people attend Cannes every year. Of those, there are about a thousand serious producers, sales agents and distributors trying to do business, about thirty thousand wannabees, and about four thousand tourists who stumble into town during the most exciting week in the film industry calendar.

Every time you meet someone at Cannes, you exchange business cards following a brief conversation. When the person turns and leaves, you jot on the back of the person's business card one of two things – 'Nutbar', or 'Call when I get back home'. Later in the hotel room, you empty your pockets onto the bed and sort them out further. I always have to buy a new bag to carry home all of the business cards, free magazines and flyers.

It is very likely that the person you are pursuing will have been to Cannes recently, and will have met many people who they made promises to, but can't exactly place.

If you can't get their birth date, or feel it is too tacky to use it, then dream up an excuse from another moment in their career. The first time they appeared in, directed or produced a film that opened in Leicester Square, or Times Square, the anniversary of their first Oscar nomination, and so on.

Your next job is to use the power file regularly.

The gatekeeper theory

The first person you speak to in any company in the world is the gatekeeper – a lowly paid person or intern who also has their own career aspirations.

Treat this person as you would a god, for they control direct personal access to the person that you are pursuing.

Suppose you have written a script that you feel is suitable for Clint Eastwood. You discover that his production company is called Malpaso Productions (from noting the credits in the cinema or on TV). By dialling directory information you can get his telephone number – directors from the Directors Guild of America (or in Great Britain, the Directors Guild of Great Britain), and the Screen Actors Guild in New York or Los Angeles (for an American actor), Equity for a British actor. The guild will give you the telephone number of the agent or personal manager for the person that you are pursuing, and from them you can get the address of the production company.

The first person you will deal with is the gatekeeper. The gatekeeper should get their own page in your power file. You call, send them a treat, a card, anything legal that will get you noticed. Each time you place a call, mark it on your power file. If you call Malpaso Productions at midnight on a Sunday to sell your script to Clint Eastwood (purpose), you will get the answering machine (result) and note to call back this company when it is open 10 to 5pm Pacific Coastal Time Monday to Friday (action). But give yourself a reward. Get a box of little gold stars and paste one in.

Selling your screenplay is a very lonely business and a few days or even weeks later, when you are skimming through your power file, that little

If you want to see how serious you are about writing and selling a script, you can do your own private onanism test in the privacy of your own home. If after six months of reading this page, you do **not** have at least a hundred names in your power file, then it's official – you are an onanist with no intention of writing or selling your script.

gold star will give you a reminder of the burst of positive action you made, and it will cheer you up.

If you call and call and call, maybe one day the assistant to the head of production at this company will call you up to arrange for an appointment a week Tuesday. If that ever happens, empty the rest of the gold stars on the table and cover the page. This is the whole intent of the power file – to get the one-on-one meeting.

Now, how do you find people to add to the power file? How do you know whether or not they are interested in buying scripts – your script?

Adding to the Power File

Here are some ideas of how you can fill your power file to overflowing:

1. Read the trades

The American trades are *Hollywood Reporter* and *Variety*; the British trades are *Screen International*, *The Business of Film* and *Screen Finance*; in Canada there is *Playback*; and in France there are *Film Français* and *Ecran Totale*.

Buy any copy of a trade magazine and they are organized like this:

- Front-page story, to remind you what is currently the hot topic.

- Inside front, three to five pages, production notes from around the world about films in production. Here you would note any projects either similar to the one you are working on, or would like to start.

- The centre of the trade magazines generally covers topics of interest to filmmakers, exhibitors, distributors and other executives, for example a focus on Icelandic cinema.

- The end pages have a production survey where all of the films from around the world are listed and tracked through the production process. The first time they appear in the trades, they have a complete cast and crew list, the name of the writer and producer, contact details and a synopsis of the film which can either be short, like 'Thriller' or long (three to eight words) like 'Three school boys chase the same girl'.

Again note any projects that might be of interest to you and track the producer and/or writer, or any other relevant people from the production listing that you think might be useful to you.

- All trade papers publish the box office charts, and this is another source of data that can be useful, if treated in the right way. The box office charts will give you an idea of what is commercially successful and the decay rate of films once they have been released. For example, a horror film opens strong, and curves down after about two weeks. Comedies build for several weeks, before peaking and tapering off.

2. Read the product guides

There are three film markets during the year – and they are attended by most of the filmmakers, film sellers and film buyers. It is obvious that this is a tremendous resource to a writer in order to ascertain the types of genre or story that are easiest to sell.

The three film trade markets occur mid February in Los Angeles at the American Film Market (AFM); the Marché du Cannes during the Cannes Film Festival in May; and the MIFED market in Milan in October. There are also several television markets during the year. For each market, the major trades publish a thick product guide with all of the films (product) on sale, as well as the film buyers attending.

It is a good idea to attend as many markets as you can. The one easiest to access is the Marché du Cannes in France. Because it runs simultaneously during the Cannes Film Festival, attendees are spoilt for choice for parties, networking, screenings, free magazines and so on. Cannes is also near some spectacular countryside which makes a great diversion for a day or two when you tire of the hustling of the market.

The trade papers publish a product guide prior to each market. Listed in the product guide are the key market players – buyers of films and sellers. Pages from product guides list the home address of the company, along with the names and titles of executives attending.

The product available at the market is listed in one of three categories:

- Completed, or screening now, or cassette available. This means that the film is completed and the representative of the film is eagerly seeking a sale for the film to the territory represented by the buyer.

- In production, or 'Delivery scheduled for…' (date three to ten months in the future) which means that the representative of the film is attempting to create a buzz about the film prior to completion, or the production company is suffering from a cash flow crisis and is attempting to sell the film rights to a territory to raise the completion budget.

- The film is listed as in pre-production. At this stage, the production company is attempting to raise the production budget of the film by selling the rights to the film at a discount over what the film would command in their territory when completed. This is called a pre-sales agreement. The producer will then take the contract back to their home nation and give it to a film financing bank, who will assess the credit worthiness of the buyer, and then use the agreement as collateral against a loan to the production company to enable the film to be made.

This is a golden opportunity for writers to sell their script, and to pull this off, a great deal of pre-planning is necessary. By preparing your power file, ascertaining the different film companies attending and ascertaining the types of product which they purchase, you will eliminate irrelevant companies and make sure that you will shoot with a rifle and not with a shotgun, and have a better chance of hitting the target.

3. Promote yourself

Every time you meet anyone, tell him or her about your movie and ask them if they know anyone who would be interested in the script. Everyone wants to be in the movies, and even if they aren't personable, interested or able to, advance your project, and in this way you expand your circle of influence.

You are also using the 'six degrees of separation' rule – that you are only ever six contacts away from anyone else in the world. Guy Ritchie may have married Madonna. Even without her contacts, he is considered to be one of the best-connected people in the UK.

Packaging Your Screenplay

Packaging is the process whereby you add talent or expertise to your screenplay. The more you add to your screenplay, the easier it is for a production company to say *Yes* to your script.

1. Find a producer

This is the hardest task a writer has to do. The wrong producer will leave you in a pile of jangled nerves and so bitter and twisted that you will probably abandon a career as a screenwriter.

The right producer is a joy to work with, and someone you can bounce ideas off, and who helps pick you up when you are down.

To go to a film market as a writer, your goal is to raise money for the production of the film. The right producer will assist you in closing the deals necessary to get your film into production. Within that budget will be an amount for your screenplay.

2. Marketing tools

The most successful sales at a film market have resulted from some cheap printed marketing materials. In the same way that you would not market your home, without a sheet of details and a floor plan or photo, or even worse, attempt to get a job without a one-sheet (CV), so, too, it is pertinent to create a one-sheet for your movie.

Hire a graphic designer and give them the pitch, or allow them to read the screenplay. It is instructive to see what the designer comes up with. Do they or do they not 'get' it? If they don't, perhaps your screenplay is not clear enough.

Roger Corman has used this approach successfully for decades. Much of his inspiration comes from juxtaposing newspaper headlines. If he comes up with a title, for example *Teenage Werewolf in Paris*, he creates a one-sheet and takes it to the film markets. If the poster arouses enough interest, he returns to LA, hires a screenwriter to create a script that represents the poster, and then shoots the movie.

A one-sheet is a cost-effective way to test market your idea.

If it is so easy to go and pitch and sell your film or script at a film market, why isn't everyone doing it?

The answer, as with most things in the film industry, boils down to money. It costs approximately $20,000 to join each market, plus the cost of a stand, staff, travel and advertising will set back a company at least $50,000. Most writers cannot afford that.

Instead, a new breed of industry professional was born. The sales agent – someone with the financial ability to set up at a film market and who is able to amortize the cost of attending the market over several projects, some completed, some in post-production, and some, like yours, in development, or pre-production.

A sales agent will charge the producer of the film a commission for any pre-sales agreement achieved during a market. Armed with your one-sheet, try to get a sales agent to represent you at film markets.

This doesn't prevent you from sitting around in the lobby of the Majestic Hotel, one-sheet in hand, ready to pounce on a celebrity financier or producer when they walk through! Indeed, film lore is rife with tales of success from the lobby of the Majestic!

Let's deconstruct the one-sheet shown in figures 11.2 and 11.3

Title

Two or three words which start to sell the story. Commercially successful films have titles that sum up the entire movie in two or three words. *Meet the Parents*, *Castaway*, *Traffic*, *Airplane*, *Analyze This* all sum up the story of the movie. Choose words that make your film resonate with emotion and action.

Logline

The log line is an expansion of the title of the movie – usually no more than eight words. Although filmmakers often look to the writer for ideas for the log line, it usually is the marketing department of the distributors who come up with the log lines. Be prepared to wince.

Visual image

A strong visual image that represents the movie, or scenes from the movie if shot. Whatever the image, it should fire the imagination. As you preview the artists' ideas, you will start to see the first visual images of your script.

Credits

These are usually placed at the bottom of the page. Here you would add any people that you have committed to the project. Don't worry if you don't have anyone signed up yet. Just make it look strong and confident. Make certain that you place your contact details in legible type.

Movie titles

Reservoir Dogs had a very different meaning for us farmboys growing up in America. You city slickers, or Europeans probably thought that this title was a cutesy arty title. And it is. But to me it had a different meaning which summed up the movie in two words.

As a kid we were told never to go into a dry reservoir. They did a lot of open quarry mining for gravel near where I grew up. There were two types of quarries – some quarries would hit a spring and fill up with water. We used to dive off the sides of these in the summer. Other quarries were dry quarries. There would just be a puddle in the bottom after a rain shower. Dogs and rats would fall down into the quarry, and be unable to get up. The only way they could survive was by eating each other. And every summer there would be a sad story about some kid who went down into a dry quarry and was ripped to shreds. Knowing that now, isn't that the story of *Reservoir Dogs*?

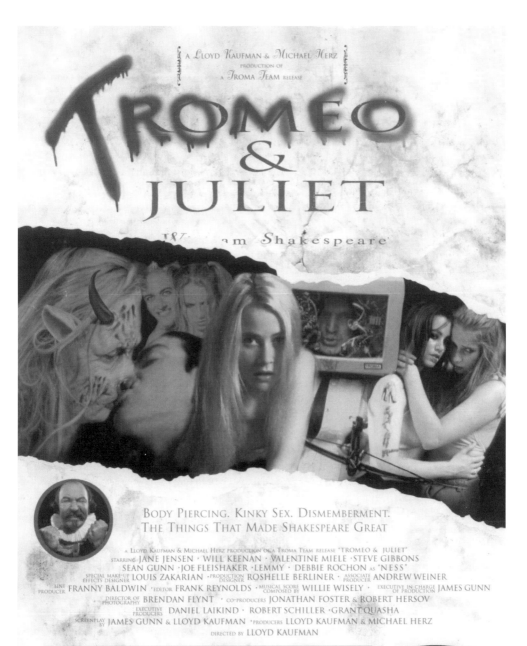

A LLOYD KAUFMAN & MICHAEL HERZ
PRODUCTION OF
A TROMA TEAM RELEASE

TROMEO
& JULIET

by ... m Shakespeare

BODY PIERCING. KINKY SEX. DISMEMBERMENT.
THE THINGS THAT MADE SHAKESPEARE GREAT

A LLOYD KAUFMAN & MICHAEL HERZ PRODUCTION OF A TROMA TEAM RELEASE "TROMEO & JULIET"
STARRING JANE JENSEN · WILL KEENAN · VALENTINE MIELE · STEVE GIBBONS
SEAN GUNN · JOE FLEISHAKER · LEMMY · DEBBIE ROCHON AS "NESS"
SPECIAL MAKE-UP EFFECTS DESIGNER LOUIS ZAKARIAN · PRODUCTION DESIGNER ROSHELLE BERLINER · ASSOCIATE PRODUCER ANDREW WEINER
LINE PRODUCER FRANNY BALDWIN · EDITOR FRANK REYNOLDS · MUSICAL SCORE COMPOSED BY WILLIE WISELY · EXECUTIVE IN CHARGE OF PRODUCTION JAMES GUNN
DIRECTOR OF PHOTOGRAPHY BRENDAN FLYNT · CO-PRODUCERS JONATHAN FOSTER & ROBERT HERSOV
EXECUTIVE PRODUCERS DANIEL LAIKIND · ROBERT SCHILLER · GRANT QUASHA
SCREENPLAY BY JAMES GUNN & LLOYD KAUFMAN · PRODUCERS LLOYD KAUFMAN & MICHAEL HERZ
DIRECTED BY LLOYD KAUFMAN

| FEATURING THE MUSIC OF |
| MOTORHEAD · SUPERCHUNK · ASS PONYS · SUBLIME · THE MEATMEN |
| UNSANE · SUPERNOVA · WESLEY WILLIS FIASCO · SUSAN VOELZ |

figure 11.2
Sample One-Sheet (Front)

figure 11.3
Sample One-Sheet (Reverse)

The back of the poster contains the following:

Top paragraph
Here's an application for the basic premise that has been driving you crazy: those twenty-five words or less which sum up the movie.

More images
How well did your screenplay inspire the graphic artist?

Naked self-promotion
Finish off with a well-written paragraph or two explaining why your script is this year's hot topic. You are the writer. You are the genius. Stop blushing and market yourself (this is blatant self-aggrandizement).

Other Ways to Add to Your Power File

Your power file is only as good as the information you put into it. And the more information you put into it, the better chance you have of developing a truly good power file. Successful writers are always adding to their power file.

Hint The film industry is people business – it's not what you know, it is who you know.

---

1. Start with people you know

Call up every single person you know. Tell them you have finished your script. They will already know what it is about, because you will have been talking to them so much about it. Ask them if they know anyone who could buy your script, or would know anyone who would be interested in buying your script. Even if they do not know anyone they probably will know someone who does know someone. Apply the 'six degrees of separation' rule and expand your circle of influence.

I found out yesterday that I am one person away from Bono, Woody Allen and the editor of *Wallpaper*. Of course I'm still debating which script to send to whom!

2. Watch movies

This is the fun part. See every single movie that you can. If possible, try to see it in a cinema – it is useful to gauge the audience's reaction, and it is generally a more pleasurable experience than seeing everything at home on the television.

Every time you see a movie similar to the type of film you want to write, or have written, capture the production company details (they are always in the credits). Note everyone in the production that might be interested in working with you – the writer, the director, the producer. Maybe you can get in touch with the script editor.

If you want to get in touch with a star, a director, a writer, there is a secret telephone number that you, as an aspiring writer, can use. It is 411 (in North America), and 192 in the UK. Directory Information. For an American actor, you call the Screen Actors Guild in New York or Los Angeles, for a British actor, call Equity. For directors, call the Directors Guild of America, or the Directors Guild of Great Britain, and for writers, the Writers Guild of America, or the Writers Guild of Great Britain.

How you make this call is important. These Guilds are extremely busy and understaffed. Limit your request to three names per telephone call. The telephone numbers they supply will not be the personal home telephone numbers of the stars that you are pursuing. You will get their agents' telephone number. Call the agent and try to ascertain whether or not the person you are pursuing has a production company (if you can't find out any other way) or ask them for the production company telephone number (if you can't find out any other way).

3. Read magazines

In addition to the filmzines and fanzines, you should subscribe to the excellent newswire services. In the UK there is 6degrees.co.uk and in the USA indiewire.com and filmthreat.com which provide quick, reliable information on what is happening in film. And they are free.

More fun work! Reading magazines on a regular basis, however, can be gruelling. Nonetheless you must keep abreast of the developments in the industry. Trade magazines like *Variety* publish invaluable information on what is happening at the moment and who is looking for what.

Magazines can also offer information on who is doing well, and who is heading for their next session in rehab. This information may not have a direct use, but it helps make you industry-smart and savvy.

4. Surf the net

The internet offers unparalleled opportunities to research films and filmmakers. Don't ignore this amazing tool.

Summary

1. Try to relax as you suck in all of the information from the various trades and markets. There is no science as to what works best – you just sort of get a feel for it.

2. Try to get a feel for the business side of the industry as you build up your power file.

You've got your power file in shape, suppose someone calls you up and asks you to come into a meeting. You're ready to pitch!

12　Pitching

When someone asks you what your screenplay is about, and you tell them, you are verbally pitching your script to them. If they ask you for a written summation – a treatment – you are submitting a written pitch.

The word pitching is really a misnomer as it conjures up visions of snake-oil salesmen peddling questionable wares to an unsuspecting public. Yet if you took pitching out of the film business, the entire industry would collapse. Every movie ever made was made as a result of pitching. And the film industry is a people business, which means that your communication skills are very important.

Pitching, as defined for the film industry, is described as the process which you as a writer, director or producer, use in order to impart your passion for your project to others – cast, crew or financiers. One of the ironies of living and working in the UK is to see how undeveloped British filmmakers' pitching skills are compared to their colleagues in America. While some British producers like Nik Powell and Steve Wooley are legendary in their pitching abilities, most British filmmakers ignore this skill – unlike their associates in the retail trade. Just look at the window display of any shop in London and you will see what I mean.

Pitching is the fundamental foundation of the film business, and if you took pitching away from writers, directors and producers, you would not have any film industry. If you are unable to pitch properly and effectively you are doomed as a writer (unless you can align yourself with a director or producer who can pitch for you).

Hint Pitching is the single most important skill anyone, including writers, must acquire in order to succeed in the film industry.

In our everyday life, we pitch all the time. When your best friend or dearest relative calls up, they will ask you 'What's new?' You will then pitch them either a problem at work (to elicit sympathy) or prospects in love or work (to gain support or admiration). People who can't succeed at this elemental task are often referred to by others as 'cold' or 'loners'.

The Structure of a Pitch Meeting

In order to pitch properly it is important to understand properly the structure of a pitch meeting and the various signs and clues of the meeting, how to read them, and how to capitalize on them.

Any pitch meeting has three parts (just like your screenplay): Beginning Middle and End. Here, the elements of a pitch meeting are broken down, along with a list of the goals you must achieve, in order to sell your screenplay. I also list some tools you can use in order to help you achieve your goals:

Beginning

Most pitch meetings are fifteen to twenty minutes long, and the first part can take anywhere from twenty-five to fifty percent of the time, depending on variables beyond your control.

Your task in the first part of the pitch meeting is to schmooze with the person you are seeing so that they can get to know you, and so that you can get to know them. Remember that the person you are meeting is nervous too.

We do the same thing in our everyday life – when we see a friend in the street we say 'How are you? What's new? How did the job interview go?' and in the UK we usually comment on the weather. At the start of a pitch meeting, both sides are trying to figure each other out, and both parties are nervous. The only difference is that the person to whom you are pitching is usually more experienced at pitch meetings and therefore better able to cover up their anxiety.

If you have been able to do some proper research, then you might start off by commenting on their recent television interview, the news article on a current project or the success of one of their projects which is similar to your own.

Your first goal in a pitch meeting is to see whether you are pitching a left brain or a right brain person.

Our minds are divided into two. The left side controls rational thought, the right side controls the subconscious and the emotions. While you are schmoozing, cast a glance around the office to see if you can ascertain clues about the type of person that you are meeting. Do they have wall charts with circled deadline dates hanging next to profit and loss statements, (left brain – numbers man)? Or are there award certificates and photos of themselves shaking hands with celebrities (right brain – pictures man)?

No one is totally left or right brain, but most people lean one way.

A good tool for determining whether or not you have a right brain or left brain person is to place two items on their desk a few minutes after you start the meeting – a neatly typed one page synopsis of your script and an object from the script, maybe the revolver, a photograph, or a map of the enchanted island. Observe which one the person picks up.

Author, producer, director and publisher Michael Wiese, while working at Viacom, had the good fortune to stumble across the home video rights to boxing fights in the forties and fifties. His innovative approach to this worn material was to edit out the knockout rounds from the films and edit them together for home video and call it 'Boxing's Greatest Hits'. In order to enhance the value of the product, he decided that Don King would be a great cover jacket.

Through his observation and networking, Michael ascertained that Don King was a right brain person – carried away with the emotion of the event. A video jacket with Don King's face was prepared in advance of the initial pitch meeting. Michael went with an assistant who was told that when cued (approximately half way through the start of the meeting) they should sit the box upon the desk where Don King could see it, leave it there for exactly five minutes, and pull it down, but to count the times Don King made direct eye contact with the image of himself for a period longer than three seconds. King did this an incredible thirty-seven times during the meeting. Needless to say, he did the deal.

You will know when you are at the end of the first part of the meeting when the person you are pitching says 'How can I help you?' or 'What do you have?' You are now in the second part of the meeting.

Middle

Start with your basic premise, the so-called twenty-five words or less. Do not read from notes. Reading from notes is the kiss of death at any pitch meeting. You want to establish direct eye contact with the person you are pitching. If you read from notes, it will appear that you do not feel totally comfortable with your material, or that you will be unable to emit appropriate passion for your project.

See if you can gauge their interest. If their head is going 'Yes, Yes, Yes' then you have the time to give an expanded, more detailed pitch.

You are waiting for them to say 'Could you have your agent or representative contact our head of business and legal affairs?' Kerching! You have done the deal.

Often, however, after you have finished your short introductory pitch, you will hear instead 'No thank you.' Your task now is to discover why. Is it because you are pitching to the wrong person? Maybe the circumstances of the company's finances have changed drastically since your appointment was made. Maybe they just don't like your idea.

Whatever the reason, you then reach back into your quiver and select another arrow and fire it off. It is a good idea to take at least three fully developed pitches to a meeting. Maybe you start with a pitch other than the one you were asked to bring, just to warm up. Do whatever makes you feel comfortable.

Often too, after your initial twenty-five words, you will hear a 'No' expressed in a different phrase – a phrase that will strike terror into your heart like 'Stop, please, we have something exactly like that.' More commonplace is something like 'Isn't it amazing about the common currency of ideas in circulation?'

If that happens to you, make a positive choice. Yes, it is a *bummer* that the company you are pitching to already has something similar to your idea. But hey, at least you have proven that your ideas are commercially viable! It is extremely rare that film companies steal ideas from writers. What does happen, however, to beleaguered story development executives is that they think they have heard your idea from someone else. Development executives can hear dozens of story pitches in a week and it is likely that they have heard something similar to yours in the last month, or in the last one hundred pitches.

So move one.

Reach back into your quiver and pull out your next pitch, which brings up the next point of pitching – go with at least three fully prepared pitches to your meeting. It would be a shame to go to a one-on-one meeting, especially considering all of the time and effort it takes to set one up, with just one pitch.

Hint Development people are nervous about meeting you and hearing your pitch too. They just have more experience than you do. So relax.

The End

You will know when you are in the third part of the meeting when you either hear 'No thanks' or what you are dying to hear 'When can you get your agent or representative to contact our head of business and legal affairs?' Kerching! Congratulations. You have done a deal. But regardless of the outcome of the meeting you are then automatically in the third part of the pitch meeting.

However you arrive at the third part of the pitch meeting your task is to leave as quickly as possible. Do not make small talk, do not comment on the weather, the news, the jukebox in the corner. Just leave. If you linger before leaving you overstay your welcome and the minute you leave will be the minute that your contact details are destroyed.

Film people are notoriously insecure – so insecure in fact that they seem over-polite. If you make small talk in the third part of the meeting, don't mistake the person's interest, even affection for anything other than a pained effort to lean over and push the eject button.

Three Golden Rules of Salesmanship

These rules work for a pitch meeting for a screenplay, or just about any situation where you are trying to get the deal, film industry or not.

1. Never say a number

He or she who says the first number loses. Think back to the times that you had to negotiate payment for a job. Do you remember having to answer the question 'Make me an offer?'

For research or for a laugh, walk into any car salesroom anywhere in the world. Car salesmen are trained to get you to say a number. And they are not beyond lying to get that number out of you. A car salesman will always ask you what your budget is, what you want to spend. If you resist naming a price, the salesman will badger you until you say a number, using phrases like 'We'll work with you/Let me paper you into this deal/I'll speak to the manager, but you have to give me something to work with'. And before you know it you are saying something like $200 per month.

The minute you say a number, you lose. If you say a hundred to a hundred-and-fifty a month – do you think for a minute that the salesman heard the number one hundred? And the irony is, in the car sales showroom context, the car salesman has already lost the argument by virtue of the fact that the cars all have huge red price stickers on them.

Similarly, in a pitch meeting, the person you are meeting, be it a producer, agent or story executive will often ask you what you are looking for money-wise from your script. Never say a number! You may over-price, or under-price yourself. Always make it very clear that the person they need to speak to regarding money, or price, will contact them later. You will make yourself look more professional, and can restrict the energies of future meetings to the creative issues involving them and you. If you don't have an agent or representative, now is the best time to get one. Other alternatives are to use a friend, or a solicitor.

Hint Never talk money with a producer. Not only will you come out short changed, but that could scuttle the deal.

---

2. Never go to money

By this I mean that you should try to get the person who you are pursuing with your script to come to your place of work. If they don't ever come to you, you essentially are dealing with an onanist. The theory is that, if the person will not leave their yacht, penthouse or mansion to come to visit you, then they will never take you seriously.

This rule definitely applies to producers attempting to raise money, but as a writer, it is always more difficult to get a story development person out of their office – they are simply too busy. You try, however, to get them onto neutral territory: a coffee shop, or park bench.

Never suggest lunch. A lunch meeting can take an hour or more. If you have not met this person before, and they don't take to you, or if your pitch is wrong, they will feel totally trapped by you.

If, on the other hand, you simply suggest a coffee across the road, you get them out of the office, away from the telephones, and a coffee meeting can be anything between eight and forty minutes – without the person you are with feeling trapped or rude.

Hint When they start calling you, when they start trying to hang out with you – then you know you are getting hot.

---

3. You don't ask, you don't get

If you are ever in the second part of a pitch meeting and you notice that the person you are meeting glances at their watch, and you have yet to ask for the deal, you are automatically in the third part of the meeting.

You must ask for the deal the minute you are in the second part of the meeting. Of course you don't blatantly ask if they want to buy your script – that would be tacky and an ineffective marketing approach. However, you can ask 'I hear you are looking for a thriller' or 'Now that your most recent film was a hit, isn't it true that you are entertaining romantic comedies?'

You basically try to build accord with the person you are selling to. If they say 'No' remember there are three kinds of 'No'.

Believe it or not, when I was really broke, I became a professional debt collector. My job was to call up corner stores who had defaulted on their loan payments for wet/dry vacuum cleaners and get them to settle their bills, either by rescheduling their payments, or by repossessing the goods. It was on this job that I learned the three kinds of No.

No number one means 'The house is on fire. Emergency! No! I can't speak to you for another second.' Fair enough. They're busy. Maybe I can call later. When you are pitching a script, the equivalent might be that the company has just been bought out, and no one knows what the new owners want to fund. Put the contact to one side to age for a few weeks, and call back later.

The second type of No, the No I hate, is the maybe No – the 'Can you put some details in the post and we'll review your material and get back (if we are interested)'. No way. You bet. Sure thing. That's the huge pile of stuff beside the desk that nobody looks at. I got so that I didn't even bother sending stuff out to the maybe Nos – they just never responded, and I as a commissioned salesman was charged for postage.

The third kind of No was the 'Tell me more' No – the No with reservations. This was a joy to hear because it meant that they wanted more information. It meant that you had a chance to close. The way to handle this situation was to learn to recognize objections and then offer alternative information to make them feel comfortable with the transaction.

Trial closings

The final aspect of 'If you don't ask, you don't get' is the trial closing. You have to ask for the deal. You say things like 'I understand you are looking for a thriller' if that is what you have. If you haven't asked by the time they look at their wristwatch, you are automatically out of there – in the third part of the meeting.

Can you remember talking to someone who is really boring, and you have an important meeting to go to. Remember how you go into all sorts of convoluted gestures in order to see what time it is without this boring unfortunate recognizing what you are doing?

In your pitch meeting you have to start asking for the deal as soon as you are in the second part of the meeting. 'Is this the type of thing you are looking for?' or 'Did you find that scary?' And so forth.

Pitching Tools

The trick with pitching is to inspire a visual image in the recipient's mind. There are several tools you can use to accomplish this. Practice each of them until you get comfortable with each one. Then you will be able to use the tools appropriate for the person you are pitching.

Hint Make your movie come to life so everyone witnessing your pitch can visualize it.

The first few seconds of your pitch are really important. It is in these vital few seconds that you set up the pitch and establish your pitching style.

1. The camera angle

We see the park, it's autumn. There's the park bench. It's cold. Leaves are falling. And there's the body. Oh no. Both eyes have been gouged out. Is this what you have been waiting for?

In this pitch we start with a wide shot, and then zoom into the eyes of the victim. By using the camera angle, we involve the person in the first few frames of your movie. Of course this takes up a few seconds of time, but you also sneak in a rather ambiguous trial closing.

What if?

What if everything you have heard about extra terrestrials is true and you find out that your husband/wife is from outer space?

The advantage of the *what if?* is that it allows you to condense your premise into a few lines, and tests it out. If at the end of your *what if?* you can't get any accord from your target, then you are in trouble.

2. The movie cross

Comparing your movie to one or two other movies is called a movie cross – 'My story is a cross between *Castaway* and *Bladerunner*.'

The advantage of this technique is that your target immediately gets a feel for the style of the movie. The disadvantages may be too dangerous to justify the use of this technique. If your target has not seen one of the movies you mention, then the movie cross is meaningless, and your target is flustered. Or your target may not agree that your pitch has anything to do with the movie you have compared it to. Be careful with this one. *Aliens* was successfully pitched as '*Jaws* In Space'.

3. Pop a question

When you ask a direct personal question of your target at the start of a pitch, you immediately focus the target's attention on you and your story. And it becomes intensely personal. You have to be careful not to make it too personal, like this opening sprung on me at one of our pitching events in front of two hundred people.

Have you heard of the death watch? You haven't? Well that's a shame, because it's watching you! This is the story…

Better was this pitch:

Did you know that there was, in fact, a fifth child of the Royal Family? This is the story of Norma…etc.

The question still personalizes the story to the target, but in a more usable, less intense way.

Tips for Pitching

1. Reading notes

This is a surefire way to bomb in a one-on-one pitching session. If you read from notes, you will be unable to make direct eye contact and you will not look like you really know your story. I have interviewed many film producers and I always ask them what they are looking for. Passion is the one thing that tops every single one's list. You cannot look passionate if you are reading from notes. If you need to, refer to a few notes made on an index card if you freeze during your pitch.

2. Be brief

Time is money. And you won't have much of either if you ramble on and on. Get straight to the point. Don't waste time.

3. Be entertaining

Nik Powell is one of the most successful practitioners of the art of the pitch. Having produced the Monty Python films, *Mona Lisa* and *The Crying Game*, Nik has had a hand in the launch of many new writers in the British film scene. I asked him how many times he has pitched *Back Beat* – the story of the fifth Beatle – before he got the money. He said about four thousand times. I asked him if he could give me a sample pitch. He said he couldn't because it was different every time. He tailored each pitch to the individual he was pitching.

4. Sell the sizzle not the steak

Your pitch should describe the elements of your story with salesmanship in mind. When you call up a travel agent for details on a tropical holiday what do they send you? The plumbing, wiring and electrical diagrams of the hotel they want you to stay in (the steak), or the glossy photo with the swimming pool and tennis courts (the sizzle)?

The common error many writers make is they pitch their story as 'this happens, then this happens and then that happens' – a surefire bore.

Pitch Repair

Below are listed two pitches from the Writers Lab. Try to pinpoint their strengths and weaknesses and think about how you could fix them:

Pitch #1
A thirty-five year old ex-barmaid named Betty Jackson discovers that she is wasting her life and wants to move out of London and get a better life.

The character description is too specific.
The goal of the character is too vague – we all would like a better life.

Repair
An unemployed barmaid rediscovers her gift of gardening and enters her tomatoes in the country's biggest fair.

Pitch #2

Three high school friends get involved in a drug ring and have to flee when one of them betrays them to the local Mafia boss.

There is no hero – no point of perspective – in this story. Choose one of the characters. Stories about drugs and the Mafia are too unbelievable and are very overworked. Often exaggeration for effect is good, so why not make the boys supermarket clerks, or after-school toilet attendants.
There is no story only setting.

Repair

The dullest boy in high school persuades the quarterback of the football team to steal grocery receipts only to discover that…

Summary

1. Passion is everything.

2. Be persuasive.

3. Be clear and concise.

How can you get a film company to consider your script when you don't have an agent? Write the eight-line letter.

13   Eight-Line Letter

Ask and ye shall receive. Well, maybe not every time.

But ask in the correct manner, and your chances of success start to soar, be it a request for funding, for a favorable equipment rental deal, or for interest in your screenplay.

The first rule of successful begging is to ascertain exactly what it is you require. Then, it is necessary to quantify the need in a simple, straightforward sentence that is clear, yet entertaining to read.

If the first item on the agenda is film stock, find out where there are advertising production companies and quantify a request as follows:

We are attempting to create the world's first 35mm feature film (ninety minutes long) with a budget of absolutely zero. We wonder if you have any redundant 35mm film stock that you would allow us to utilize in exchange for a credit on the film.

Let us analyze this simple paragraph. Notice how often that key words such as '35mm', and 'feature film' are repeated emphasizing the precise goal we were trying to achieve. Nobody would mistake our request for a donation to the local sports centre.

The choice of words is also important, for example, we asked to 'utilize' film stock. We discovered early on that we had a very negative response to the term 'give us'. And if you think about it, once a roll of film stock is utilized, it is pretty much utilized.

The next task is to ascertain who the actual person is in the company you are pursuing. Simply ring them up and ask, for instance, for the person responsible for script development – if you are trying to sell a script. If you are seeking financing, you would ask for the person responsible for clients' discretionary income (within an accountancy firm). Of course, you could ask for the person responsible for redundant film stock, if you are blagging film stock, and so on. Once you have this person's name, you are nearly ready to go into battle.

The last piece you need is a simple paragraph that describes yourself. Try to do this in an interesting way, even if you have a boring day job – 'I am a singing bus conductor who writes screenplays in my spare time.'

Film people are paranoid that they will miss the low-key individual that really has talent, and they also know that many now-successful film-makers started as very shy individuals.

You now have a choice. You have the target names, why not try a cold call telephone pitch. Try to get the target on the telephone and persuade them with your charm that you are worth helping or worth meeting.

If that fails, or if a film company tells you that as a screenwriter, they will only speak to you through an agent, you can try the eight-line letter.

Often, the only way to present you script to a production company is through an agent or entertainment attorney known to the company. Here's how can you get that elusive company to call you.

The secret is to compose a well-written letter, exactly eight lines long. Send it by post, or by fax or email to an actual human being at the production company. You target the person whom your research has shown is the person responsible for deciding whether or not their company should purchase your screenplay, or will decide whether or not they want to meet you for a one-on-one pitch meeting.

The reason that your letter must only be eight lines long is because you want that person to read it. When you write the letter understand that the person to whom you are writing is most likely to be extremely busy, and therefore an eight-line letter which is clear and concise stands, by reason, a far better chance of being dealt with.

If the letter is ten lines long, or, heaven forbid, twenty lines long, your letter will require too much of the person's time, and since you are not known to that person, your letter will probably be consigned to the same paper shredder as your script was.

If you haplessly send a letter to a film company marked 'To the person in charge of script acquisition' your letter will also go straight into the rubbish. If you, as screenwriter, are too lazy to call and discover whom the appropriate person in the company is to send a letter to, they may assume that you paid as little attention to your script. You, as a writer, will be attempting to approach the head of story development, sometimes called head of acquisitions. If you are writing to the local firm of accountants seeking an introduction to the most wealthy clients in their office block, then somehow you want to find out if that firm has a person employed who is responsible for clients' discretionary investments.

Elements of an Eight-Line Letter

1. A good visual style

The paper does not need to be expensive, but should be crisp and clean. Avoid the use of fancy colours. Plain white is difficult to beat.

You should design a logo or graphic image, along with the name of your company. The image should say, very simply, why you are hot, or why you are going places.

The Raindance logo says film, yet it shows the wear and tear similar to a piece of film that has gone through a projector or editing table over and over again.

Next, try to invent a company name for yourself, but don't get silly – with titles like '20th Century United Artists'. Rip-off names like these garner little respect, especially if an aged relative of yours answers the telephone. You should make certain that you have a reliable answering machine as well.

It is also advisable to get a second dedicated fax line. If you physically cannot get one, try and find a friend who has a fax machine at the office that you can use. If you have a second dedicated fax line, you are one big step away from rank amateur first timer: A tel/fax number just doesn't carry a sense of success to it.

The company name should be fresh and simple and, above all, shouldn't sound pretentious. You can register a company and become a limited company, either by buying an off-the-shelf company (£100 to £125) or by setting one up yourself. The actual fees are just £20.00. The drawback of registering a limited company is that you have to keep records and file annual tax returns. Failure to do this can get you into all sorts of problems with the authorities. If you anticipate that your trading is going to start on a more limited basis, then consider starting a proprietorship – a company under your own name. For example, Joe Bloggs trading as Hot Shots. You can get a bank account in the name of your company and type the company name on your letterhead. Either way, come up with a smart, simple and clean look to a letterhead.

If you are pursuing any company in America, put in these two words somewhere in the letterhead – *Thatched* and *Royal*. North Americans are very impressed with the 'low-budget' films like *The Crying Game*, *Four Weddings and a Funeral*, *Notting Hill*, *Full Monty*, and *Sliding Doors* that have come out of the UK, and in this fiercely competitive business, you must learn to take advantage of every situation.

2. The text of the letter

The first three lines describe yourself, and what you do as your day job, even if it's boring. It is here in the first few lines that you must grab the attention of the reader. It is also an opportunity to bend the realities of your life. You should exaggerate for effect here, when you are talking about yourself.

If, for instance, you are a butcher, then state 'I am a butcher, recently made redundant by the BSE crisis, who writes scripts in my spare time.'

The point is that you must grab the reader's attention.

A film development executive will be just as intrigued about your ability to write a screenplay if you are a disgruntled housewife, as they would be if you were a stylish trendsetter.

3. Twenty-five words or less

Next, you should outline your screenplay in twenty-five words or less. Many new writers get this wrong, and you will find this the most difficult thing in the world to do. You must sell the story, not tell the story.

Try to imagine yourself as the proud owner of a chalet in the south of France. If you got a request for information on renting your chalet for the summer, what would you send? The blueprints and heating plans of the building, along with the surveyor's report? Or would you send the most flattering photo you could take?

Logo and address

Mr Bigshot
Film Producer
Address

dd/mm/yy

Dear Sir or Madam,

The first three lines are when you describe yourself, your day job and what you do for your day job, even if it is boring. It is also your chance to create a mystique about yourself.

The next three lines are the basic twenty-five word pitch for your project. Try to recreate the little paragraph on the back of the video jacket, and remember, you only want them to call you for more details!

I would like to submit my project to your company for consideration. I look forward to hearing from you.

Yours faithfully,

Your name

The twenty-five words should read as follows:

My first [second, forty-third, etc.] *feature script is the story about* [here you describe your hero – young man, beautiful girl, depressed athlete] *who* [put in what they want most in the world] *but* [here you describe their worst nightmare, or allude to the opponent who will prevent them from getting their goal] *and* [tease us with the ending].

The last two lines are *I would like to submit my screenplay to your company for consideration. I look forward to hearing from you.*

Sign your name.

Remember that the sole task of this letter is to get this person to call you. And it is a lot cheaper than sending an entire script.

What Happens to Your Letter

Let us look at what physically happens to your letter once it reaches the offices of any film production company in the world. Travel with your letter, leapfrog the receptionist and sit on the other side of the table.

Whether it arrives by fax or post, the development executive's assistant will place your letter in a letter tray along with the rest of the correspondence of the day. People in the film industry work notoriously long hours, and at the end of the day, there is an unwritten rule that all calls and letters must be responded to.

It is a long-standing joke in the film industry that calls are returned at the end of each day. Call late and try to get the answering machine. In that way they can say that they tried to get back to you, but hey! it wasn't their fault you were out. As they are returning calls (many film people process in excess of a hundred calls per day) they start going through their mail with a Dictaphone where they can record their written instructions to their assistant.

When they come to a fourteen-line letter it gets immediately placed into the nutbar category. They don't have time to read it, and besides, their date is waiting at the bus stop, and it's now 7:15 p.m. and they're irritated.

Next is your letter. It's short and concise. If you write a good first few lines, and especially if you make them respond, winch or smile – you are seventy-five percent home. Then it's down to those twenty-five words or less. How good are they? How fresh are they? How original are they? It's really up to you to figure that out. But I do know this – if you send your letter to the right company, and if it is well written, they will call you. And that is what it is all about.

I know the eight-line letter works. We always use this form of a letter when we want to set up a meeting for sponsorship, or to get a celebrity to attend one of our events at the film festival.

However, I met a former student of mine on the street a few months ago and she told me that the eight-line letter didn't work at all. She showed me the letter, and it looked pretty good. In order to sell her screenplay, she needed to find a production company in the south eastern United States. She did her homework and found thirty-eight companies that were just the right size to produce her film. She told me that she had sent her eight-line letter to all of them, and only had four requests for her script.

I had always thought that a success rate of one in ten was pretty good. The day I met her she was returning from the post office where she had mailed her scripts to America. I haven't seen her since, but I am certain that she was successful.

Summary

1. Make your eight-line letters entertaining.

2. If the letter isn't working, rewrite it and make it better.

3. Don't expect every letter to work.

Now, let's talk the deal.

14   **The Deal**

The laws covering the sale of screenplays are strikingly similar to the laws covering the sale of property.

There are only three ways that screenplays are bought and sold. They are outright purchase, option deal and step deal.

1. Outright Purchase

A producer who reads your script may want to purchase your script outright. He/she will negotiate with you, or your agent, and agree a cash price for your screenplay. You then get a cheque. The copyright for the screenplay passes to the producer, and the deal is done.

Within the body of the contract, you may have certain rights and privileges expressed in the contract. A simple one might be that you are reimbursed for any travel expenses to meetings, or a salary might be included to cover the cost of your time for any rewrites, or polishes that the producer may want you to do.

When the demands of a writer become too harsh or onerous for a producer to bear, or if the writer is unwilling to compromise, it is referred to as 'holding your script hostage'.

The theory is that if the producer wants your script so badly (because it's hot) then he/she will be a much easier target to extract concessions. Writers who want to direct their own script most frequently use this tactic – 'I will only allow you to purchase my script if I can direct.'

This is a perfectly legitimate marketing ploy, but understand that the chance of selling your script decreases with the number of encumbrances you attach to the sale.

2. Option Deal

Sometimes a producer will want to buy your script, and after agreeing a purchase price, will offer to option the script from you. By making a down payment (usually ten percent) the producer effectively rents the copyright from you for the agreed period of time (usually twelve months). This allows the producers to complete financing, casting, and other pre-production details, and conserves cash flow. By signing an option contract, you agree not to show the script to any other party. The producer can represent that they own the copyright to their investors.

The balance of the purchase price is due and payable either on the anniversary of the option contract, or the first day of principal photography – whichever comes first.

At the end of the option period, one of three things may happen. Firstly, you receive a cheque for the balance. Secondly, the producer may say he/she is no longer interested (in which case you keep the deposit, and the copyright reverts back to you). Thirdly, the producer may feel that they need more time to complete the financing. In which case they will offer you an additional deposit, in return for an extension of the option for an agreed time. This additional deposit may or may not be applied to the purchase price depending on the terms of the agreement.

These points are usually made at the opening negotiations. In other words you may be asked to sell your script on a one-year option, with a ten percent down payment, with the right of two further twelve-month extensions, each with a pre-agreed payment.

The terms of an option agreement are all negotiable. I have known options to be as short as three months, with payments as high as fifty percent (for a hot script).

Option payments can also be considered a useful revenue source. Even if your script is not produced, you can represent that it has been sold. This elevates your stature to a writer with a script in pre-production. If the copyright reverts back to you, then you can re-market the script, knowing that it has already gathered serious attention.

Sometimes a producer will ignore step and option deals and try to persuade you to 'let them try to stir up some interest' on your behalf. When you agree, the producer picks up the telephone and verbally pitches it, and effectively is using your script without the legal right to do so. Worse, later on, when the producer has tired of your project, when you attempt to call someone, they tell you that your project has already been submitted and rejected, leaving you in no-man's land.

A producer can ruin the sale prospects of a screenplay in an afternoon.

A good producer will pay you for the script, either as a purchase or as an option, and then develop a marketing strategy for the screenplay. To attempt to sell a script without a marketing strategy is commercial and career suicide.

The Writers Guild of America prohibits shopping in its agreement with producers, and producers who ignore this are subject to heavy fines. Unfortunately, this practice continues to be widespread.

Here is an example of a deal memo letter between a writer and a producer that I have used. All people and titles are fictitious.

Option strategy

You can continue to market your screenplay after you have signed an option agreement, although you must inform the producer with whom you signed the option, of each person to whom you have marketed (or intend to market) your screenplay.

Producers understandably take a dim view of this practice, and may attempt to get you to sign a clause in the option agreement that prevents you from doing this.

If in doubt, consult the Writers Guild of America, or the Writers Guild of Great Britain for advice.

This sample agreement is provided for educational and information purposes only. To protect your own interests I highly recommend that you use the services of a qualified entertainment attorney who will advise you on the specific terms and conditions in your contract that will satisfy your needs.

Entertainment attorneys

When you sell a script, or are hired to write one, there will be deal points to negotiate and contracts to sign. An entertainment attorney is your employee who is trained specially to anticipate your problems and cover you with a warm layer of protective language.

Entertainment attorneys are well-connected players who are totally consumed by the movie business. A good one will know all of the latest gossip, will know to the penny who is getting paid for what, and ultimately, if he/she likes your script, will be able to push it in the right directions for you.

When you are looking for a lawyer, make certain that you obtain the services of an entertainment attorney. Someone who specialises in property conveyancing, or divorce law will be worthless to you as lawyer.

An entertainment attorney is hard to find and elusive, like top agents. The best way to get to one is by personal recommendation. Try to find someone in the industry who can put you in touch.

Lawyers' fees are not cheap: from £100 ($150) per hour to £300 ($500) per hour. Sometimes a lawyer will agree to defer their fees against a percentage of your future earnings. The usual rate is five percent, half of what an agent will charge.

Mr Bigshot
Film Producer
Address

dd/mm/yy

Re *Table 5* by Elliot Grove

Dear Sir or Madam,

This letter shall confirm the agreement between AEC Ltd (Purchaser) and Elliot Grove (Author) for Producer to acquire certain motion picture, television and allied rights in and to the screenplay titled *Table 5* (Property) for the purpose of producing a theatrical motion picture, a television motion picture or mini-series (Picture).

I understand the terms of the agreement are as follows:

1. Option

A. Commencing on May 1, 2001 the Purchaser shall have an exclusive and irrevocable six month option to acquire certain motion picture, television and allied rights in and to the Property. As consideration for such option, Purchaser shall pay Author £1,000 immediately. The foregoing option shall be applied against and in reduction of the purchase price.

B. Purchaser shall have the right to extend the option for a further six-month period by giving written notice and paying the Author a further payment of £1,000 on or before the initial six month option expires. Said payment will not be applied against a reduction to the purchase price.

2. Cash purchase price

If Purchaser exercises the option to exploit the Property as a television movie or mini-series, then the purchase price shall be £15,000 (less option monies paid to the Author pursuant to Paragraph 1A).

If Purchaser exercises the option to exploit the property as a theatrical motion picture, the purchase price shall be: £30,000 if the total budget of the film is less than £2,000,000, or £40,000 if the total budget of the film is greater than £2,000,000.

Payment will be made to the Author in full on the earlier:

A. Exercise of the option on or before the end of the option period; or

B. The first day of principal photography.

3. Contingent compensation

If the Author shall have sole screenplay or teleplay credit then the Author shall receive 5% of 100% of the net profits from the picture and all elements thereof, from all sources and all media. If Author receives no credit or shared credit, Author shall receive 2.5% of 100% of the net profits.

Net profits shall be calculated and defined per Purchaser's standard definition of net profits, subject to good faith negotiation within standard industry practices.

4. Television mini-series

Purchaser shall not have the right to exploit the property as a television mini-series without first negotiating per episode royalty and other payments as may be feasible.

5. Credit

Author shall receive credit on all Pictures produced from said Property, as opening title single card credit and in paid ads under the Purchaser's control, included in any otherwise excluded ads if the director receives credit.

A. Subject to arbitration the credit shall read 'Screenplay by Elliot Grove'.

B. Author to receive credits on all other versions, DVD, VHS, remakes, sequels, Internet broadcasts, etc.

6. Theatrical release

If the Purchaser exploits the Property as a television movie and there is a UK theatrical release for the picture or any portion of it before the television release, then the Author shall receive full payment as per Paragraphs 2 and 3.

If there is a subsequent theatrical release in other territories then the Author shall receive 50% of the compensation paid in Paragraphs 2 and 3 per territory released. These additional monies will be paid to the Author upon the date of release in said territory.

7. Sequels and remakes

The Author shall receive 50% of compensation payable in Paragraphs 2 and 3 for each sequel, and 33.3% for each remake of the Picture. These additional monies to be paid to the Author upon the first day of principal photography.

8. Reserved rights

All rights not granted to the Purchaser are reserved to the Author. The author reserves the following rights, without limitation: live stage Author written sequels and prequels, audio cassettes, live television, live dramatic tape, radio and all publication rights, and all digital Internet transmission rights.

The Purchaser shall be entitled to publish summaries and synopses of the Property not attributable to the Author, not exceeding 7,500 words. Purchaser shall not be allowed to publish a novelization or photo-novelization without Purchaser and Author negotiating the terms thereof in good faith.

9. Miscellaneous

A. The parties shall negotiate in good faith the compensation for the Author for any other exploitation of the Property. The Author shall also receive a free video

Possible deal points for writers seeking additional control over their work

The Writers Guild of America has a Minimum Basic Agreement (MBA) which covers basic rights for writers. The following is a list of additional rights a writer may want to add to the MBA. Producers will fight and fight against these deal points, but if you can, try to get them:

1. Sale/Option – the writer should be given the first reasonable opportunity to rewrite a script. If a new element (i.e. director/actor) has been added to the package within three years of the sale/option then the original writer should have right of first refusal to rewrite/revise the script.

2. Step deal – where a writer is hired to write a treatment or script and the purchaser contemplates replacing the writer, then ample time and opportunity should be made available
for all parties to meet and discuss the continued services of the writer.

3. The writer should have an opportunity to view the director's cut of the film in time to allow suggestions by the writer to be incorporated into the film.

4. The writer should be included personally in any press junkets, press kits, premières, previews, trips to festivals or award shows.

5. Screen credit, if due, to be included on all posters, film titles, press kits, all advertisements for the film, regardless of medium, in a size and placement no less than that of the director.

cassette of each program based on the property, and further agrees to sign a customary letter prohibiting duplication.

B. The Purchaser shall name the Author as an additional insured on the errors and omissions policy for the Picture.

C. There shall be no relief of the purchaser's obligations under this agreement should the Purchaser assign its rights and interest in the property.

D. Should the Purchaser enter into an involuntary arrangement with its creditors, or become bankrupt, then all rights under this agreement shall revert directly to the Author.

E. The Purchaser shall pay all pre-approved personal travel expenses in connection with the Author's services.

F. The Author represents that he has the sole right and authority to negotiate and enter into this agreement and is able to convey the rights expressed herein without restriction or limitation.

G. All payments and notices from the Purchaser are to be made to

Elliot Grove
c/o Raindance
81 Berwick Street
London W1F 8TW

10. Other terms

Other terms and conditions incorporated by reference in this letter herein are those that are customary in agreements of this type in the United Kingdom television and motion picture industries, subject to good faith negotiation within customary industry parameters. The parties intend to enter into a formal long form agreement incorporating the terms and conditions herein.

Please contact me immediately if the above is in any way inconsistent with your understanding of the agreement.

Otherwise this letter shall constitute a firm and binding agreement until such time, if any, as a more formal document is executed by all parties. If all is in order, please sign this original and the enclosed copy and return them to me.

Yours sincerely,

Elliot Grove _____ Date _____

Agreed and accepted by _____ Date _____

Mr Producer, Any Entertainment Company (AEC) Ltd

For documents signed in the UK add the following:

In the presence of _____ Date _____

Name
Occupation
Address

3. Step Deal

Far more common than an outright purchase is the step deal. A producer will read your writing sample spec script and call you in for a meeting where they will tell you that as much as they love your descriptive writing and the way you handle dialogue, they do not want to make your script. Instead you will be required to write their story. The writing process is divided into a number of steps – thus step deal.

Producer/Writer Agreement

The following sets forth the principal terms of the agreement between

Producer _____

and

Writer _____

in connection with the project currently titled [insert name of screenplay]

1. The Producer hereby engages the Writer to write a first draft screenplay and a first set of revisions (the Work) of the project currently titled [insert name of screenplay] intended as a theatrical motion picture (the Picture). The Work shall be based upon the story and ideas agreed between the Producer and the Writer.

2. The first draft shall be delivered no later than [insert date]. The Producer shall thereafter have a four week reading period. The first set of revisions shall be returned no later than [insert date].

3. In consideration for the services of the Writer, the Producer shall pay the Writer a guaranteed sum of [insert fee] payable as follows:

A. The sum of _____ upon the execution of this agreement

B. The sum of _____ upon delivery of the first draft

C. The sum of _____ upon commencement of the first revision

D. The sum of _____ upon delivery of the first revision

4. The Producer shall have exclusive rights to present this Work to any studio or third party financiers as seen fit subject to the following terms and conditions:

A. The terms of any third party option and acquisition shall be negotiated between the Writer's representative and third party in good faith.

B. The Writer shall be entitled to the same conditions of employment with a third party as offered to the Producer.

C. Terms and conditions to be negotiated include an optional rewrite and polish, sole and shared credit bonus, passive payments for sequels, remakes and TV productions, a first opportunity to write subsequent productions, representations and warranties, credit, anti-injunctive relief, notice, suspension,default and termination.

5. The Writer agrees to execute a certificate of Authorship as well as all other documents reasonably necessary to effectuate the purposes of this agreement.

6. The Writer shall give the Producer the first negotiation right in connection with [insert name of project]. If and when the Writer is prepared to exploit said project the Writer shall first offer the Producer the right to produce the picture on terms then to be negotiated in good faith. If terms cannot be agreed within fifteen days then the Writer shall have no further obligation to the Producer for [insert name of script].

7. If the Producer has not financed the Picture within twenty four months after the Writer delivers the first set of revisions, then the Writer shall have a non-exclusive right to attempt to finance the Picture without the assistance or involvement of the Producer provided that:

In the event that the Writer succeeds in financing the Picture, then the Producer shall be

A. Reimbursed the monies advanced to the writer plus interest, plus a bonus of [insert figure] percent.

B. Pay to the Producer an amount of 5% of 100% of the net profits of the first motion picture which net profits shall be defined, computed, accounted for and paid to the Producer in the same manner as they are to the Writer.

This agreement shall be covered by and construed under the laws of [state or country suited for you].

Writer   _____   Date   _____

Agreed and accepted by   _____   Date   _____

Mr Producer, Any Entertainment Company (AEC) Ltd

For documents signed in the UK add the following:

In the presence of   _____   Date   _____

Name

Occupation

Address

Upon contract, you will be paid a fee for the completed script, which will be broken into several performance-related steps.

The first step is the treatment. You will attend a meeting where the story will be outlined. You will then have a deadline, usually three weeks, to write a treatment, and when you deliver it, a second payment will be made, according to the payment schedule in the contract. Then follows a cooling-off period where the producer may decide that your services are not required. In which case, you keep the money, and the producer keeps copyright of the treatment. You will be unable to market the treatment, because you will not own the copyright. You cannot own the copyright because you are a writer for hire.

Or they may like your treatment, call you in for notes, and send you off to write the first draft. The minute you are commissioned to write a first draft, another payment is due. Like the treatment stage, there is a contractual deadline, and upon completion, the next payment is due. There then follows another cooling-off period, when the producer may decide not to continue with you (you have effectively been fired, but in the nicest possible way), followed by the second draft and polish steps. The payments, in total, would represent the total amount of money you agreed in the opening stage of the negotiations. The Writers Guild of Great Britain and the Writers Guild of America both have recommended minimum amounts which production companies, who are signatories, have agreed to pay.

Writing a Treatment

There are two types of treatments. The first is a step outline, which writers often prepare for their own use. It is simply a 'This happens, this happens, and then this happens' outline of the entire story. A treatment that you write as part of a step deal or as a tease for your own screenplay is structured differently. Essentially you are writing a sales tool for your idea. A Hollywood phrase is 'Sell the sizzle, not the steak' or tell me your idea in twenty-five words. By that, your challenge is to distil your idea into a tightly knit essay, which may or may not be in the chronological order of the actual finished screenplay. Compare yourself to the owner of a chateau in the South of France you want to rent for the summer to holidaymakers. A request from a jaded northerner, or curious North American comes in. What do you send to the prospective client? The plumbing and wiring diagrams? Or the glossy brochure with the artist's rendering of the swimming pool, yet to be finished?

Hint Writers are exploited – 'Write me a treatment for a script/star that I have interested' says the producer. He hopes you'll effectively partner with him but in reality is using you to jumpstart his producing career!

Writers Guild of Great Britain Film Rates

Please note that these fees are not buyouts. There are considerable additional use payments. For full details, buy the PACT/WGGB Agreement at £10 from the Guild office.

	Features Budgeted at £2 Mill +	Features Budgeted £750K to £2 Mill +	Features Budgeted at under £750K
Treatment			
Commencement Payment	£2,500	£1,000	£1,000
Acceptance Payment	£1,500	£1,000	£1,000
First draft			
Commencement Payment	£4,800	£3,500	£3,500
Delivery Payment	£4,800	£3,500	£3,500
Second draft			
Commencement Payment	£2,400	£1,200	£1,200
Delivery Payment	£2,400	£1,200	£1,200
Principal photography payment	£4,800	£2,600	£2,600
Total minimum payment	£23,200	£14,000	£14,000
Additional use pre-payment	£8,000	£5,000	*
Total guaranteed payment	£31,200	£19,000	£14,000

*The terms for films in this category to be exactly the same as for films budgeted at £750,000 and up to £2 million, except that the producer is not required to make the £5,000 advance payment against additional uses. The Total Guaranteed Payment is therefore the same as the Total Minimum Payment of £14,000, for the fee the Producer opts, before the first day of principal photography, to take either worldwide theatrical rights or two UK network television transmissions.

Writers' Guild of America Film Rates – Theatrical Compensation

		Period effective 5/2/99 to 5/1/00	
		Low	High
A.	**Original Screenplay, inc. Treatment**	$45,490	$85,330
	Installments:		
	Delivery of Original Treatment	$20,614	$34,134
	Delivery of First Draft Screenplay	$17,916	$34,134
	Delivery of Final Draft Screenplay	$6,960	$17,062
B.	**Non-Original Screenplay, inc. Treatment**	$39,822	$74,035
	Installments:		
	Delivery of Treatment	$14,928	$22,758
	Delivery of First Draft Screenplay	$17,916	$34,134
	Delivery of Final Draft Screenplay	$6,968	$17,143
C.	**Original Screenplay, exc. Treatment or Sale of Original Screenplay**	$30,570	$62,571
	Installments for Employment:		
	Delivery of First Draft Screenplay	$23,608	$45,511
	Delivery of Final Draft Screenplay	$6,962	$17,060
D.	**Non-Original Screenplay, exc. Treatment or Sale of Non-Original Screenplay**	$24,877	$51,195
	Installments for Employment:		
	Delivery of First Draft Screenplay	$17,916	$34,134
	Delivery of Final Draft Screenplay	$6,961	$17,061
E.	**Additional Compensation for Story inc. in Screenplay**	£5,692	$11,377
F.	**Story or Treatment**	£14,928	$22,758
G.	**Original Story or Treatment**	$20,614	$34,134
H.	**First Draft Screenplay with or without Option for Final Draft Screenplay (Non-Original)**		
	First Draft Screenplay	$17,916	$34,134
	Final Draft Screenplay	$11,940	$22,758
I.	**Rewrite of Screenplay**	$14,928	$22,758
J.	**Polish of Screenplay**	$7,468	$11,377

Reality Check – Negotiating the Sale of Your Script

The prices mentioned above are the going rate for established writers with opening title single card credits as screenwriters.

And the Writers Guild of Great Britain mentions the words 'Suggested Minimum'. Can you imagine how I feel about the word 'suggested' when I am producing?

Producers working with unproduced writers will try to get the lowest possible price for a screenplay. In the UK it is about a thousand pounds. Roger Corman told me in 1996 that he pays on average $15,000 to $25,000 for screenplays, even though the WGA minimums started at about $35,000.

Has the writer been exploited? It really is up to you to answer this.

If you feel uncomfortable with any deal, you should walk away.

On the other hand, if your film can be made and if the producer you are negotiating with has the ability to make your film, and make it well, then you will enhance your marketability on your next film.

Many writers have sold their scripts cheaply in order to get a screenplay by credit. Future scripts are then marketed on the basis that the writer achieved one screenplay credit, and therefore the subsequent screenplays are more valuable.

Is it possible to get a percentage of the profits?

Never. It only happens for a handful of movie personalities such as Harrison Ford and Jack Nicolson. When a producer convinces you to accept a percentage of profit in lieu of payment, they are fairly certain they can reduce your payments to next to nothing using creative accounting. This is not to say that you shouldn't form a partnership with a producer in order to get your film made. This deal requires that you vend your script into the company for a percentage of the shares, making you an effective partner with the producer. These deals typically have a time bomb guaranteeing the return of the copyright should the production of the film hit certain milestones relating to financing, casting and production. Neil Jordan and Steve Wooley operate their production company – In The Company of Wolves – along these lines.

Again, choosing the right producer is difficult and a writer should always ask whether a producer is capable of getting the project off the ground and completed. After all, getting that first elusive credit as a screenwriter will enhance your career, and increase your value in the marketplace.

What if you want to direct as well?

A writer who declines an offer of purchase for their script unless they are allowed to direct is considered an egomaniac with delusions of grandeur in the film industry.

Not only does the industry recognize the mental and physical stamina required to direct a movie (did you know that directors must pass a physical test conducted by the financier's physicians?) but writing a screenplay is very difficult.

A writer who 'holds their script hostage' is announcing to the world that they are taking two of the most difficult and demanding jobs in the film industry and combining them into one – the writer/director.

True, this is certainly the most glamourous job in the film industry, but as a writer, you must recognize that your script is much more difficult to sell or finance when you encumber the deal with the fact that you want to direct.

Again the low-budget independent filmmaking route beckons aspiring writer/directors. Remember to get a professional outside opinion on the merits of your script before you start filming. Otherwise you stand the chance of leading a host of private investors off the cliff with you. This basic reality is one of the few advantages of seeking traditional industry financing for your project.

More Reality Checks

This is where we go into *bummer* in a serious way. Let's do a reality check on the deals and monies that screenwriters are paid. In order to do that I need to put my producer's hat on.

1. Outright purchase

UK producer Paul Brooks, now living in LA, once told me that he had never paid more than one thousand pounds for a script – and he had produced six UK features at this point. Each of the writers he has worked with has gone on to bigger things, notably Vadim Jean and Gary Sinyor whose film *Leon The Pig Farmer* launched the British film revival in the early 1990s.

I'm a producer. You are a screenwriter? As a producer, do I love the word 'suggested'? How many times was the word 'suggested' used in the section above? How many opening title credits as 'screenwriter' do you have on a feature length movie that got theatrical distribution in more than one cinema and not at a film festival? None? I thought so. Do you want an opening title credit? And you want to be paid? I'm going to suggest you take $1,000 for your screenplay. As producer, I'm going to turn your screenplay into a movie in the best way possible, not give you a penny of the profits, but you will have that elusive first opening title credit. In other words, you will only be paid $1,000 for your script.

If you take this deal have you been exploited?

Firstly, you don't need to take this deal and you should never take any deal that you are not totally comfortable with.

Secondly, if you seriously consider a low money deal, you should ask yourself if you are likely to get any other offers, and then weigh up the probability that this producer will make your script into a great movie. You are in effect partnering with this producer – who is likely to be starting out as well.

Hint Always ask yourself who is likely to make the best movie of your screenplay. This is the producer you should sell your screenplay to.

---

2. Option deals

A producer will attempt to option your screenplay from you for a very modest sum against a low purchase price (or even against a 'suggested' price in this depressingly common scenario). What you are really doing in this case is becoming a business partner with the producer. In certain situations you may know the producer very well and this type of partnership can work. But like any personal relationship, two people can very easily fall out under the stress and strain of a business deal.

Producers used to attempt an option payment for as little as $1. Cases like this are less common because of recent commercial litigation. In several cases, producers took writers to court because the writer had signed a $1 option with them and then sold the screenplay to someone else. In all cases the producers lost because they were unable to prove the payment or 'consideration' needed to solidify the transaction. Not many writers I know would bank a check for a dollar or a pound! Now producers offer a payment for as little as they can. Fifty to a hundred dollars or pounds seems to be the going rate.

Hint Use this deal to bolster your CV – 'I have sold my first script. Here is my second.'

---

3. Step deals

Everything is negotiable. A step deal I did in London several years ago was with a single Australian mother of three children. Because she was on the dole, I couldn't pay her any money. I met her every Friday afternoon at a supermarket, where she would give me the sides she had written that week, and I would give her two bags of shopping worth no more than £40 ($60).

After a few months she fell in love with her ex-lover and moved to New Zealand. I now have sixty-seven pages of a script that I don't know how to finish, but I use page thirty-seven as the script format guide which can be found at the end of this book.

Everything is negotiable.

Hint Never sign any deal that you don't feel comfortable with.

---

4. Playing God

Lawrence Bender optioned the screenplay *Reservoir Dogs* from Quentin Tarantino for a small sum and got the budget together. It was their first picture, and they both launched brilliant careers from the success of that film.

Games they play in the movie business – suppose your agent calls with a 'good news, bad news' call. Which would you like to hear first? The bad news? It's an option deal. And the good news is that your screenplay has been sold for $75,000. This means, under the standard deal, your agent will receive a total of $7,500, deduct their ten percent and remit to you the balance, $6,750 (minus any expenses).

This is actually a good deal for you. Although your movie may not get made for a long while, you have actually earned some money, and what is more, if you get a second script written and optioned, you are earning about twenty percent of what you would earn if you sold one.

I know several writers who make a good living from their option fees. Whenever I see them, I ask them about such-and-such a script and they respond by saying 'I've just got that one back, and my agent thinks someone else is interested.'

But back to the deal your agent has done for you.

What you don't know, and what your agent didn't know, was who was really interested in your script. Your script was optioned by an independent producer in LA, priding themselves at being a creative producer and an expert in doing lunch.

Let's suppose that the producer who bought your screenplay had a direct contact to a company like Icon Entertainment (Mel Gibson's company) and know exactly what sort of product this company was looking for, for the next Mel Gibson vehicle. Your script fits the bill exactly. But major stars don't star in scripts by first timers, and they especially don't pay minimum rates for them.

Have you been exploited? Or do you feel cheated? Why didn't you, or your agent, approach the star directly. Now stop crying, and remember that your marketability has been greatly enhanced by this transaction.

What this producer did was sell the company an option for $750,000, and accepted a down payment of $75,000 from which your payment of $7,500 was made. The way you find this out is not from your agent, but from a telephone call from your best friend with a copy of *Variety* in front of them. All of your friends are delighted. They now know someone who has sold a script for $750,000 to the company of a major Hollywood star. What they don't understand is why you are not out at the pub buying everyone drinks. You can't. You only have a cheque for $6,750.

Hollywood is full of producers who make a speciality of 'doing lunch' and trying to find material for studios and production companies. Often the producer will have multiple deals and yet not have these scripts produced due to the vagaries of the movie business. However, they earn a good living. Understand that they have costs too, and often underwrite the costs of rewriting the script themselves, trying to get the right vehicle for the company or star they are pursuing.

What usually happens near the end of the option period is the copyright reverts back to you. The star has lost interest. You wouldn't tell anyone would you? And your agent would quietly market your script elsewhere.

5. Sharks

Sometimes you will run across a producer who will option your script under the standard option deal, and then manage to get the film into production. You are expecting your cheque on the first day of principal photography, but in the excitement of production, the cheque is not forthcoming. Perhaps you lack the confidence to make sure the money is paid, or are unaware that your cheque was due on this deadline. As a first-time writer you are further disadvantaged by your ignorance.

Typically, the producer may fob you off with various promises, until at some point you lose patience and bring up the grubby issue of money. At this point the producer will tell you to sue, knowing that the cost and time involved is prohibitive.

Instigating a court action for payment involves a lawyer – who will demand a hefty deposit for legal fees. It also involves waiting months and years for a court date. Even if the producer loses, he/she could still appeal the decision, adding another lengthy delay with more legal fees. After a time, the producer hopes you will become so weary of the litigation process that you will then be willing to accept a nominal payment and abandon your court action.

Sharks are not that common, but are known within the industry. It is a good defensive action to enquire about the credibility of any producer who purchases your script. Network with other writers and filmmakers. The film industry is quite small, and if a producer has treated other writers badly, their reputation will follow them.

If you discover that you are dealing with a shark, you have two options: either abandon the deal and hope for another purchaser; or, deal with the shark, knowing you will not be paid but safe in the knowledge that your script will get made and win you the elusive opening title credit.

6. Finder's fees

Occasionally you will run into a producer who will offer to take your script to specific people in exchange for a fee.

You will be looking for a producer who is well-connected with the type of production companies that will be interested in the type of story you have written. You also want to be aligned with a producer who has a good working relationship with these various companies.

Certain producers are expert at presenting scripts, and they earn their money from you, the writer, and often are also paid by the company to whom they sell your script. As producers they are better at this aspect of the business, and have little inclination or aptitude for the actual production process.

Be wary that they are not shopping your script, and ask them to sign an agreement like the one over the page.

Finder's fee agreement

As an inducement to [name of person or company name] for presenting [name of story, book, manuscript or screenplay], [your name or company name] agrees to pay the sum total of [x percent] of any or all monies or other consideration earned or received by [your name or company name] at any time in connection with the name of story, book, manuscript or screenplay, if [name of person or company name] delivers one or all of the following:

A. If the material is optioned in any form and/or

B. If [your name or company name] is hired on a development deal.

This fee is to be paid in less than fourteen days from the date the monies are received by [your name or company name].

I, [your name or company name] and [name of person or company name] agree that if any legal action takes place because of a violation of the terms of this agreement then the prevailing party shall be entitled to full recovery of legal and court fees.

This agreement shall be covered by and construed under the laws of [state or country suited for you].

Writer _____ Date _____

Agreed and accepted by _____ Date _____

Mr Producer, Any Entertainment Company (AEC) Ltd

For documents signed in the UK add the following:

In the presence of _____ Date _____

Name
Occupation
Address

Summary

1. Credit = credibility = power = career = money.

2. Writers say – 'If we work as writers for hire (for money) we are hacks, if we work for nothing we are chumps.'

Next we discuss the Life of a Screenwriter.

15   The Life of a Screenwriter

Writing a screenplay is very hard. Writing a good screenplay involves a good amount of fortune, and a strong belief in the first biblical reference. But like everything else, I believe that there can be a plan. And with a good plan you stand a better chance of succeeding. The key to becoming a successful screenwriter is really very basic – get great ideas, write them down in a distinct personal style, circulate each finished script in the film community and as soon as one script is finished, start the next.

If it is so basic, why isn't everyone doing it? Because writing a screenplay is difficult. Writing a truly great screenplay is very, very difficult.

My first suggestion is not to try to write the world's greatest screenplay every time. Write according to the structural details I have outlined. Yes, so write stories from the heart. Write stories that you are familiar with, and appeal to you. Make sure that the characters are well developed and that you really know them. Write the screenplay knowing that it is a screenplay. A saleable screenplay in fact. But not your best work. Every couple of years, try to write the world's greatest screenplay. Write it in a timeframe that you believe is reasonable, workwise. If you feel yourself getting writer's block (lack of confidence) then you know it is time to set it aside for a while and get on with one of the journeyman pieces that might be able to help you pay the rent. If in the writing of this great screenplay, you solve one of your inner problems and truly become a better person – then I believe that the act of writing a screenplay has already been worthwhile for you.

Understand Genre

Genre is really the key to a successful career. Choose a specific genre and study it inside out. Then learn another. Writers should specialize in two or three genres. Hollywood only buys genre, and prefers genre mixes like romantic comedy, sci-fi horror and thriller love.

Hint John Truby's Writers Studio (www.truby.com) is the most advanced place to study genre in the world.

The Screenwriter and Creativity

Have you ever been walking down the street and had a great idea for a movie? Have you noticed how these great ideas seem to pop into your head as you are doing something mundane? As a writer you need to understand the greatest tool that you have – your mind. Knowing how your mind operates will give you the knowledge to utilize your mind even further.

Our minds are divided into two parts. The left side and the right side. The left side controls rational thought and the motor control of our muscles. It is this side that keeps our hearts beating, allows us to do repetitive work, like walking, without having to dwell on it, and is the side that calculates our bank balance. The right side of the brain controls emotion. The panic if the bank balance is too low, the bursts of sadness or happiness when you see the news, and the subconscious.

When you are doing something boring, like walking or vacuuming, the left side of the brain is occupied, freeing the right side of the brain. That's why all those wonderful ideas for a movie come bubbling up.

But notice how quickly they vanish? If the telephone rings, and you walk over to answer it, within seconds that wonderful idea has vanished. When you finish the telephone call, you then remember you had a great idea, and now spend the next hour or two in agony trying to pull it back.

Much has been made of the great artists of the last century. Picasso and John Lennon, to name but two. I do not believe that any artist was more talented than any other mortals on this planet were. What I do believe is that these great artists were in touch with their alpha state.

The great artists of all time are not more talented. They are simply better at accessing the ideas that come to them in alpha state.

But how do you capture those great ideas?

Alpha State

Capturing ideas in alpha state is easy and fun. But like a muscle, it improves with practice.

Identifying alpha state

The moment you do any physical movement you will be in alpha state. You may not realize it. Tasks like walking, driving, cycling, ironing and cleaning send me into alpha state in seconds. Here is a simple exercise that you can perform to put yourself into alpha state.

Close your eyes and roll your eyes upwards until you feel your eyelids flutter. The effort of keeping your eyelids fluttering will put you in alpha state. If you want to take this exercise a step further, close your eyes, roll your eyes upwards for exactly a minute. Can you see the first minute of your movie? Are you aware of a color? An image? An emotion? If yes, perhaps these ideas can give you an idea for your movie. If not – perhaps this is just too crazy for you, or you were distracted by a noise.

Capturing the moment

The only way to capturing those wonderful alpha state ideas is to jot them down as they happen.

How you jot them down is important. You should carry a small pad and pencil with you all the time. If you are a frequent driver, perhaps a Dictaphone is a safer idea. When you have an idea, whip out your pad and jot down a couple of words that will jog you back to the moment when you are next at your computer. I never write down more than eight words. The words you write should just be enough to jog your memory, and allow you to return to the moment that you had the idea. You will then be able to finish off your alpha state daydream and experiment with different possibilities.

I discovered alpha state by accident.

I live with a dog, and walking the dog every morning is my responsibility. It is a task that takes twenty minutes, rain or shine. I used to hate taking the dog out, until I discovered alpha state. Now I look forward to those precious twenty minutes at the start of each day where I can see what the solutions are to the problems at hand.

Leonardo da Vinci was a great walker and filled hundreds of notebooks with thousands of drawings, poems and ideas while he was walking.

I can't assign tasks to alpha state, tasks like 'I'm two hundred short for the rent today – what am I going to do?' But solutions to the problems and opportunities in my life get answered every single morning. I just don't know which ones – which is why I always carry a notebook.

Hint If you utilize alpha state while writing your movie make sure you really get to know your characters inside out. If you do they will actually talk to you during your alpha state moments.

While I was writing *Table 5*, I was struggling with the relationships between the girl and her ex. I had a scene that just wasn't working. One morning, while walking the dog, I realized I had rewritten this scene at least a dozen times. At that moment I thought I felt a hand on my shoulder. I turned around, and heard Ramona's voice saying 'Elliot, I wouldn't ever say that. I would say this.' 'What would you say instead?' I asked. And she spoke the lines. I scribbled down a few key words, raced back to my desk and finished the scene in under an hour.

Alpha state will work for you like this as long as you don't ask it to solve mechanical problems like your overdraft!

Getting an Agent

Having an agent is wonderful. A good agent offers moral support, handles all your professional correspondence, gives feedback on your work, and drums up new business. For this an agent charges ten percent of the money you make – a very reasonable deal. But finding an agent who is able to satisfy your requirements is very difficult. Any good agent will have a client list packed with screenwriters, and will be reluctant to take on a new writer, especially if existing clients are selling well.

By reason, the best time to get an agent is when you have someone interested in your screenplay. By using your power file and writing the eight-line letter, you can get serious interest in your screenplay. Then contact an agent and see if they will represent you and close the deal. For this you will pay them ten percent.

It is a popular misconception that agents will continue to market your work. In fact, marketing yourself and your screenplay is your responsibility. It is a certainty that an agent will sell your script if they see a buyer for it. But with dozens of other writers on their books, they cannot be expected to think solely of you. So keep selling yourself and your scripts. But conduct all the business and refer the leads to your agent. This will make you look professional to the script buyers and, of course, to the agents. But what if you haven't got a deal? What other routes are available to get an agent?

Hint Having an agent is desirable and preferable. But it doesn't mean that you need an agent. Do not let the lack of an agent encumber your marketing program.

The Four Routes to Getting an Agent

1. Make friends with someone in the agency

Get your script to them and ask them to read it. If they like your screenplay, they will recommend it to someone else. The theory of this technique is that this employee wants to move up the ladder and will use your screenplay as a demonstration of their ability to discover hidden talent, and expand the revenue of the agency.

2. Research existing agencies

See if they are looking for new writers. Find an agency that is willing to consider new writers, submit three screenplays – a half-hour script for episodic TV for an existing show; a ninety-page script suitable for a low-budget production; and a two hour script whereby you really let loose.

A reality check, please. Put yourself in the shoes of the agent. You are very busy. You don't have time to read scripts at the office, so you bring them home. Despite your intention to read them during the week, at night, you haven't. Now it is Saturday morning. You have three scripts to read by an unknown writer, plus a new script by an existing client. The existing client's previous script was sold for three times Writers Guild minimum, earning you a hefty commission. Which script would you read first? And one more thing – you have to get ready to go to a family wedding in three hours.

The film industry is fiercely competitive.

Back to your three scripts. Suppose the agent has time to devote to you. The three scripts are lying on a pile, next to the wedding clothes you have to put on. Which script would you read first? Of course you would read the short script. And if it were great you would read the ninety pager. And if that were fantastic, you would probably read the two hour script in the back of the taxi on the way to the wedding. Any agent in the world would want to work with you. Not only are you prolific, but you are versatile and the agent can see getting you work (and earning money) from your television as well as film scripts.

If the first script the agent reads is boring, if it has clumsy descriptive passages, or dialogue without moral argument, do you think they will bother with your second script? Of course not.

Hint Never send a script out until it is as good as you can get it.

---

3. Specialize in other areas

Many screenwriters start in dramatic radio, especially in Britain where the BBC produces about 1,000 hours of drama per year. Radio doesn't pay as well, but it does pay. Once you have been produced, you can add that to your CV when you approach agents you would like to represent you.

Another route is theatre. This is accessible to anyone with a stage play. Simply hire a room and put on your show. Invite agents to your show, and see if they see a spark of talent there that they can sell. If you write a stage play that is produced by an established company, then you will almost certainly get an agent on the strength of that.

4. Start your own agency

I don't recommend this route but I know several people who have started their own agencies. In the UK you can start an employment agency by paying a £50 ($75) fee to the local municipal government office. You get a license to run an employment agency – in this case, for screenwriters. The theory of this route is that the agency will allow you to get around the barriers put up by film companies who will only accept screenplays from agents. The difficulty is that your agency is still unproven. A tactic to combat this is to get someone already in the industry to be a patron – someone who will agree to allow you to put their name on your letterhead but who has no legal or financial responsibility for your company.

Another tack would be to team up with other writers, directors and actors and form a co-operative agency. The drawback here is that as the company grows in size someone has to raise operating capital to pay for an administrator, computers, office rent and so on. But it still is an interesting proposal. Why not start the next United Artists?

Researching the Marketplace

You need to keep abreast of your industry. The more you know about current trends, the better able you will be to see the future. Reading the trades, networking at film festivals and industry events, and keeping up to date with the various film magazines, e-letters all takes time. But it can be fun. Learn to enjoy! And remember to devise a filing system that will allow you to retrieve the information you put into it with ease.

1. Story ideas

Discovering commercially successful story ideas is the mother-lode for a screenwriter. But writing for the market is risky and dangerous. It takes two to three years for a screenplay to go through the writing, production and marketing process. To estimate the public's taste in two or three years from the time you sit down at your typewriter is impossible. The first source of stories must come from your own life, and if you write that which you know, you are more likely to write with passion. And the passion will be appealing to your audience.

2. Cannes, festivals and markets

The Cannes Film Festival is the largest film festival in the world. It is also free to enter as a filmmaker, writer or director. Every year, thirty-five thousand people descend on the sleepy town of Cannes to attend the festival. Of the thirty-five thousand, about a thousand are film sellers, three or four thousand are film buyers, and the rest are cinema fanatics, wannabees, and tourists.

By tracking films at the Cannes Film Market, which runs parallel to the film festival, you will be able to see what sorts of films sell. Attending Cannes is also advantageous for the networking opportunities, and after one pays for airfare to Nice, can be very inexpensive. While in Cannes, you can arrange to meet sales agents, directors and producers from around the world. I go to Cannes each year for a few days and discover that I end up forming alliances with people that I use for the coming year.

Hint Never take a screenplay to Cannes. Take a one-sheet and treatment. People are too busy to read a script at Cannes.

Attending other festivals, smaller than Cannes, has the advantages of a smaller group: it is much more intimate. You will also be able to get relatively close to the festival programmers and filmmakers which will enable you to see what sort of films work in the festival. If you have a feature or short in a smaller festival it will be very easy for you to gauge the audience reaction. Probably the quickest way to learn how to write is to sit in a non-partisan audience and watch how your script plays.

3. Book fairs

Book fairs are a great place to see what is going to be commercial. Here books are sold from everything from galley proofs to a poster. In fact my publisher first touted this book at the Hamburg Book Fair in October 2000. She attended with a mockup of the jacket and a two-paragraph synopsis. When she got back to London, she was able to tell me that the book had a favorable response from book buyers and started saying the word 'Deadline' to me.

4. Style magazines

Being a writer is fun. You can always justify the expense of some beautifully produced glossy style magazines as your contribution to keeping in touch. Here you will read stories planted by PR companies, and journalists all vying to identify the next trend. But why not? It is showbiz.

Perhaps you can get a feel for what trends are developing and use this instinct to help plot the content of your next script.

5. Do you have to live in Hollywood?

No, but it helps if you are dealing with a company based in Los Angeles. If you don't live in LA, but want to deal with an LA company, you could treat your out-of-town address as exotic. Everyone I have met in LA is desperate to leave.

When you sign a deal with a major Hollywood company, don't be surprised if a condition of the deal is you physically moving to LA for the duration of the project.

And despite what many LA executives might tell you there are many film companies in cities other than LA!

Map of the Film Industry

Yes it is true. There is a blueprint of the film industry building – a giant warehouse in a secret location. I can't tell you where it is, or show you the blueprint, but I can tell you about it. I hope that you will be able to use this information to get into one of the many doors in the film industry and sell your screenplay.

From the front, the film industry building is vast. It is one of those massive Victorian buildings built at the turn of the last century, and it has large pillars with a long flight of steps in front of it. In front of the film industry building is a very busy road. Directly in front of the entrance there is a loading bay, and a bus stop. Across the road there is a train station. Every morning at nine a.m. dozens of office workers alight at the bus stop and train station and race up the steps to go to work. A little later, you might see a limousine pull up, and disgorge some bodyguards and a star and see them run up the steps and into the film industry building. Everyone seems very busy. Oddly enough, most days you can see several hundred people waiting on the steps of the film industry building. When a star comes out, these paparazzi snap away like mad and hound them for autographs.

If you spent a complete twenty-four hours there, you would be amazed at how late some people left, and how early some people arrived. The film industry is noted for the long, hard hours people work.

I came back today from a meeting with the new owners of Hammer Films. Despite a media blitz when they bought the back catalogue to the company in Britain and in America, they received a princely total of six spec scripts.

The new CEO had even cleared several bookshelves to accommodate the rush of scripts! And they had let it be known that they were looking for another Hammer House of Horror film!

But before you get your screenplays and stamps out, remember, by the time you see it in this book, it's too late! I am sure they have enough scripts by now to last them a lifetime.

Turning to look at the front of the building, the first thing that springs to mind is the fact that there is no threshold guardian. No one is checking the credentials of people scurrying into the film industry building. Unlike the medical industry building, or the aerospace building or the legal building where threshold guardians closely check documentation, it would appear that anyone can enter the film industry building.

Moving up the steps and through the front doors, the first thing you notice is the size of the place. The corridors stretch ahead of you as far as you can see. Doors line both sides of the hallway. And unlike the medical industry building, each of the doors is unique. In the medical industry building, there are only a few doors: general practitioner, pediatrician, surgeon, dentist, holistic medicine, and gynaecologist. But every single door in the film industry building is totally different.

The first door on the right is covered in cobwebs and there is a huge padlock on the lock. On first glance, it would appear that the doorway hasn't been used for years. Closer inspection reveals a fresh nick in the keyhole. Hammer Films, one of the great names of British filmmaking, which has lain dormant since 1981, has just been taken over and the new owners are planning to go into production.

If you look up the hallway you will see hordes of people walking up and down. Some are hurrying up to doorways, pulling out a set of keys and letting themselves in. Others stop at high-security doors, press a PIN

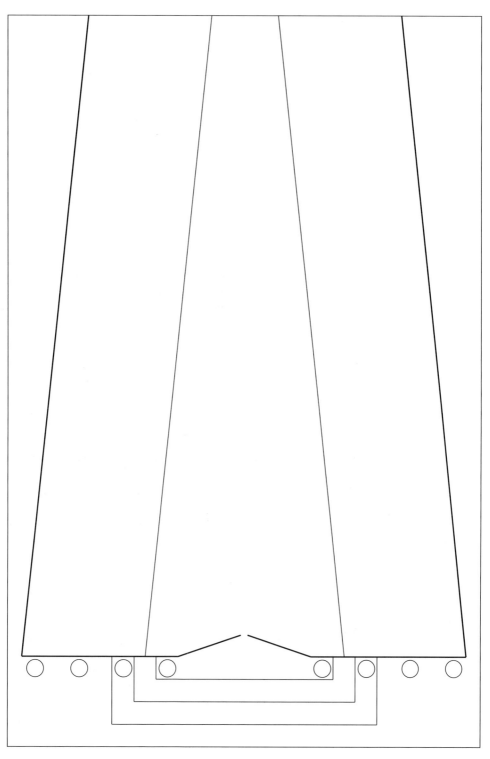

figure 15.1
The Map of the Film Industry

number into the lock and get zapped inside. That's something we must do – get the right set of keys or figure out which buttons open doors.

Of course if you spend more than a few hours in the hall you will see lots of people suffering from the dreaded onanist's rash walking aimlessly up and down the hallway. They rarely get into a doorway, unless it's like the one over there. Here there is actually an open doorway, with an attractive shrub in a pot outside. In this office there is a comfortable couch, a coffee table with free magazines and an urn with free coffee – a government agency or film society dispensing free information. These doorways are nice on a day when you have suffered a lot of rejection.

Maybe you are walking up the hallway and you see one of the doorways that is guarded by security men and infrared light beams. Standing there you notice the doorway is made of stainless steel, like a bank vault. To the right-hand side there is a key pad where you enter a secret code. As you are peering at it, trying to figure out the combination, the security men (who are dressed in black, naturally) toss you rudely aside. You look up as a group of people scurry in and you think you recognize a star. Not just any star, but the star who would be perfect for your script. You leap to your feet and race to get inside, but the door clangs shut in your face. So, you are back in the corridor.

Hint Your job is to get out of the hallway and into the rooms. Keep your power file up to date and never stop networking. Find out where the keys to the doors you want are kept.

You see another door is ajar. You peek in and see that they are looking for screenplays. You walk in and observe the plush trimmings and the telephone bench with not two, but three telephone receptionists. You befriend one of them and discover that the person you need to see with your screenplay works in the office directly behind you. Hell, she even got her to read your screenplay. And you have an appointment a week Thursday at 4 p.m. That is a glorious week. Every time you pass an onanist in the corridor you can brag about your meeting.

This is the story of Miramax in the early years. Rumour was that you wouldn't get a meeting with one of the brothers until you had been cancelled, without notice, for ten times. Not very funny, if you have saved up your last shilling to get a cheap ticket to New York from London. Apparently this is the way they tested your passion.

You arrive fashionably early on the day, are greeted by your friend on the switchboard and invited to sit on the white leather couch. A telephone with free outgoing calls sits temptingly beside you. But you will resist. An hour passes. Your friend keeps beckoning reassurance to you. Another hour. 6:15. Still no meeting. Your friend comes over to you, very apologetically and tells you that your appointment has been cancelled due to an unexpected but lengthy transatlantic conference call that is still in progress. Of course you reschedule for a week Tuesday.

The same thing happens again and again. You finally get into the room, meet the big cheese. You pitch your guts out, she is nodding 'Aha, Aha, tell me more' when suddenly it hits you. This isn't the big cheese, this is the threshold guardian for the real big cheese in the next room.

Back in the corridor. Walking a little further along you come to another door with a simple letterbox. Suicidal after your rash of cancellations and other nobler forms of rejection, you take the plunge, form a good solid knuckle and rap the door for what might be your last sales pitch ever. To your amazement, someone says 'Come in!' Suspiciously you push open the door, and there, in a single, small room, lit by no more than a naked light bulb sits an independent producer. Surrounded by scripts, red-letter notices, a fax machine and a worn-out photocopier rests, quite possibly, the best chance you have to get your first script made. Don't overlook this option. But don't be bullied by a producer. You will know when you meet the right one. It will just leap out at you.

Allow me the indulgence of telling you a true story about a particular adventure in the film industry building.

In 1998 I had the idea of creating a film award show to honour British filmmakers, writers and actors. We called it the British Independent Film Awards. In the second year, Diana Ross actually showed up and we got miles of coverage. Coming up to year three I asked the William Morris Agency to represent the Awards in order sign a television deal for the event.

We arranged for a meeting at the prospective broadcasters, and I attended with my assistant, Fred Hogge, and our agent. We arrived, were given a choice of expensive drinks, and ushered straight into the Big Cheese's Office, from where we were taken into the Super Big Cheese's office. The room was a classic British library room, with wooden floors, expensive tapestries and hunting prints on the wall. The window overlooked London's Green Park, and in the distance Buckingham Palace. Facing the window was a floor to ceiling wall of expensive original edition books.

The Super Big Cheese sat at a desk with his back to the window. On the desk were copies of the contract, bound with red legal ribbon in the quaint British tradition. Our agent reached to pick one up, but the Super Big Cheese reached out and said 'Let's wait for a minute. We like to keep things professional.'

The three of us retreated to our leather wing chairs in front of the bookcase. We ran through the main points of the contract and were in total agreement. As we were about to get up and sign – I even had my pen out, the Super Big Cheese's assistant, Big Cheese came in and said 'Excuse me, sorry to interrupt, but Harrison Ford is on the line.' Naturally we shrugged as if a call from Harrison Ford was totally routine for us.

I am not sure if the call from Harrison Ford was real or not. I suspect it was. My fantasy is that Harrison Ford was in on it too. What I do know is that as Big Cheese nodded to get our consent to take the call, he turned towards the window. And what I hadn't noticed then, but remember now with painfully accurate recollection, is that at our feet was a semicircular groove around our chairs and the bookshelves. And as Super Big Cheese turned to talk to Harrison Ford, he reached under his desk and pushed a button. Suddenly the whole bookshelf started to revolve and we were spun out of the office and into the corridor. It was so sudden. And we were back in the corridor.

The deal, so tantalizingly close, vanished before our eyes without a single explanation. The only thing I can say is that my last glimpse of the office was of Big Cheese mouthing the word *onanist* at us as we were turned out of the office. And it all happened so fast. That took a few days to get over, let me tell you! My agent said that these things happen sometimes, and to get on with the next deal.

Hint Never take anything personally. Of course it is almost impossible not to take it personally. But try not to.

Summary

1. Remember that you are a professional. Act like a professional and you will be treated like a professional.

2. Be creative when you approach your career.

Next, how you present your script to the industry is an important part of looking professional.

Screenwriters have an ideal entrepreneurial opportunity, if they consider themselves as a manufacturer of product – take a ream of paper, available from any stationers, and turn it into a screenplay worth thousands using just a few pennies' worth of ink, your time, and your mind.

If you treat your writing like a business, then it follows that you are a professional, and certain rules apply to your profession – as they do to any other profession. What follows is both a format and style guide which attempt to give the reader an idea of the different choices and strategies involved in the craft of screenwriting.

Screenplays must be submitted in the correct format, or the industry personnel you are pursuing will ignore them. By ignoring the simple formatting rules will make your script look amateurish.

The film industry has become institutionalized to the point where scripts follow one set of rules for screenplay, and another for television. This chapter explains the basic rules for screenplay.

Basic Principles

1. Twelve-point Courier typeface

Screenplays and teleplays are written in 12 point Courier typeface, which has evolved from the old manual typewriter's typeface. A script set in 12 point Courier, properly formatted, will roughly equal a minute of screen time. A similar script set in a more pleasing font like Helvetica will confuse the reader – they will not know how long the screenplay is. Use A4 paper, or in the US use $8\frac{1}{2}$" by 11" white 3-hole paper.

2. Don't use camera directions

Scriptwriters should not use camera directions in their scripts – this is the job of the director. Unfortunately, beginning writers often see produced film scripts with camera angles and scene numbers, and assume that this is how a script should look.

It is important to understand that the author's script is the beginning of a creative process, and that a produced script goes through many different stages of appearance, with the input of producers, directors, and technicians who mark the script with scene numbers and camera angles as an organizational tool. Writing a presentation script for a sale should not include scene numbers.

The best way around using camera directions in a script is to write the script in a very visual way with descriptions that imply camera directions. This strategy also works to make the script more readable, since camera descriptions are often clumsy and break up the flow of the script. Consider, for example, the following from *The Shawshank Redemption* by Frank Darabont:

```
He reaches for the glove compartment, opens it, pulls
out an object wrapped in a rag. He lays it in his lap
and unwraps it carefully --

-- revealing a .38 revolver, oily black, evil.

He grabs a box of bullets. Spills them everywhere,
all over the seats and floor. Clumsy. He picks bul-
lets off his lap, loading them into the gun, one by
one, methodical and grim. Six in the chamber. His
gaze goes back to the bungalow.
```

3. Don't break scenes up into shots

Use master scenes only in your script which describe the whole action in one setting. Remember that the person reading your script for the first time must be able to understand what is going on – clearly.

4. Don't number your scenes

Scripts are only given scene numbers when they are budgeted and scheduled to be shot. An author's version of a script (presentation script) should never have scene numbers.

5. Length

Each script page is generally considered a minute of screen time. In order to appear professional, it is important that your script be of a proper length. Feature film scripts have some flexibility, but they should generally be within the 100 to 120 page range. Television programmes are necessarily more precise, with shows varying to some degree in how they divide up the commercial time, with teasers at the beginning and short epilogues or tags at the end. For a writer looking to write a spec script (speculative, without pay) for an established show, it is strongly advised that you watch the show carefully, and if possible, obtain the bible for the show – where the characteristics of the main roles are detailed.

You can make a script of 122 pages appear to be 120 by simply calling three pages within the script 62a, 76a etc. The final page count will then number 119 or 120.

6. One-camera film format vs. three-camera tape format

One-camera feature films and filmed television shows have a different format from taped, three-camera television shows. TV shows with a great deal of action or exterior scenes tend to be filmed. Sitcoms, variety shows, game shows and talk shows are mainly shot in a video studio using a three-camera script format. The feature film script uses single spacing for both the dialogue and scene description. In the three-camera format, both the dialogue and scene direction are double-spaced.

7. Acts

Feature films are not formally broken down into acts. The creation of acts comes from theatre where the curtain would fall after each act. Cinema is a much more fluid medium and not subject to a curtain.

Television scripts, with the blocks of time set for commercials, are structured by distinct acts. Movies-for-television are generally broken into seven acts, sitcoms into two acts, and one-hour programs into four acts. Again, television programs vary with the use of introductory teaser scenes and short epilogues.

8. Make it perfect

Although it may sound trivial, correct spelling and grammar are a must. Good grammar and spelling won't sell your script, but you don't want to give potential buyers another reason for rejection. The finished product should be clean and neat. Make certain that the final spell check is done manually to eliminate the errors that computerized spell checking can lead to.

The Screenplay

1. Covers and binding

Stay away from the green neon metal flake covers. The last thing that a writer wants is for their script to look like a vanity press publication.

Screenplays are bound with beige, white or grey card.

The title page should contain nothing more than the title and the author's name. The title should be typed in capital letters, but in 12 point Courier. Your name should be typed in upper and lower case. If you type your name in caps, you say to any industry person who picks up your script that you are a megalomaniac. See figure 16.1 over.

figure 16.1
Incorrect Script Title Page

AIRPLANE THAT LANDS SAFELY

By

Budding Author

© 4th Draft, 17th Revision

Lawyer	Budding Author
Address	Address
Home	Home
Office	Mobile
Fax	Office
Email	Email
	Website

figure 16.2
Correct Script Title Page

LAST BUCK

By

ELLIOT GROVE

Copyright Control
Raindance Ltd
81 Berwick Street
London
W1F 8TW

Include nothing within the covers other than the title page and the screenplay itself – no cast of characters, casting suggestions, related articles, previous correspondence, autobiography or illustrations.

In America, the traditional binding for scripts is three-hole punch on the left side with brass brads in the top and bottom hole (to facilitate copying). In Europe, A4 with a wire clip through two holes is adequate. In America, double-sided copying is acceptable, and greener.

2. Title page – drafts, dates, WGA registration

Conventional wisdom varies on this point, but for a beginning writer, it is generally best not to number drafts or type the date of completion. This information is only important once the script is purchased and it goes through a series of rewrites. It is not necessary for you to mark your script with the WGA registration number in order for it to be protected, and many people view this practice as amateurish – it is common for beginning writers to be overly concerned about their ideas being stolen. The title page should have nothing more than the writer's name, address, phone number, and the title of the script.

3. First page

The first page is not numbered. Centre the title in caps and quotes. For television shows broken down into acts, type in the act, centered, in caps, and underlined, three spaces down from the title. Four spaces down, all scripts begin with FADE IN:

4. Scene Headings

Scene headings, or slug lines, indicate whether the location is an interior (INT.) or exterior (EXT.), the location, and whether it is day or night.

Occasionally, a scene is both interior and exterior, as in a doorway or at a window, and this is expressed as INT./EXT.

INT./EXT. APARTMENT WINDOW – NIGHT

If the location encompasses a large area, such as a football field, then the writer needs to specify a certain area, such as ON THE BENCH or AT FIFTY YARD LINE. The time has to be either day or night, not morning, dusk, or twilight. The day or night designation is for shot scheduling purposes and needs to be straightforward. Subtler distinctions in time should be indicated in the text of the scene description.

Sometimes extra information must be included in the scene heading such as the season or year. Put this in parentheses after the location.

EXT. LOS ANGELES (1939) – DAY

When scenes continue to another page, you can type (CONTINUED) in parentheses at both the bottom right margin of the first page and

CONTINUED:

without parentheses and a colon at the top left margin of the second page. But this practice is really for scene numbering, which comes later when the script is broken down for production, and isn't really necessary. Some writers use CONTINUED, others don't.

5. Scene endings

Scene endings are always in caps at the far right tab with a colon. FADE OUT is followed by a period, ending the act or the entire script. It is not necessary to put a scene ending at the conclusion of each scene.

6. 'Cut to:'

Some writers never use CUT TO: arguing that moving from one scene to another implies the transition. Other writers use CUT TO: after almost every scene liking the way it sounds when read aloud. Still other writers reserve CUT TO: for sudden changes in location, or for cutting back and forth from different locations during an action sequence. I prefer the latter.

7. 'Dissolve To:' and 'Fade To:'

These endings have become less and less popular in filmmaking with the emphasis on hard cuts. In addition, the photographic look of scene transitions is really a choice for the director to make.

8. Fade out

Used to end all scripts.

9. Scene description

Always double-spaced down from the scene heading, the scene description or direction indicates in the most economical terms what the setting is, who the characters are, and what action is taking place.

10. Paragraphing techniques

The greatest flexibility in format for the screenwriter is in the style used in scene description. The particular form that a writer uses to describe the setting and the action in a scene has a great impact on the way it reads. Some writers format scene description in paragraphs like one would see in a novel, one sentence after another in long blocks.

Other screenwriters break their scene description into short one- and two-sentence paragraphs. Whichever paragraphing form you use, it is important to develop a strong individual writing style that is clear, concise and visual.

Here are some examples:

Racine tries the door. It's locked. Racine shakes it
hard, but it's solid. Racine looks to his left.
There's a window down the wall there. He moves to it.
It goes into the dining room. Matte watches him from
the same spot, through the dining room door. Racine
pushes up on the window. It won't budge. Racine moves
to his right, past the front door, to the large
window off the living room. He pushes at it as his
eyes lock with Matte, who watches from the hall. The
window won't move. Racine spins and picks the nearest
object, a wooden rocking chair. He lifts it, turns
and smashes the big window. Glass showers into the
living room.

(Lawrence Kasdan, *Body Heat*.)

NICOLI staggers down the street, unarmed.

DOYLE is waiting at the foot of the stairs.

NICOLI sees him, turns in desperation to run back up.

DOYLE has his .38 drawn. He fires three shots into
NICOLI's back.

NICOLI stiffens and falls backward at DOYLE's feet.
DOYLE collapses next to him.

(Ernest Tidyman & William Friedkin, *The French Connection*.)

This technique has the advantage of isolating separate actions and
images. It also tends to prevent the reader from missing the key story
information, which can get buried in a long paragraph.

A third method, which is becoming increasingly popular, is to set key
images in short sentence fragments, capitalized, on a single line.

GITTES' HEAD SLOWLY CLEARS THE SOFA TOP

and he looks.

GREEN SMOKE CURLS

up lazily from his desk drawer.

REACTION GITTES

sees he's been had.

(Robert Towne, *The Two Jakes*.)

Used properly, this style is very visual, economical, and readable.

Many writers use a combination of these three paragraphing styles, for various effects at different moments in their stories. Developing an understanding of the particular effect of each of these styles is an important part of the craft of screenwriting.

11. Capitalization

When characters are first introduced their names need to be capitalized. Thereafter, in the descriptive passages, their names appear in upper and lower case. This serves as an organizational device to assist casting directors, script supervisors and performers and tells them the size of their parts.

When sound cues are used the first word in the cue needs to be capitalized to alert the sound technician skimming the script that his expertise is going to be needed here.

If a scene is to be shot mute, the proper abbreviation is M.O.S. This confusing looking stage direction comes from the early days of sound picture when a German director bellowed through a megaphone 'Mit Out Sound'.

Although for the screenwriter, camera cues are to be avoided like the plague, if an occasional camera direction is used it should appear capitalized (ANGLE WIDENS, CAMERA DOLLYS, IN CLOSEUP). Even better, if the writer can use a term which implies a camera angle (SEE, FOLLOW, and LOOK), then it too must be capitalized.

There are three camera directions that are commonly abbreviated – foreground is f.g., background is b.g. and off screen is o.s. When these abbreviations begin a sentence the first letter is capitalized.

12. Character cues

The character cue is simply the name given to the character that speaks the line of dialogue that follows. Always capitalize character cues. The abbreviations for VOICE OVER (V.O.) and OFF SCREEN (O.S.) are used with the character cues to denote two different things.

VOICE OVER is used when dialogue is put over a scene either through narration, a character thinking out loud, or when a tape recording is played in a scene.

OFF SCREEN is used when a character is heard but not seen, as when a character talks from another room in a house, or is simply out of the camera frame.

Both (V.O.) and (O.S.) appear abbreviated, capitalized, and in parentheses directly after the character cue.

Characters with small roles are sometimes given numbers such as FAN No 1 and FAN No 2. Or, the role that a certain character plays is sometimes put in parentheses next to the character cue as in JOSEPH

(CARPENTER). Some writers feel that one should try to give every character in the script a name in order to help define the character. Others think that since the viewer often has no occasion to learn a minor character's name, there is no point in mentioning it in the script.

13. Character direction (parentheticals)

Character directions are special instructions to the actor, pertaining to the specific dialogue that follows. Generally, the use of these parentheticals should be avoided. Character directions in a script can seem to be an attempt by the writer to tell the actor how to act. Actors generally will strike the parentheticals from a script.

In most cases, the tone should be clear from the dialogue.

Some writers use character directions to pace the dialogue using the term beat, meaning a pause.

```
                    DENYS
          There's a woman there, Tania.
          He's been with her some years now.
          (beat)
          She's Somali.
          (beat)
          The comfort you'd bring is less
          than his pain if you knew. You
          mustn't go.
```

(Kurt Luedtke, *Out of Africa*.)

Occasionally, a writer might use dialogue in an ironic or comic way, going against the expectations of the situation, and the character direction then becomes necessary. Some writers also use parentheticals for directing the movements of a character during a particular passage. But for the most part, this is best left in the scene description.

Another use of a character direction is to make it clear to the reader that three people are involved in a conversation:

```
                    JOANNE
                  (to Ben)
          How old is Elliot? I'll bet he's...

                    BERNICE
          ...thirty-six.
```

14. Format

Personal direction always appears under the character cue in parentheses. If the dialogue of a single character is broken up by scene description, when the dialogue resumes a parenthetical is used with the word continuing.

```
                         HACKETT
                       (continuing)
              I suppose we'll have to kill him.

    Another long contemplative silence.

                         HACKETT
                       (continuing)
              I don't suppose you have any ideas
              on that, Diana.
```

(Paddy Chayefsky)

15. Dialogue

Unlike in plays and novels, dialogue in the screenplay is as short and economical as possible. Many screenwriters see dialogue as another form of action, putting characters at odds, driving the plotline.

A helpful tip is to consider a two-character scene as one where character A asks something of character B, who misunderstands the question (or maybe ignores it) and answers another question. When done skillfully, this type of dialogue can be followed by the audience and creates the 'reading between the lines' that is considered 'sub-text' in many screenwriting manuals.

A large part of rewriting a screenplay, especially for beginning writers, tends to consist in large measure of simply cutting down unnecessary lines and fragments of dialogue.

16. Dialogue format

– Spell out two digit numbers, personal titles, and indications of time.

– Do not hyphenate long words, breaking them from one line to the next.

– Never break sentences from one page to the next.

– When a long passage of dialogue needs to be continued onto another page type (MORE) at the character cue tab and then (cont'd) after the character cue on the following page.

– Omit these shooting script devices – scene numbers, capitalized sound effects, the word continued at the bottom of each page whenever a scene extends to the next page; numbers or dates of successive drafts, or any other indications of rewritten or revised material.

– Type a character name all in caps when that character is first introduced into the screenplay. Do this is in the action/description paragraph, never the dialogue.

– All scenes begin with a new scene heading, followed by an action/description paragraph; never begin a scene with dialogue.

– In a new scene, mention character names before giving them dialogue.

3"
→→ COREY (cont'd)
one suitcase. That leaves you out
of it. I'm going to shoot Blazers'
mouth shut.

She fondles an ashtray

EXT. JERSEY STREET - DAWN

But Blazer isn't available right now, because
he's rollerblading towards the flapping door
of a circus tent.

CUT TO:

INT. TENT - DAY

1½"   **1"**
→→ Blazer glides into the tent and comes to ←——
a perfect stop right under the nose of PHIL,
the Balloon King. It's taken the FALLADY
about two seconds to realise where she's
seen his face before.

4"
→→ PHIL
What do you want?

His voice breaks out in an audible sweat.

BLAZER
I'm looking for a couple of high wire
boys - Elliot Groveski and Paul Berchardini.

The swinging overhead light shatters into
a million pieces.

BLAZER
3½"
→→ (continuing)
I want to show them new ways to fly.

figure 16.3
Script Format Guide

New writers that I work with love to debate the finer points of script format. I believe it such a popular topic because it prolongs the moment until they actually have to touch a typewriter.

And if you are typing a fantastic screenplay, does anyone actually care whether or not the word gunshot is all upper case, underlined or not?

Summary

1. Take the time to format your script properly.

2. Don't be intimidated by the formatting rules – it will just make you delay the writing process.

Are you ready for the moment of truth? Try my troubleshooting guide.

17   Troubleshooting Guide

This useful guide should be referred to whenever you get stuck.

Ask yourself the following questions, and see if you can unlock your story, and discover the fractures in your story.

Premise

- [ ] the premise is fractured
- [ ] the premise is not spoken to in enough scenes
- [ ] the premise doesn't speak to a larger theme
- [ ] the premise is not commercial

Hint Is your film high concept or low concept?

Action

- [ ] the action is not integrated to the story
- [ ] the action is contrived
- [ ] there is no action

Hint A well-written script should be composed of visual stimulation.

Ghost

- [ ] the story has no ghost
- [ ] the ghost is not painful to the hero
- [ ] the hero overcomes the ghost too quickly

Hint Examine your ghost for the unique characteristics of each genre.

Hero

☐ the hero is too passive
☐ the hero is too reactive
☐ the hero is cold (audience cannot sympathize or empathize with hero)

Hint Review your character essays until you know each one intimately.

Hero's goal

☐ there is more than one goal (the story is fragmented)
☐ the goal arc begins too late
☐ the goal arc is not specific
☐ the goal arc does not build in intensity or importance
☐ the goal is unimportant
☐ the goal arc is reactive/too negative

Hint Most stories fail because the hero does not have clearly defined goals and needs.

Hero's Needs

☐ there is no psychological weakness
☐ the psychological weakness is not painful to the hero
☐ the moral need is vague
☐ the moral need doesn't affect/hurt other characters
☐ the hero has no moral need

Hint A good hero has two problems to solve – an outer problem (goal) and an inner problem (need). There are two types of inner problems – psychological (personal weaknesses) and moral weakness (how your hero reacts with other characters).

Backstory

☐ the backstory is redundant or starts too soon
☐ the backstory relies on hackneyed devices like flashback
☐ more of the action should be included in backstory

Hint Most scripts start the story too early.

Opponent

- [ ] there is no main opponent in the story
- [ ] the choice of main opponent is wrong
- [ ] the story lacks conflict
- [ ] the main opponent is internal
- [ ] the main opponent is an organization
- [ ] the opponent is flat or one-dimensional

Hint The development of the opponent character is the most important in your screenplay.

Scene writing

- [ ] the scene has no climax
- [ ] the scene has no conflict
- [ ] there is no point to the scene
- [ ] the scene does not move the story

Hint Scenes contain their own structure – a beginning, a middle and an end.

Descriptive passages

- [ ] the descriptive passages are overwritten
- [ ] the descriptive passages are too static
- [ ] the descriptive passages are not visual
- [ ] the descriptive passages do not contain movement

Hint Great descriptive passages describe people and objects moving with emotion.

Dialogue

- [ ] does not sound like different people talking
- [ ] is on the nose
- [ ] is overwritten

Hint A picture is worth a thousand words. Show your characters doing things as much as possible.

Setting

☐ the social stage is not appropriate to the story
☐ the choice of social stage is unclear
☐ there is no social stage

Hint The choice of setting (social stage) will predetermine the qualities of the hero.

Summary

1. The more time spent planning your script at the first draft stage, the fewer flaws your script will have.

2. Remember that you are an intuitive storyteller, and this troubleshooting guide may not apply to your story.

To be a successful writer, you must follow the three golden rules of screen writing.

18   **Three Golden Rules**

Syd Field taught me the real meaning of downloading. It was so refreshing to talk to an amazing writer like Syd and hear him say that he didn't write. He spent half of his writing time each day downloading the alpha state ideas he had from the previous day, and then spent the rest of his daily writing time evaluating and polishing the ideas he wrote down from the day before. Syd says that he 'Throws his ideas onto paper' and then worries about whether or not they are any good.

Becoming a successful screenwriter means following a few simple rules. Of course the usual mental and physical health rules apply. The biblical golden rule – *Do unto others as you would have them do unto you* – is also a pretty good rule to follow. A successful screenwriter needs, I feel, a few more specific rules that outline a plan to attack the specific problems that a screenwriter faces.

Rule Number One – Quantity, Not Quality

Just throw it down on a piece of paper. Every day. Write for half an hour. Don't even worry if it's any good. Just throw it down on a piece of paper, and determine at a later date whether what you have written is any good.

Ernest Hemingway used to say that you must relax. And write down everything that you have dammed up in your alpha state. Throw it down. You can always polish it later.

Hint Chances are that ninety-nine percent of what you write is rubbish. The important thing is not what you write, but that you do write.

Rule Number Two – Discipline

Thinkers think, joggers jog, writers write. If you can get paid for thinking or jogging, fantastic. But writers write. They move their fingers for about three hours a day.

I know, discipline is a nasty word. It implies physical pain and mental anguish to get your screenplay written.

But rather than overlook this second golden rule of screenwriting, let's try and make the very thought of discipline palatable.

First of all, you must write every single day.

But rather than start with an eight-hour bash on your Saturday off, why not try a half-hour a day, five days a week to start. The half-hour works like this – the first half (about fifteen minutes) is spent downloading from the alpha state. The second half is spent polishing what you have written from the day before.

After four weeks of this, see if you can gently raise your writing time to forty-five minutes, then to an hour. Professional writers that I know rarely work more than three hours per day unless they are on a deadline.

If you plan to write Monday to Friday, then you must pick a time of day when you know you can write every single day. If you plan to write at night and are used to spending Wednesday nights out, then you have to compensate by writing on a Saturday or Sunday for a half-hour.

The important thing is that you write for the same length of time every single day.

You will be amazed at how prolific you will be writing just a half-hour a day. And by spreading your writing times out by twenty-four-hour intervals, and utilizing the alpha state opportunities that you may have travelling to work or walking the dog, your work will have a freshness and vitality that will distinguish it.

A friend of mine has been commissioned to write a how-to filmmaking book for Focal Press. He works on this book on three- and four-week spurts, burning the candle at both ends, leaving himself in a state of physical and emotional exhaustion. Following these workathons, he does nothing for months on end, suffering increasing tension from pent-up guilt and frustration. This attacks his confidence to the point where he is seriously contemplating abandoning his excellent project after spending hundreds of hours on it. His (and mine) poor editor is reeling from the dozens of missed deadlines to the point where it appeared that the book would be abandoned.

When I saw him recently, I asked him how much longer his book would be, and he estimated three to four months of round-the-clock work. I convinced him to try an hour a night and he suddenly realized that three to four months of sixty minutes a day would probably suffice to get the book delivered.

We all live very different lives from each other. But no matter what life we lead, we all have a rhythm, or a routine to our daily existence. Programming oneself to write for a set time each day is just another of the habits that we must form if we want to work as a writer.

Hint If you find yourself avoiding the discipline of writing, stop 'writing' and try downloading from the alpha state. You will soon have so much raw material that you will suddenly feel the urge to write.

Rule Number Three – Reject Rejection

Writing is a lonely business. Filmmaking is a crazy business. Putting the two together means that you are faced with heaps and heaps of rejection. Nothing is more competitive than the film business. You will face untold amounts of rejection, and unless you develop a plan to deal with rejection, you will never make it as a screenwriter. And rejection will get you down to the point at which it affects all areas of your life – if you do not learn how to follow this third golden rule of screenwriting. There are three types of rejection:

1. Physical rejection

Three years after I started Raindance, I suffered both physical and moral rejection to the point where I couldn't imagine continuing. I packed up all the files, gave notice to the landlord, and called the telephone company to disconnect the telephone. A good friend of mine called me, listened to my sorry state of woe and said – 'Quitters never win, and winners never quit.' I sat on the packing boxes for an hour, and unpacked them. That was seven years ago.

Announcing your ambition to write a screenplay, and then announcing that you will actually start to write a screenplay, have the same effect on your personal life as announcing a marriage, or divorce. It is cataclysmic, and unless handled properly will totally ruin your writing career.

When you first announce your ambition to write a movie, you will be swept away by a riptide of enthusiasm and approval for your chosen goal. There is, after all, nothing like a glamorous daydream.

However, fail to deliver an Oscar-winning script on your first foray into the movies, and your friends will desert you. 'Why don't you get a real job, a real hobby, why are you always dreaming?' will be the chorus that rings in your ears at every social gathering, or stabs you in the back every time you leave the room.

Worse yet will be the words from your loved ones who will try to get you to abandon your screenwriting career because they see your hurt from all the rejection you will suffer. They are truly just trying to help, and again, if not dealt with in a loving and caring way will destroy your writing, and if you are not careful, your relationships as well. I don't have a solution for this, but I do know lots of people with the rash who fall at this hurdle.

And the reason you will give up writing at this stage is because you will lack confidence in yourself and will not be able to have the belief in the biblical quote 'in the beginning was the word…' which will mean you will not be able to take the screenwriter's leap of faith which means you will see your whole dream, your goal, as entirely worthless. Which would be a pity. Since you have talent.

2. Moral rejection

You will beat yourself up if you are not aware of the destructive power of moral rejection. Sometimes you will read the facts in such a way that you will be unable to continue. Discouragement will reign supreme.

You might start looking at the statistics of the film industry. Reading the trade papers, you will be horrified that about 40,000 screenplays are

Before you give up, I implore you to perform a simple exercise. Look in your correspondence file. Find out how many letters of rejection you have. If you have none, it means you haven't been trying to sell your screenplay. If you have dozens, have you exploited them properly? Have you found out why they said 'No'? Have they said No because the office is on fire, and they must leave in time to save themselves? Have they said No because they are out of the business? Have they said No because they want you to sell them more? Is there any useful advice they can give you regarding your story concept, characterization, scene description and dialogue? Always try to find out why someone says No.

registered every year for copyright, yet only a few hundred are actually produced. If you aren't careful, this statistic will send you to the rooftop of the tallest building in your neighbourhood.

___

Hint Reject rejection means being true to your goal. Follow golden rules one and two and this makes rejecting rejection much easier.

___

You have to remember that statistics can be bent to suit any political voice. Rather, analyze the meaning behind the statistics. Of all the scripts registered at the Writers Guild, it isn't the ratio that counts, it is the percentage of great scripts to clankers. It is also true that the Writers Guild admits about 500 new writers per annum. The only way that you can join the Writers Guild is if you have sold a screenplay to a company that the Writers Guild recognizes. In other words, to reframe the statistic, why not say that despite the number of screenplays sent to the Writers Guild every year, an average of one writer per day sells a screenplay under WGA terms and conditions!

___

Hint Reframe the statistics. This will breed confidence.

___

3. Psychological rejection

Sometimes you will suffer such a humiliating amount of rejection that you will feel like giving up. You will enter your own page seventy-five, your personal Big Gloom. You are beating yourself up. You have lost the light at the end of the tunnel.

There is really nothing I can say to you, except at this point you are probably suffering from the one disease from which no doctor can cure you – self pity. There is only one person that can help you – you.

In closing, let me tell you a true story. After high school, I went to art school in Toronto. In order to support myself, I needed to find a summer job. In my middle year at art school, I left it too late to get a good job. All my classmates (who were less talented than me) found the great jobs with high pay – driving Post Office vans, filling in as PAs in the financial district, or working up north as park rangers.

The only job I could find was working for a real estate company going door to door trying to get the owners to give me instructions to sell their property. For this I was to be paid a commission relative to the value of the property.

I spent the first two days suffering every form of rejection known to mankind – I was chased by the snapping guard dog, saluted by drugged out housewives, threatened by irate night shift workers I had woken, and greeted by the stony silence of the locked door. On top of that, the elements were very unkind. It was the hottest heat wave in living memory, and I developed blisters.

I went back to the owner of the agency and told him I couldn't do this any more. I was prepared to do anything but. I would carry out the trash, mow the grass, and paint the shutters, anything but go door to door. Unfortunately, his was the only job available. And I needed a job desperately, or I wouldn't be able to finish art school.

I timidly asked him how many doors I would have to knock on until I got a yes. I already had forty-seven rejection slips. He looked at the map on the wall, scratched his chin and said about a hundred. A hundred! I couldn't imagine that.

Still desperate for a job, I asked him how much commission I would get for that. Again he studied his chart, pulled out some sales figures and said 'About $3,000' (£2,000).

So I decided that the only way this would work for me was to reframe the problem in my mind: 'You mean, $3,000 divided by a hundred means $30 [£20] for every no?'

I raced around the neighborhood. I knocked on door after door. You want to sell your house? No? Great! And I would earn another $30! I could hardly wait for someone to say no, because I knew I was one closer to my payoff. Sure enough, after one hundred and seventeen, I had my first instruction. The next was eighty-seven and it really did average around a hundred a yes. I had the best summer job I had ever had.

However you do it, you have to be able to depersonalize rejection. Try to make it fun.

Which is why Raindance has teamed up with Focal Press to offer writers struggling with rejection something positive. Whenever you get a rejection letter, send me a copy, c/o Focal Press. I will instantly send you a letter of acceptance to the Raindance Gallery of Rejection. And you know what I am going to do, don't you?

When you are famous, and have a hit film, I will advertise the fact that when you were unknown, you read this book, and in your moment of deepest despair, you wrote me a letter. And I have the proof right here in the Gallery of Rejection. I will market the fact that you read this book!

I will send you a personalized letter of acceptance to the Gallery of Rejection, so you will have at least one yes in your file.

Happy screenwriting.

Elliot Grove
June 2001

19 Resources for Screenwriters

Screenwriting Books

Adventures in the Screen Trade: A Personal View of Hollywood and Screenwriting
by William Goldman, Warner Books (May 1989)

Alternative Scriptwriting: Writing Beyond the Rules
by Ken Dancyger and Jeff Rush, Focal Press (August 1995)

How to Write a Movie in 21 Days: The Inner Movie Method
by Viki King, Harper Collins (March 1998)

Opening the Doors to Hollywood: How to Sell Your Idea, Story, Book, Screenplay, Manuscript
by Carlos De Abreu, Howard Jay Smith, Random House (December 1997)

The Screenwriter's Workbook
by Syd Field, DTP (September 1998)

The Complete Guide to Standard Script Formats: The Screenplay
by Hillis R. Cole and Judith H. Haag, CMC (December 1989)

Successful Script Writing
by Jurgen Wolff, Kerry Cox, Writers Digest Books (February 1991)

Which Lie Did I Tell: More Adventures in the Screen Trade
by William Goldman, Pantheon Books, (March 2000)

The Writer's Journey: Mythic Structure for Storytellers and Screenwriters
by Christopher Vogler, Michael Wiese Productions (November 1992)

Writing the Short Film
by Pat Cooper, Ken Dancyger, Focal Press (October 1999)

Screenwriting Guides and Directories on the Internet

Screenwriters network
Meet other screenwriters, read biographies of producers and
directors, or look through the film script bank.
www.screenwriters.com

Screenwriters online
Insider's guide to the industry includes news, features and gossip,
as well as networking resources for writers.
www.screenwriter.com

Spec Screenplay
Extensive screenplay directory dedicated to the art of screenwriting.
Includes writing tips, news, interviews, articles, archives, and FAQs.
www.hollywoodlitsales.com

About.com – Screenwriting
Articles about and ruminations on the screenwriting process, film
reviews from a writer's perspective, chat, and more.
www.screenwriting.about.com/arts/screenwriting/index.htm

American Screenwriters Association
Nonprofit screenwriting organization offering networking meetings,
seminars, newsletter, competition, critique service, and more.
www.asascreenwriters.com

Dave Trottier
Dave Trottier, author of *The Screenwriter's Bible*. Courses and advice.
www.davetrottier.com/

Drew's Script-o-Rama
Claims to be the most comprehensive index of movie and TV scripts.
www.script-o-rama.com

Qwertyuiop.net
Interviews of screenwriters and screenwriting news.
www.qwertyuiop.net

SU: for screenwriters and screenwriting
Interviews with professional screenwriters, screenwriting articles,
newswire, screenplays, and tons more, over 1600 pages.
www.screenwritersutopia.com

Pro Screenwriter
Links for professional screenwriters and people looking for
screenwriters and plays.
www.members.aol.com/linkwrite/profwrt.html

Scriptocinetv
Help for screenwriters and playwrights in French.
www.scriptocinetv.com

The Writers' Website
Links for screenwriting.
www.writerswebsite.com

ScreenTalk
Numerous articles on everything to do with screenwriting. A great site for screenwriters based in Denmark. Lots of scripts for downloading.
www.screentalk.org

Done deal
Information on screenwriting and screenwriting tips. Also, the latest script sales section.
www.scriptsales.com

EuroScreenwriters.com
A good European site. Links and screenwriting articles.
www.euroscreenwriters.com

Wordplay
Everything to do with screenwriting.
www.wordplayer.com

FilmUnlimited.co.uk
The Guardian's film website. Information about international writers.
www.filmunlimited.co.uk

Writers Guild of America
Everything to do with screenwriting. Lists of agents and information.
www.wga.org

Script Secrets – William C. Martell
My personal favorite writer's website. Packed with tips and scripts by a screenwriter with seventeen produced films.
www.scriptsecrets.com

Essential Scripts

Reading these screenplays will give the ability to study the successes of others. Read any of these screenplays and you will see great story-telling, each written with a strong and unique personal style. Make a special note of the descriptive passages and the dialogue and ask yourself how you would feel if you were a development executive or financier presented with one of these scripts.

As Good As It Gets by Mark Andrus and James L. Brooks
Witty, human, biting, and romantic.

Chinatown by Robert Towne
Possibly one of the most stylistically influential screenplays.

Goodfellas by Martin Scorsese & Nicholas Pileggi
That wacky Mafia.

Good Will Hunting by Matt Damon and Ben Affleck
Read the magic on the page, and see if some of it rubs off on you.

L.A. Confidential by Brian Helgeland & Curtis Hanson
A perfect fusion of tight plotting and vivid characterization.

The Last Seduction by John Dahl
A haunting and chilling thriller.

Leaving Las Vegas by Mike Figgis & John O'Brien
Bleak, hard-hitting, unflinching look at alcoholism as suicide.

The People Vs. Larry Flynt by Scott Alexander & Larry Karaszewski
Excellent character study of a consummate outsider.

The Piano by Jane Campion
One of the most layered, thoughtful, and haunting stories on film.

The Shawshank Redemption by Frank Darabont, based on the short story by Stephen King
One my favourite screenplays, and a most uplifting tale of redemption.

Sling Blade by Billy Bob Thornton
Inevitable, predictable, yet still utterly fascinating to see unfold.

Swingers by Jon Favreau
The real rules to dating.

The Truman Show by Andrew Niccol
A solid piece of scriptwriting with well-executed ideas.

Internet Research

General research

Writers Guild of Great Britain
Hundreds of links to research websites.
www.wggb.demon.co.uk

Refdesk.com
Refdesk is basically a reference portal of impressive scope. From this
site you can link to a mind-boggling number of resources, from news
to finding the best '10–10' long distance phone rates.
www.refdesk.com

Librarian's Index to the Internet
Though designed for use by public librarians, this 7,000-site directory
is a useful resource. With links to sites related to the arts, education,
geography, literature, law, medicine, sports, and many other subjects.
www.lii.org

MagPortal.com
A categorized index of links to some of the latest magazine articles.
www.magportal.com

Art, music and theatre

AllMusic.com
A complete online database of recorded music.
www.allmusic.com

Aria-Database.com
Designed for both singers and fans, this site indexes information on
1,200 arias from 170 operas, with some 380 translations and texts.
www.aria-database.com

Fine Arts Museums of San Francisco
With over 65,000 works of art, this is currently the largest searchable
art image database in the world.
www.thinker.org

Film and TV

Cyberspace Film School
Official website of indie guru Dov S-S Simens. Includes useful info on
how to produce, find agents, contact stars and direct your first feature.
www.webfilmschool.com

Greatest Films
Plot summaries, reviews, commentary, film history per decade,
posters, trivia quizzes, famous scenes, all manner of 'best films' lists.
www.filmsite.org

The Internet Movie Database
Current and future releases, box office stats, quotes, news, and more.
www.imdb.com

Indiewire.com
The definitive daily report on independent filmmaking.
www.indiewire.com

Filmthreat.com
Left-of-centre weekly film newsletter.
www.filmthreat.com

Shootingpeople.org
The UK's popular newsgroup with daily postings.
www.shootingpeople.org

Scriptshop.co.uk
Services for writers and buyers of scripts.
www.scriptshop.co.uk

Netribution.co.uk
Web film magazine with local news stories, reviews and newsletter.
www.netribution.co.uk

Aint-it-cool.com
Harry Knowles' famous review site.
www.aint-it-cool.com

Moviejuice.com
Provocative film reviews from Mark Ramsay.
www.moviejuice.com

Government

CIA Factbook 2000
The newest version of the CIA's very useful global guide. Contains
facts on every country in the world.
www.odci.gov/cia/publications/factbook/index.html

Rulers
Lists of heads of state and heads of government of all currently
existing countries and territories.
www.geocities.com/athens/1058/rulers.html

History

The Historical Text Archive
Historical materials, links to other sites, and electronic book reprints.
www.msstate.edu/archives/history/index.html

TheHistoryNet.com
Comprehensive resource for information on national and international history, including eyewitness accounts, personality profiles, battles.
www.thehistorynet.com

Women in American History
An online guide to the women indicated by the title.
www.women.eb.com

Science and medicine

SciCentral.com
A gateway to over 50,000 sites pertaining to over 120 specialities in science and engineering.
www.scicentral.com

WeatherNet
Thousands of forecasts, images, and a huge collection of related links.
cirrus.sprl.umich.edu/wxnet

Achoo.com
Comprehensive health care directory of 5,000 sites.
www.achoo.com

Reference

Biographies
Includes more than 27,000 notable men and women.
www.s9.com/biography

Encyclopedia Britannica
Now online in its entirety, and it's free.
www.britannica.com

Carl.org
Searchable index to 17,000 periodical titles and online articles.
www.carl.org

Bloorstreet.com
Links to scores of websites for writing and research.
www.bloorstreet.com

The 50 Top-Grossing Motion Pictures at the Domestic Box Office in Nominal US Dollars as of March 8, 2001

	Title	Release	Gross ($M)
1	*Titanic*	Dec 97	600.8
2	*Star Wars*	May 77	461.0
3	*Star Wars Episode I*	May 99	431.1
4	*E.T.: The Extra Terrestrial*	Jun 82	399.8
5	*Jurassic Park*	Jun 93	357.1
6	*Forrest Gump*	Jul 94	329.7
7	*The Lion King*	Jun 94	312.9
8	*Return Of The Jedi*	May 83	309.1
9	*Independence Day*	Jul 96	306.2
10	*The Sixth Sense*	Aug 99	293.5
11	*The Empire Strikes Back*	May 80	290.3
12	*Home Alone*	Nov 90	285.8
13	*Jaws*	Jun 75	260.0
14	*How the Grinch Stole Christmas*	Nov 00	260.0
15	*Batman*	Jun 89	251.2
16	*Men in Black*	Jul 97	250.1
17	*Toy Story 2*	Nov 99	245.7
18	*Raiders Of The Lost Ark*	Jun 81	242.4
19	*Twister*	May 96	241.9
20	*Ghostbusters*	Jun 84	238.6
21	*Beverly Hills Cop*	Dec 84	234.8
22	*The Lost World*	May 97	229.1
23	*Cast Away*	Dec 00	224.3
24	*Mrs Doubtfire*	Nov 93	219.2
25	*Ghost*	Jul 90	217.6
26	*Aladdin*	Nov 92	217.4
27	*Saving Private Ryan*	Jul 98	216.1
28	*Mission: Impossible II*	May 00	215.4
29	*Back To The Future*	Jul 85	208.2
30	*Austin Powers*	Jun 99	205.4
31	*Terminator 2*	Jul 91	204.8
32	*The Exorcist*	Dec 73	204.6
33	*Armageddon*	Jul 98	201.6
34	*Indiana Jones And Last The Crusade*	May 89	197.2
35	*Gone With The Wind*	1939	191.9
36	*Toy Story*	Nov 95	191.8
37	*Gladiator*	May 00	186.6
38	*Dances With Wolves*	Nov 90	184.2
39	*Batman Forever*	Jun 95	184.0
40	*The Fugitive*	Aug 93	183.9
41	*The Perfect Storm*	Jun 00	182.6
42	*Grease*	Jun 78	181.5
43	*Liar Liar*	Mar 97	181.4
44	*Mission: Impossible*	May 96	181.0
45	*Indiana Jones*	May 84	179.9
46	*What Women Want*	Dec 00	179.8
47	*Pretty Woman*	Mar 90	178.4
48	*Tootsie*	Dec 82	177.2
49	*Top Gun*	May 86	176.8
50	*There's Something About Mary*	Jul 98	176.5

Oscars for Best Screenplay

2000	Adaptation	*Traffic* – Stephen Gaghan
	Original	*Almost Famous* – Cameron Crowe
1999	Adaption	*The Cider House Rules* – John Irving
	Original	*American Beauty* – Alan Ball
1998	Adaption	*Gods And Monsters* – Bill Condon
	Original	*Shakespeare In Love* – Marc Norman, Tom Stoppard
1997	Adaption	*L.A. Confidential* – Brian Helgeland, Curtis Hanson
	Original	*Good Will Hunting* – Ben Affleck, Matt Damon
1996	Adaptation	*Sling Blade* – Billy Bob Thornton
	Original	*Fargo* – Ethan Coen , Joel Coen
1995	Adaptation	*Sense And Sensibility* – Emma Thompson
	Original	*The Usual Suspects* – Christopher McQuarrie
1994	Adaptation	*Forrest Gump* – Eric Roth
	Original	*Pulp Fiction* – Quentin Tarantino, Roger Avary
1993	Adaptation	*Schindler's List* – Steven Zaillian
	Original	*The Piano* – Jane Campion
1992	Adaptation	*Howard's End* – Ruth Prawer Jhabvala
	Original	*The Crying Game* – Neil Jordan
1991	Adaptation	*The Silence Of The Lambs* – Ted Tally
	Original	*Thelma & Louise* – Callie Khouri
1990	Adaptation	*Dances With Wolves* – Michael Blake
	Original	*Ghost* – Bruce Joel Rubin
1989	Adaptation	*Driving Miss Daisy* – Alfred Uhry
	Original	*Dead Poets Society* – Tom Schulman
1988	Adaptation	*Dangerous Liaisons* – Christopher Hampton
	Original	*Rainman* – Ronald Bass, Barry Morrow
1987	Adaptation	*The Last Emperor* – Mark Peploe, Bernardo Bertolucci
	Original	*Moonstruck* – John Patrick Shanley
1986	Adaptation	*A Room With A View* – Ruth Prawer Jhabvala
	Original	*Hannah And Her Sisters* – Woody Allen
1985	Adaptation	*Out Of Africa* – Kurt Luedtke
	Original	*Witness* – Earl W. Wallace, William Kelley, Pamela Wallace
1984	Adaptation	*Amadeus* – Peter Shaffer
	Original	*Places In The Heart* – Robert Benton
1983	Adaptation	*Terms Of Endearment* – James L. Brooks
	Original	*Tender5 Mercies* – Horton Foote
1982	Adaptation	*Missing* – Costa-Gavras, Donald Stewart
	Original	*Gandhi* – John Briley
1981	Adaptation	*On Golden Pond* – Ernest Thompson
	Original	*Chariots Of Fire* – Colin Welland
1980	Adaptation	*Ordinary People* – Alvin Sargent
	Original	*Melvin And Howard* – Bo Goldman
1979	Adaptation	*Kramer Vs. Kramer* – Robert Benton
	Original	*Breaking Away* – Steve Tesich
1978	Adaptation	*Midnight Express* – Oliver Stone
	Original	*Coming Home* – Nancy Dowd, Waldo Salt, Robert C. Jones
1977	Adaptation	*Annie Hall* – Woody Allen, Marshall Brickman
	Original	*Julia* – Alvin Sargent
1976	Adaptation	*Network* – Paddy Chayefsky
	Original	*All The President's Men* – William Goldman
1975	Original	*One Flew Over The Cuckoo's Nest* – Bo Goldman, Lawrence Hauben
	Adaptation	*Dog Day Afternoon* – Frank Pierson
1974	Original	*The Godfather Part II* – Francis Ford Coppola, Mario Puzo
	Adaptation	*Chinatown* – Robert Towne

1973	Adaptation	*The Excorcist* – William Peter Blatty
	Original	*The Sting* – David S. Ward
1972	Adaptation	*The Godfather* – Mario Puzo, Francis Ford Coppola
	Original	*The Candidate* – Jeremy Larner
1971	Adaptation	*The French Connection* – Ernest Tidyman
	Original	*The Hospital* – Paddy Chayefsky
1970	Adaptation	*M*A*S*H* – Ring Lardner Jr.
	Original	*Patton* – Francis Ford Coppola, Edmund H. North
1969	Adaptation	*Midnight Cowboy* – Waldo Salt
	Original	*Butch Cassisy And The Sundance Kid* – William Goldman
1968	Adaptation	*The Lion In Winter* – James Goldman
	Original	*The Producers* – Mel Brooks
1967	Adaptation	*In The Heat Of The Night* – Stirling Silliphant
	Original	*Guess Who's Coming To Dinner* – William Rose
1966	Adaptation	*A Man For All Seasons* – Robert Bolt
	Original	*A Man And A Woman* – Claude Lelouch, Pierre Uytterhoeven
1965	Adaptation	*Doctor Zhivago* – Robert Bolt
	Original	*Darling* – Frederic Raphael
1964	Adaptation	*Becket* – Edward Anhalt
	Original	*Father Goose* – S.H. Barnett, Peter Stone, Frank Tarloff
1963	Adaptation	*Tom Jones* – John Osborne
	Original	*How The West Was Won* – James R. Webb
1962	Adaptation	*To Kill A Mockingbird* – Horton Foote
	Original	*Divorce: Italian Style* – Alfredo Giannetti, Ennio de Concini, Pietro Germiv
1961	Adaptation	*Judgment At Nuremberg* – Abby Mann
	Original	*Splendor In The Grass* – William Inge
1960	Adaptation	*Elmer Gantry* – Richard Brooks
	Original	*The Apartment* – Billy Wilder, I. A. L. Diamond
1959	Adaptation	*Room At The Top* – Neil Paterson
	Original	*Pillow Talk* – Russell Rouse, Clarence Greene, Stanley Shapiro, Maurice Richlin
1958	Adaptation	*Gigi* – Alan Jay Lerner
	Original	*The Defiant Ones* – Nedrick Young, Harold Jacob Smith
1957	Adaptation	*The Bridge On The River Kwai* – Pierre Boulle, Michael Wilson, Carl Foreman
	Original	*Designing Woman* – George Wells
1956	Adaptation	*Around The World in 80 Days* – James Poe, John Farrow, S.J. Perelman
	Original	*The Red Balloon* – Albert Lamorisse
1955	Story	*Love Me Or Leave Me* – Daniel Fuchs
	Original	*Marty* – Paddy Chayefsky
	S'play	*Interrupted Melody* – William Ludwig, Sonya Levien
1954	Story	*Broken Lance* – Philip Yordan
	Original	*The Country girl* – George Seaton
	S'play	*On The Waterfront* – Budd Schulberg
1953	Story	*Roman Holiday* – Dalton Trumbo
	Original	*From Here To Eternity* – Daniel Taradash
	S'play	*Titanic* – Charles Brackett, Walter Reisch, Richard Breen
1952	Story	*The Greatest Show On Earth* – Frederic M. Frank, Theodore St. John, Frank Cavett
	Original	*The Bad And The Beautiful* – Charles Schnee
	S'play	*The Lavender Hill Mob* – T.E.B. Clarke
1951	Story	*Seven Days To Noon* – Paul Dehn, James Bernard
	Original	*A Place In The Sun* – Michael Wilson, Harry Brown
	S'play	*An American In Paris* – Alan Jay Lerner
1950	Story	*Panic In The Streets* – Edna Anhalt, Edward Anhalt
	Original	*All About Eve* – Joseph L. Mankiewicz
	S'play	*Sunset Boulevard* – Charles Brackett, Billy Wilder, D.M. Marshman Jr.

1949	Story	*The Stratton Story* – Douglas Morrow
	Original	*A Letter To Three Wives* – Joseph L. Mankiewicz
	S'play	*Battleground* – Robert Pirosh
1948	Story	*The Search* – Richard Schweizer, David Wechsler
	S'play	*The Treasure Of The Sierra Madre* – John Huston
1947	Story	*Miracle On 34th Street* – Valentine Davies
	Original	*The Bachelor And The Bobby-Soxer* – Sidney Sheldon
	S'play	*Miracle On 34th Street* – George Seaton
1946	Story	*Vacation From Marriage* – Clemence Dane
	Original	*The Seventh Veil* – Muriel Box, Sydney Box
	S'play	*The Best Years Of Our Lives* –- Robert E. Sherwood
1945	Story	*The House On 92nd Street* – Charles G. Booth
	Original	*Marie-Louise* – Richard Schweizer
	S'play	*The Lost Weekend* – Charles Brackett, Billy Wilder
1944	Story	*Going My Way* – Leo McCarey
	Original	*Wilson* – Lamar Trotti
	S'play	*Going My Way* – Frank Butler, Frank Cavett
1943	Story	*The Human Comedy* – William Saroyan
	Original	*Princess O'Rourke* – Norman Krasna
	S'play	*Casablanca* – Julius J. Epstein, Philip Epstein, Howard Koch
1942	Story	*The Invaders* – Emeric Pressburger
	Original	*Woman Of The Year* – Ring Lardner, Jr., Michael Kanin
	S'play	*Mrs Miniver* – Arthur Wimperis, George Froeschel, James Hilton, Claudine West
1941	Original	*Citizen Kane* – Herman J. Mankiewicz, Orson Welles
	Story	*Here Comes Mr Jordan* – Harry Segall
	S'play	*Here Comes Mr Jordan* – Sidney Buchman, Seton I. Miller
1940	Original	*The Great McGinty* – Preston Sturges
	Story	*Arise, My Love* – Benjamin Glazer, John S. Toldy
	S'play	*The Philadelphia Story* – Donald Ogden Stewart
1939	Story	*Mr Smith Goes To Washington* – Lewis R. Foster
	S'play	*Gone With The Wind* – Sidney Howard
1938	Story	*Boys Town* – Dore Schary, Eleanore Griffin
	S'play	*Pygmalion* – George Bernard Shaw, W.P. Lipscomb, Cecil Lewis, Ian Dalrymple
1937	Story	*A Star Is Born* – William A. Wellman, Robert Carson
	S'play	*The Life Of Emile Zola* – Norman Reilly Raine, Heinz Herald, Geza Herczeg
1936	Story	*The Story Of Louis Pasteur* – Pierre Collings, Sheridan Gibney
	S'play	*The Story Of Louis Pasteur* – Pierre Collings, Sheridan Gibney
1935	Story	*The Scoundrel* – Ben Hecht, Charles MacArthur
	S'play	*The Informer* – Dudley Nichols
1934	Adaptation	*It Happened One Night* – Robert Riskin
	Original	*Manhattan Melodrama* – Arthur Caesar
1932/33	Adaptation	*Little Women* – Victor Heerman, Sarah Y. Mason
	Original	*One Way Passage* – Robert Lord
1931/32	Adaptation	*Bad Girl* – Edwin Burke
	Original	*The Champ* – Frances Marion
1930/31	Adaptation	*Cimarron* – Howard Estabrook
	Original	*The Dawn Patrol* – John Monk Saunders
1929/30		*The Big House* – Frances Marion
1928/29		*The Patriot* – Hans Kraly
1927/28	Adaptation	*7th Heaven* – Benjamin Glazer
	Original	*Underworld* – Ben Hecht, Joseph Farnham

Oscars for Best Picture

2000   *Gladiator* – Douglas Wick, David Framzoni, Branko Lustig
1999   *American Beauty* – Bruce Cohen, Dan Jinks
1998   *Shakespeare In Love* – David Parfitt, Donna Gigliotti, Harvey Weinstein, Edward Zwick, Marc Norman
1997   *Titanic* – James Cameron, Jon Landau
1996   *The English Patient* – Saul Zaentz
1995   *Braveheart* – Mel Gibson, Alan Ladd Jr., Bruce Davey
1994   *Forrest Gump* – Wendy Finerman, Steve Tisch, Steve Starkey
1993   *Schindler's List* – Steven Spielberg, Gerald R. Molen, Branko Lustig
1992   *Unforgiven* – Clint Eastwood
1991   *The Silence Of The Lambs* – Edward Saxon, Kenneth Utt, Ron Bozman
1990   *Dances With Wolves* – Jim Wilson, Kevin Costner
1989   *Driving Miss Daisy* – Richard D. Zanuck, Lili Fini Zanuck
1988   *Rainman* – Mark Johnson
1987   *The Last Emperor* – Jeremy Thomas
1986   *Platoon* – Arnold Kopelson
1985   *Out Of Africa* – Sydney Pollack
1984   *Amadeus* – Saul Zaentz
1983   *Terms Of Endearment* – James L. Brooks
1982   *Gandhi* – Richard Attenborough
1981   *Chariots Of Fire* – David Puttnam
1980   *Ordinary People* – Ronald L. Schwary
1979   *Kramer Vs. Kramer* – Stanley R. Jaffe
1978   *The Deer Hunter* – Barry Spikings, Michael Deeley, Michael Cimino, John Peverall
1977   *Annie Hall* – Charles H. Joffe
1976   *Rocky* – Irwin Winkler, Robert Chartoff
1975   *One Flew Over The Cuckoo's Nest* – Saul Zaentz, Michael Douglas
1974   *The Godfather Part II* – Francis Ford Coppola, Gray Frederickson, Fred Roos
1973   *The Sting* – Tony Bill, Michael Phillips, Julia Phillips
1972   *The Godfather* – Albert S. Ruddy
1971   *The French Connection* – Philip D'Antoni
1970   *Patton* – Frank McCarthy
1969   *Midnight Cowboy* – Jerome Hellman
1968   *Oliver!* – John Woolf
1967   *In The Heat Of The Night* – Walter Mirisch
1966   *A Man For All Seasons* – Fred Zinnemann
1965   *The Sound Of Music* – Robert Wise
1964   *My Fair Lady* – Jack L. Warner
1963   *Tom Jones* – Tony Richardson
1962   *Lawrence Of Arabia* – Sam Spiegel
1961   *West Side Story* – Robert Wise
1960   *The Apartment* – Billy Wilder
1959   *Ben-Hur* – Sam Zimbalist
1958   *Gigi* – Arthur Freed
1957   *The Bridge On The River Kwai* – Sam Spiegel
1956   *Around The World In 80 days* – Michael Todd
1955   *Marty* – Harold Hecht
1954   *On The Waterfront* – Sam Spiegel
1953   *From Here To Eternity* – Buddy Adler
1952   *The Greatest Show On Earth* – Cecil B. DeMille
1951   *An American In Paris* – Arthur Freed
1950   *All About Eve* – 20th Century-Fox
1949   *All The King's Men* – Robert Rossen
1948   *Hamlet* – J. Arthur Rank, Two Cities Films

1947	*Gentleman's Agreement* – 20th Century-Fox
1946	*The Best Years Of Our Lives* – Samuel Goldwyn
1945	*The Lost Weekend* – Paramount
1944	*Going My Way* – Paramount
1943	*Casablanca* – Warner Bros.
1942	*Mrs Miniver* – Metro-Goldwyn-Mayer
1941	*How Green Was My Valley* – 20th Century-Fox
1940	*Rebecca* – Selznick International Pictures
1939	*Gone With The Wind* – Selznick International Pictures
1938	*You Can't Take It With You* – Columbia
1937	*The Life Of Emile Zola* – Warner Bros.
1936	*The Great Ziegfeld* – Metro-Goldwyn-Mayer
1935	*Mutiny On The Bouhty* – Metro-Goldwyn-Mayer
1934	*It Happened One Night* – Columbia
1932/33	*Cavalcade* – Fox
1931/32	*Grand Hotel* – Metro-Goldwyn-Mayer
1930/31	*Cimarron* – RKO Radio
1929/30	*All Quiet on the Western Front* – Universal
1928/29	*The Broadway Melody* – Metro-Goldwyn-Mayer
1927/28	*Wings* – Paramount Famous Lasky

Glossary

Ad lib
Extemporaneous lines or phrases used by actors appropriate to a given situation. Often used in group scenes such as parties.

Adaption
The reworking of a story in a medium different from its creation.

Aerial shot
A shot taken from the point of view of an airplane or helicopter.

Aleatory filming
Filming techniques based on chance and probability.

Antagonist
The opponent to the protagonist (hero).

Anticlimax
An emotional letdown in the buildup to the climax of the story.

Backstory
That which happens to the main characters before the movie begins. Omission of backstory can make a story flat and difficult for an audience to relate to a main character. See also *Exposition*.

Beat
A plot point within the overall story structure. The analogy of screen writing to music is often made, with individual scenes broken down into beats, organized overall into acts or movements.

b.g. (Background)
Any action or prop which is secondary to the main action.

Big gloom
The moment where the main character is the furthest from their goal, and often considers abandoning their vision.

Black stuff
Industry term for descriptive passages.

Business
Technique of writing props into scenes for actors to work with, making dialogue dominated scenes more active and physical.

Character arc
Curved line tracing the changes and development of a character over the course of the screenplay.

Cinéma vérité
A filmmaking technique designed for a scene to be filmed with as little intrusion of the camera as possible.

Close-up (C.U.)
A camera shot which emphasizes some part of the actor or an object.

Complication
An unexpected situation which threatens to thwart the hero's objectives. Used to add texture to a story.

Crosscut
The technique of alternating between two scenes in different locations which have a bearing on each other.

Cutaway
A shot away from the main action. Used by filmmakers to cut between awkward shots, or to highlight specific details.

CUT TO
A scene ending which varies with use, but is often employed when cutting back and forth between two locations during a chase.

Deus ex machina
A resolution to a plot problem which is too convenient for the author, and unbelievable to the audience.

DISSOLVE TO
A scene ending which indicates that the final shot should gradually fade into the next scene.

Dolly
A camera cue used by directors indicating that the camera is to move in, out or with the actors during scene.

Epilogue
A brief unit of action following the conclusion of the story.

Exposition

The process whereby events that happened prior to the beginning of the movie are explained to the audience to they can understand the motivation of the main characters. Exposition is an area most often ignored by new screenwriters. They usually rely on hackneyed and overworked devices such as the general, the pointer and the flip chart.

EXT. (Exterior)

Used in scene headings to indicate that a scene will be shot outside.

Extreme close-up (E.C.U.)

A camera cue which is generally used to emphasize a particular detail.

EXTREME LONG SHOT

Camera cue in direction used to describe a shot taken by a long distance from the subject.

FADE IN

The first two words of a screenplay.

FADE OUT

Scene ending which is used in television at the end of an act, or at the very end of a feature film.

f.g. (Foreground)

Objects or action which is closest to camera.

Flashback

Established Hollywood wisdom is against the use of this device, but there are many successful examples of film narratives structured around flashbacks including *Citizen Kane*. The two types of flashbacks to avoid are the flipping calandar and harp music. Try to be imaginative with your use of this device. Flashback does not refer to time-line experiments where the A to B of a narrative story is chopped and changed, as in *The Usual Suspects*.

Foreshadowing

A dramatic tool where an event is hinted at early on such as *Silence of the Lambs*: 'You don't want Hanibal Lecter inside your head'.

FREEZE FRAME

Camera direction indicating that the picture stops dead and becomes a still photograph. Sometimes used to end scripts.

Genre

A story that follows certain rules pertinent to a specific type of story – horror, science fiction, comedy, love, detective, mystery, crime etc. Specializing in genre is essential to success as a writer.

Ghost

That thing or event from the past which the main character in your story fears. The ghost should be so powerful that it cripples your hero at the outset of the story – but then is overcome. Different genres treat the ghost in different ways – necessary to the particular genre, which creates specific problems the writer must deal with. See also *Nightmare, Troubleshooting.*

High concept

A phrase connected with scripts which have a premise or storyline which is easily reduced to a simple and appealing one line. *Aliens* was summed up as 'Jaws in Space'.

Inciting scene

The necessary scene at the beginning of the script which serves as a catalyst for the main action of the story.

INSERT

A shot within a scene which calls our attention to a specific piece of information such as a book, a watch or a calendar.

INT. (Interior)

A scene heading which indicates that the scene will be shot inside.

L.S. (Long Shot)

A camera cue indicating a shot taken from a distance.

MATCH CUT

A transition from one scene to another matching the same, or a similar subject within the frame.

MED. SHOT (Medium Shot)

A camera angle often used to describe a shot of character from the waist up.

Mirroring

The mimicking of a main character's actions or emotions in order to heighten drama.

MISE-EN-CADRE

Direction or staging within the camera frame.

MISE-EN-SCENE

The staging or positioning of the actors on the stage.

Montage

A rapid succession of shots. Also used as a scene heading, interchangeable with the *Series of Shots* heading.

Nightmare
The ultimate low that a hero must face if they fail to achieve their goal. See also *Ghost*.

On the nose
A phrase which describes dialogue which too plainly reveals the character, and more importantly, the author's intentions. Often, dialogue will simply repeat what action has immediately preceded it.

Option
Agreement where a writer rents the rights to a script to a producer or production company for a specific period of time.

O.S. (Off-screen)
Dialogue or sounds heard while the camera is on another subject. Typed '(O.S.)' next to the character cue, and 'o.s.' in scene description.

Over the top
A phrase used in a broad way to describe a scene or action in a script which goes too far in one direction and stretches believability.

Pan
A side-to-side camera movement.

Payoff
The necessary result of a complication for which the audience has been prepared.

P.O.V. (Point of view)
A camera positioned from the point of view of a particular character.

Premise
The basic idea for a story, often taking the form of a question or a problem.

Producer's notes
A shorter form of story analysis, without synopsis, where development executives make comments about a script, particularly in terms of commercial viability.

Protagonist
The main character (hero) in the screenplay.

Resolution
The part of the end of a script that ties up all of the story's loose ends.

Reveal
When new information is revealed to the audience.

Rising action
Notion of dramatic rhythm in which events in a story build upon one another with increasing momentum.

Scene cards
Method used by some writers to outline their script by describing each scene on an index card, then arranging and rearranging them to work out the story structure.

Script development
The process where an idea is turned into a script, with funding from a studio or government funding agency. Development financing is often the most difficult to obtain for new writers.

Second-act curtain
In *Three-act structure*, the moment of the greatest conflict.

SERIES OF SHOTS
A series of short shots, typically used to show the passing of time.

Set-up
Term describing both the function of the first act in posing of the problem which the story will try to resolve, and in a more general way, the process of laying the groundwork for a dramatic or comic situation which will later be complicated, and then resolved or paid off.

Shooting schedule
Production schedule for shooting a film with the scenes from a script grouped together and ordered with production considerations in mind.

Shooting script
The final version of the screenplay incorporating the notes of the director, director of photography, designers and producers.

SFX (Sound tracks)
Special effects which require some kind of technical reproduction.

Spine
The essential events in a story.

Stacking
A writing technique where different storylines are played on top of each other to heighten drama and suspense.

Step outline
A method used by some writers to outline their story by numbering the major scenes and the order in which they occur. Not to be confused with a *Treatment* which is a stylized version of the story used in seeking financing.

Story analyst

Also called a reader – both a full-time guild and part-time independent position in the industry, whose responsibility it is to cover feature film and television scripts being considered by a company for production. Generally included in the coverage is a one-line story description, a synopsis of the plotline, and the reader's comments, including the words 'Pass' or 'Consider' at the end.

Subplot

Sometimes called the B story, the subplot is used in various ways, weaving in and out of the main action. Often it is in the subplot that the major characters are developed more fully.

SUPER (Superimpose)

The photographic effect of showing one image over another. Typically, titles are superimposed over the opening scene.

Switch

A dramatic device where the writer plays on an audience's expectation and takes the story, or scene in a completely new direction.

Synopsis

Summary of a story told in present tense. When the synopsis is a single line, it is referred to as the log line.

Theme

What the screenplay is really about. Not to be confused with a topic. Anti-pollution is a topic, revenge is a theme. The more universal the theme is, the wider the appeal of the story.

Three-act structure

In the Hollywood storytelling tradition, the basic organizing principle of the sequence of fictional events including the set-up, the complication, and the resolution. The three-act story structure was considered the ultimate story paradigm until the early nineties. This paradigm is rooted in Greek history. In Hollywood, Syd Field's books and Robert McKee's teaching made the three-act story structure the industry standard until Chris Vogler's *The Writer's Journey* and John Truby's *22-Step Story Structure* paradigms exploded the theory. It is now considered an obsolete story paradigm in Hollywood. See also *22-Beat Story Structure* and *Vogler, Chris*

Three-camera format

Specific script style used for TV shows produced in a video studio.

Titles

Printed information to be read by the audience, either as separate graphics or superimposed over images. When an individual is mentioned in the titles, it is called a credit.

Treatment
Summary of story told in present tense. A treatment is often used as a tool to sell a writing project before it is written.

Tripling
Basic writing principle of creating action which occurs in three distinct beats over movements.

Twenty-two step story structure
A script structure paradigm created by LA-based John Truby and considered the most advanced of the story structure paradigm. Further details from www.truby.com

Vogler, Chris
Author of *The Writers' Journey*, the most influential screenwriting book of the 1990s, based on the teachings of Joseph Campbell.

V.O. (Voice over)
A character's voice heard over a scene, as in narration, a tape recorded voice, or a voice heard over the phone.

Visit to death
A plot point near the end of the movie where the hero is defeated and can foresee their own death.

Writers' credits
Writer 1 and Writer 2 – both writers worked separately on the project. Writer 1 & Writer 2 – both writers worked together on the project. In cases of dispute on a screenplay that has been rewritten, The Writers Guild of America will award a sole writer credit based on which writer's script maintains fifty-one percent of the dialogue.

ZOOM
A camera cue indicated by the inward or outward movement of the camera to the subject. Distinguished from the dolly shot in that with the zoom shot the camera itself doesn't move, the effect is achieved solely by the manipulation of the zoom lens.

Index

About Raindance

The Raindance Film Festival, founded in 1993, aims to reflect the cultural, visual and narrative diversity of the international independent filmmaking community.

Held during the important pre-MIFED London Screenings, Raindance targets the international film acquisition executives who congregate in London prior to the Milan market, and attracts an audience of leading film professionals and genuine film fans. Raindance has hosted the London premières of *Pulp Fiction*, *What's Eating Gilbert Grape*, *Wonderland*, *The Blair Witch Project* and *Memento*.

Throughout the year Raindance runs courses and provides advice on all aspects of independent filmmaking, writing, directing and producing, as well as a script-reading and script registration service.

Raindance also hosts the British Independent Film Awards.

Call 020 7287 3833 for details or visit www.raindance.co.uk

About the CD-ROM

All the files on the CD-ROM run through Adobe® Acrobat® PDF interface. To access the files you must have either Adobe® Acrobat® Reader® 4.0 or higher.

To access the MP3/MPEG-1 audio and video clips and interviews, you'll need to have a media player installed on your computer. There are many players available. For Windows we recommend Windows Media Player. Macintosh users can use Quicktime. For information regarding MP3 files and the appropriate media players for your system, check out www.mp3.com. Log on for installation instructions and troubleshooting, or to learn more about playing MP3 files.

Check out the Final Draft demo software included on the CD-ROM.

For information on all Focal Press publications visit our website at www.focalpress.com

Screenwriting Software

DreamaScript uses the latest technology for crafting award-winning screenplays that sell. It brings all of the concepts and tools in this book to life leaving you to unleash your creativity.

Not only a story development tool, DreamaScript empowers you to produce professionally formatted screenplays, protect your ideas with the Copyright Registration Service, request professional feedback on your screenplays, selling your script using the marketing tools and much more.

Simplify your life as a screenwriter – buy DreamaScript now.

It gives you the tools, the prompts, and the knowledge you need to prepare and write professionally.
Dave Herman, Independent Film Journalist

Visit www.dreamascript.com for more details.

£5 Off When You Order Now

Please rush me my copy of DreamaScript for £190 + VAT

Name _____

Address _____

_____

Email _____

I enclose a cheque payable to 'Dreamachrome Ltd' / please charge my card the sum of £223.25

Mastercard ☐   Visa ☐   Switch ☐

Card No ☐☐☐☐ ☐☐☐☐ ☐☐☐☐ ☐☐☐☐

Expiry Date ☐☐ / ☐☐   Issue No [Switch] ☐☐

Signature _____   Date _____

Detach this form and mail it to:
Dreamachrome Ltd, 153 Abbey Fields Close, London NW10 7EJ, UK

Or email info@dreamachrome.com

Tel +44 [0]7902 166744   Fax +44 [0]7092 166746